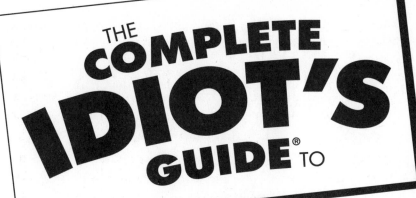

THE COMPLETE IDIOT'S GUIDE® TO

Business Letters and Memos

Second Edition

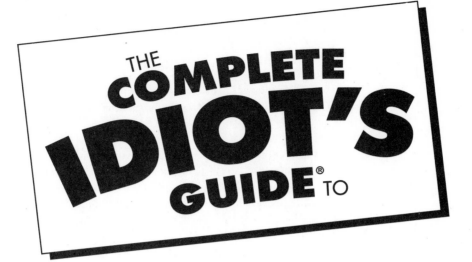

THE COMPLETE IDIOT'S GUIDE® TO

Business Letters and Memos

Second Edition

by Tom Gorman

ALPHA

A member of Penguin Group (USA) Inc.

ALPHA BOOKS

Published by the Penguin Group

Penguin Group (USA) Inc., 375 Hudson Street, New York, New York 10014, U.S.A.

Penguin Group (Canada), 10 Alcorn Avenue, Toronto, Ontario, Canada M4V 3B2 (a division of Pearson Penguin Canada Inc.)

Penguin Books Ltd, 80 Strand, London WC2R 0RL, England

Penguin Ireland, 25 St Stephen's Green, Dublin 2, Ireland (a division of Penguin Books Ltd)

Penguin Group (Australia), 250 Camberwell Road, Camberwell, Victoria 3124, Australia (a division of Pearson Australia Group Pty Ltd)

Penguin Books India Pvt Ltd, 11 Community Centre, Panchsheel Park, New Delhi—110 017, India

Penguin Group (NZ), cnr Airborne and Rosedale Roads, Albany, Auckland 1310, New Zealand (a division of Pearson New Zealand Ltd)

Penguin Books (South Africa) (Pty) Ltd, 24 Sturdee Avenue, Rosebank, Johannesburg 2196, South Africa

Penguin Books Ltd, Registered Offices: 80 Strand, London WC2R 0RL, England

Most Alpha books are available at special quantity discounts for bulk purchases for sales promotions, premiums, fund-raising, or educational use. Special books, or book excerpts, can also be created to fit specific needs.

For details, write: Special Markets, Alpha Books, 375 Hudson Street, New York, NY 10014.

Publisher: *Marie Butler-Knight*
Editorial Director: *Mike Sanders*
Senior Managing Editor: *Jennifer Bowles*
Senior Acquisitions Editor: *Renee Wilmeth*
Development Editor: *Michael Thomas*
Production Editor: *Janette Lynn*
Copy Editor: *Jeff Rose*
Illustrator: *Chris Eliopoulos*
Cover/Book Designer: *Trina Wurst*
Indexer: *Tonya Heard*
Layout: *Becky Harmon*
Proofreading: *John Etchison*

Contents at a Glance

Contents

Foreword

I used to be a terrible writer. Now I am a published author. How did I go from being a bad writer to being a good writer? I looked carefully at how successful writers write so well and I practiced their techniques. I analyzed the step-by-step processes they used to write things that I enjoyed reading and that communicated clearly.

I discovered that good writing is a skill that can be learned. I learned that the best way to write well was to copy the style of good and successful writers. It didn't matter what I was trying to write. Whether it was a book, a business letter, or a memo to my associates, I looked for a model that I knew got the job done, then used that model for my own purposes.

We write business letters and memos to get things done. They have to communicate clearly what we have in mind. We expect our readers to understand and act on the ideas and feelings we express. We want them to understand us as we intend them to. Then we will get the results we want from whatever we have written.

In *The Complete Idiot's Guide to Business Letters and Memos, Second Edition,* Tom Gorman shows you just what to do to write effective letters and memos. No matter what your present skills may be, his step-by-step method will boost your power to communicate and get things done. Using his easy, simple approach, you will learn how to write faster—and better.

This handy guide provides you with clear explanations of the general principles of good writing, along with numerous practical examples of good letters and memos. You can copy these models for your own purposes, or study them for insights on writing from scratch. Either way, you will learn how to write the best letter or memo for the occasion.

As you'll discover, being a good communicator increases your sense of personal worth and confidence in whatever you do. Before long, writing will be a pleasure instead of a chore.

Richard Heyman

Dr. Richard Heyman is professor of communication and education at the University of Calgary and Director of the Discourse Analysis Research Group, an international network of people who study language use in everyday life. He is the author of *Why Didn't You Say That in the First Place?: How to Be Understood at Work* (San Francisco: Jossey-Bass, 1994).

Introduction

Your success in business depends on your ability to express yourself in writing. Whether you're looking for a job or you're on the job—or in your own business—you have to be able to write great letters and memos and express yourself on paper—and in your e-mails—in a professional yet personal and persuasive way.

If you have problems with business writing, you found this book at the right time. That's because written communication skills have become more important than ever in business. The computer and e-mail demand that we write constantly. Meanwhile, most of us can no longer count on secretaries or administrative assistants, who are becoming increasingly rare, to correct badly written communications.

I'm a professional writer with over 25 years of business experience. I've used letters and memos to get jobs, make sales, solve problems, hire people, and then help them improve their performance. I've been a corporate writing instructor for a successful training firm, and I ran the editorial and production department for a division of a Fortune 500 company. I've written or ghostwritten a total of a dozen business books. But before I ever wrote a book, I wrote thousands of letters and memos, most of which did the job they were supposed to do.

I wrote this book because I know that it's hard to get good, practical guidance for on-the-job writing. Although business people expect you to be able to write professional-sounding documents, no one is born knowing how to do that. It often takes years to learn how.

This book will save you incredible amounts of time as you learn to write great letters, memos, and e-mails. It offers techniques for speeding up the writing process and inside tips on how to avoid mistakes—real time-savers. And the hundreds of samples and templates of letters, memos, and e-mails in this book and on the CD-ROM that came with it will make life on the job much easier for you.

Here's the approach we'll take in this book:

Part 1, "The Business of Business Writing," explains what makes a great piece of business writing and gives some practical help on solving writing problems and building communication skills.

Part 2, "Writing Is Easier Than You Think (So Please Relax)," shows you how to write quickly using a simple three-step process, how to handle punctuation, and how to use white space, bullets, and boxes to grab readers' attention.

Part 3, "Polishing Your Correspondence," helps you express your personal style in your letters, memos, and e-mails and avoid embarrassing mistakes in written English. It also shows you how to format professional-looking correspondence.

Part 4, "Letters, Memos, and E-mail for Every Situation," is about which written communication to use for different business needs, from requests to reprimands to thank-you's. It includes samples and templates that you can use as models, and shows you how to respond to difficult letters, memos, and e-mails, such as requests that you must refuse and customer complaints.

Part 5, "Writing Well in Special Circumstances," shows you how to write for your boss or a committee, how to make yourself understood to non-native speakers of English, and how to write when you face a close deadline or in a high-pressure environment.

The Appendix also tells you how to get the most from the samples and templates on the CD-ROM that comes with this book.

As you go through this book, remember to relax and take time to learn what works. Given the importance of written communication in business today, you'll find it's well worth the investment.

Signposts Along the Way

You'll find the following sidebars throughout the book. They highlight special points that I want to be sure you catch.

 FYI

These boxes give you definitions of words and terms that might not be entirely familiar to you.

 Pitfalls

These boxes warn you of problems that can occur in business writing and suggest how you can handle sticky situations.

 Tricks of the Trade

These sidebars provide professional tips on how to write better, faster, or with more impact. Some show you how to handle certain aspects of writing letters or memos.

See the CD-ROM

The "See the CD-ROM" icon ⊙ means that I'm presenting a sample letter, memo, or e-mail that you can find on the CD-ROM that comes with the book. In the book, I explain the importance of the sample in a nearby paragraph.

The CD-ROM has many more samples than we can fit into this book. Just go to the CD-ROM for a listing of the samples on the disk, and go right to any sample you want.

Acknowledgments

Many thanks to everyone who helped to make this book possible: For assistance on the second edition, I'd like to thank Renee Wilmeth, senior acquisitions editor, Janette Lynn, production editor, Michael Thomas, development editor, and Jeff Rose, copy editor. Also, my thanks go to Kathleen M. Victory for lucid and lighthearted wordsmithing on the letters and memos on the CD that accompanies this edition.

My thanks also go to the original editorial team of Dick Staron, Kate Layzer, Lynn Northrup, and Lori Cates, to John Hunt, graphics coordinator, and Glenn Larsen, designer, and to my agent, Mike Snell. Thanks also to my wife Phyllis and my sons Danny and Matt, and to my past employers, employees, trainees, and clients.

Trademarks

All terms mentioned in this book that are known to be or are suspected of being trademarks or service marks have been appropriately capitalized. Alpha Books and Penguin Group (USA) Inc. cannot attest to the accuracy of this information. Use of a term in this book should not be regarded as affecting the validity of any trademark or service mark.

Part 1

The Business of Business Writing

You go to your boss with an idea for a new procedure to solve a recurring problem in your department, and she says, "That sounds promising. Please give me a memo on that by next Monday." What's your reaction?

There's no doubt about it: Business involves business writing. That writing most often takes the form of a letter or memo. Add in the torrent of e-mails most of us have to generate and respond to, and you've got a lot of business writing to produce. Yet lots of people have trouble writing clearly, quickly, and professionally. If you're one of those people, you have a source of real help right in your hands. Please use one of those hands to turn the page, and let's get started.

Chapter 1

Letters and Memos and E-mail—Oh My!

In This Chapter

- How business correspondence moves business forward
- What makes a great letter, memo, or e-mail?
- Ways to start and close your correspondence
- How to become a better communicator

Business communication takes two basic forms: the spoken word and the written word. Of the two, the written word has a far greater impact on your career. After all, unless you're a character in a comic strip, the words you speak disappear into thin air. But the words you write stick around for a long time. They are filed, passed along to other people, and read over and over again. Whatever you write on the job becomes a permanent record of the way you express yourself.

So you want to be able to handle on-the-job writing tasks.

You also want to get the results that you're trying to produce when you write to someone. Whether you're writing to explain a task, move a sale forward, secure a job interview, or build a relationship, your letter, memo, or e-mail had better do the job. In fact, that's a good definition for effective business writing: It does the job that it's meant to do.

But you should write letters, memos, and e-mails that are better than good. You should write great business *correspondence*. How do you go about doing that? First, by understanding what makes a great letter, memo, or e-mail.

The Characteristics of Greatness

Great business correspondence …

- Grabs the reader's attention.
- Makes recommendations or requests action.

♦ Supports your position.

♦ Mentions next steps and deadlines.

Great business writing accomplishes these goals in a crisp, professional way, but with a personal touch. A great letter or memo gets results, and creates a positive impression with your bosses, co-workers, and customers—or anyone else who might be reading it. Let's take a look at each of these "Characteristics of Greatness."

Grab the Reader's Attention

Let's face it: We all have too much paper coming at us. Throw in the e-mails, and it's a wonder we ever do anything on the job besides read what people send us. With so much correspondence to deal with, how do we decide what we'll spend time reading and what we'll just skim, toss, or delete?

Often we decide based on who wrote it. If it's from our boss, we'll probably read it. But when the boss's writing is confusing, most of us would rather ask him what it's about.

Usually, we'll read correspondence if it is clear and interesting. If we can't figure out what it says, we'll move on to the next thing. If it's dull or seems to have nothing to do with us, we'll do the same. Grab the reader's attention by having something to say and stating it clearly.

The format of your letter, memo, or e-mail affects the reader also. Most readers are turned off when they see huge paragraphs and long sentences. In Chapter 8, I'll show you how your format can invite the reader into your documents.

Make a Recommendation or Ask for Action

Most readers of business correspondence want the answer to one question: What is this memo or message asking me to do? So answer that question very early in the document—in the first sentence if possible.

The following openings provide examples of this:

♦ "Many of our employees can no longer find spaces in the company parking lot. This memo presents a solution for your review and approval."

- "This memo requests your approval of $5,000 in expenses to test a direct mail campaign for our new product line."
- "Our external accountants will begin their annual audit on the fifteenth of next month, and I'd like you to prepare the general ledger for their review as outlined in this memo."
- "I have been interested in working for ABC Industries for some time and would like to meet with you to discuss how I could help your company meet its goals."

These approaches immediately tell the reader what you're writing about and why. In fact, you inform the reader about your subject and grab his attention at the same time. Isn't that efficient?

As you'll see in Chapters 3 and 4, you also can use the subject line to grab the reader's attention.

Support Your Position

It's not enough to make a recommendation or request an action. You have to explain why it makes sense. You can usually accomplish this with far fewer words than you might think, often in one paragraph or several *bullets* ().

When you make a recommendation or request an action, you should also do one or more of the following:

- Tell the reader briefly what research or "homework" you did before making this recommendation or request.
- Mention one or two alternatives and tell why your recommendation is best.
- Show the reader the positive impact of your recommendation or request; that is, what's in it for him or the organization.
- Offer the reader any help that you can.

By supporting your position, you stand a better chance of getting the reader to support your request. If you don't mention reasons for your position or benefits for the reader, you will either raise questions or objections, or risk being ignored.

Mention Next Steps and Deadlines

Be specific about next steps and deadlines. Again, put yourself in the reader's position. How do *you* direct your attention and effort on the job? How do *you* set priorities?

Most of us decide what to do on the basis of urgency. So if you tell the reader what you will do to follow up and when you will do it, you create a sense of urgency. Follow-up steps—and deadlines—drive things forward.

FYI

A **bullet** is one of a series of items arranged as a list, with each item preceded by a dot or other symbol. Use no more than five or six bullets in one set.

Tricks of the Trade

You can call a deadline a deadline if you are writing to a subordinate. But most bosses and peers don't like the term "deadline" from a subordinate or co-worker. In those cases, use the term "time frame."

Tricks of the Trade

Mentioning specific follow-up steps and time frames may get you a definite refusal. That's not all bad. A refusal signals that you should change your approach, ask someone else, or move on to something else.

Pitfalls

Don't make the mistake of thinking that e-mail isn't "written communication," because it surely is. People have to read it, and they often print it out, save it in folders, or send it along to other readers. While you can often take a more casual tone in e-mail, it is most certainly a reflection of your business writing skill.

For example, you can close by saying:

◆ "I'll phone you by the end of next week to get your reaction to this proposal."

◆ "To do the mailing by our target date, Jim and I need your approval by the tenth. If I haven't heard from you by the eighth, I'll call you."

◆ "I realize you're busy, so I'll call next Thursday afternoon to arrange a meeting at your convenience."

At the least, these kinds of closings allow you to follow up. This is key to getting results. Often one memo or e-mail doesn't succeed because people are busy and overworked. Many people dislike change and drag their feet. When you politely tell the reader how and when you will follow up, you plan future actions aimed at getting results.

Strive for Greatness

These "Characteristics of Greatness" apply to almost all written business correspondence. This book covers many types of communication for a variety of purposes in assorted formats. Most of the suggestions you'll read have one thing in common: the goal of getting results—whether you need someone to follow your suggestion, approve your recommendation, or take the requested action.

You will achieve this goal only if the reader reads what you wrote, understands what you want, sees the reason for your request, and feels a sense of urgency about it. A great letter, memo, or e-mail does all of these things. And your letters, memos, and e-mails can all be great.

The Importance of Written Communication Skills

Because a reader might forward correspondence to someone else or file it for future reference, you really don't know who will see it. That document becomes a permanent reflection on your ability to think clearly, express yourself professionally, and get things done.

Write badly, and the people playing a role in your success will notice, which will hold you back. On the other hand, if you write well, your correspondence will be read and will produce results.

What People Mean by "Communication Skills"

What does the term "communication skills" mean to you? Do you think of some silver-tongued devil who can talk anyone into anything? Do you think it's about the size of your vocabulary—the more words you know, especially big words, the better? Does it involve impressing people with your brains and schooling?

Some believe these define "communication skills," but they're wrong. Instead, good communication …

- ◆ Puts mutual interests first.
- ◆ Makes the message clear.
- ◆ Shows sensitivity to others' feelings.

Let's examine these issues in the following sections.

Put Mutual Interests First

If you write to puff yourself up rather than move the business forward, people will know it. They will see that your agenda is yourself, your position, and your interests. However, business is based upon mutual interests. To write compelling correspondence, you must identify mutual goals. This doesn't mean your goals come last. It means that everyone's goals have equal importance, or you can't do business.

Let's take an example that at first seems one-sided—a *collection letter*. Your goal is simple: You want your money. You sold something on credit, and the customer hasn't paid you as agreed. But even here, readers have goals that mesh with yours—maintaining their cash flow, credit rating, business reputation, peace of mind, freedom from legal action, and (probably) sense of honesty. By mentioning some of these in your collection letters, you create shared goals.

To get results, to get agreement, to get people to take action, you have to get them to see what's in it for them. Whether you're writing a sales letter, policy announcement, or deal memo, you have to keep *mutual* interests front and center. Good communicators show that they understand the other person's goals.

FYI _____

A **collection letter** is a written request to a customer to pay a past-due bill by a certain time. It's also called a "dunning letter."

Make the Message Clear

A lot of business writing lacks clarity. Sometimes a muddled memo reflects the writer's muddled thinking. Many writers in business try to impress the reader rather than express an idea. Others, especially when writing e-mail, dash off their ideas as they pop into their heads, which almost always short-circuits communication. Still others bury their main point somewhere in the fifth paragraph. Will the reader get that far? Doubtful.

If you want your writing to get results, first decide what you want the reader to think or do and then say it, as clearly as you can and as early as you can in the document. Then support what you say with a few key facts.

Pitfalls _____

Many people think that the more words they write, the clearer their message becomes. In fact, the opposite is generally true: The fewer the words, the clearer the message.

Show Sensitivity to Others' Feelings

In our daily dealings, too many of us display insensitivity to others' feelings. If your writing comes across as arrogant, angry, flippant, or uncaring, you will not only fail to get results, you'll make enemies along the way.

Professionalism, not to mention good manners, demands that you conduct yourself with an awareness of others' views and feelings. This holds particularly true in business writing.

Displays of anger or inappropriate humor on paper or in e-mails have scuttled many a career. A sarcastic tone, even for laughs, has no place in a business document (although some bosses seem to get away with it). Comments that might sound witty if delivered in person with a certain tone of voice or facial expression often come across as demeaning or immature in writing. Worse, you're not around to see the reader's reaction so you can apologize.

Sensitivity to others is the positive side of "politics" in business. The negative side is conforming to policies you feel are wrong, flattering people to gain favor, playing the yes-man (or -woman), and other forms of "apple polishing." While some people still employ such tactics, these forms of politics are now valued far less than the ability to get things done. Good communication helps you to get things done.

The Reader Is King

This all adds up to one thing: In business writing, the reader is king, just as the customer is king in any business. Think of your readers as your customers.

If your readers are going to buy your ideas and help you to get the results you want, you have to focus on them, on *their* goals and needs and on *their* feelings, about what you're proposing. Even if you're the CEO, you can't order people to be cooperative. You have to win their cooperation. That's what you can achieve with truly great letters, memos, and e-mails.

The Least You Need to Know

- Great business correspondence grabs the reader's attention, makes a recommendation or asks for action, supports your position, and mentions next steps and deadlines.

- Good business communication calls for a focus on mutual interests, clarity, and sensitivity to others' feelings.

- To get results, you have to show people what's in it for them or for the organization.

- Letters, memos, and e-mails move business—and careers—forward, as long as they are clear, concise, and well-written.

Business Writing Problems— And Solutions

In This Chapter

- ◆ Common difficulties in business writing
- ◆ What you can do to make writing easier
- ◆ A self-assessment of your writing skills

Many people find business writing difficult. To understand this better, we'll look at common business writing problems in this chapter.

First, however, you should understand that everyone has trouble now and then with a specific writing situation or a certain type of correspondence. For example, nobody enjoys writing letters of reprimand or rejection (except mean people—not people like us!). Many people are shy about writing to request an action. Perhaps they fear they will be rejected or they don't believe they have the authority to make the request.

When you have trouble with a specific type of document or message, you should review the chapter on that kind of correspondence in Part 4. You'll find the models and outlines useful as "thought-starters" and blueprints for your letter. The chapters in Part 4 also include advice that can help you understand your role as a businessperson in each writing situation.

Few of us in business can avoid writing. But there's no reason to avoid it, especially if you've confronted any general problems you have.

Here are the most common problems I've heard from people in my years as an editor and corporate writing consultant.

Problem: "I Hate to Write"

Some people make "I hate to write" their mantra. After years of repeating this, they really do hate writing.

Tricks of the Trade

Writing about your writing problem will actually help you address the problem. If you hate to write or can't get started, write about that for 20 minutes every day for a few days. Often the problem will disappear as you discover the reasons for it and find that writing won't kill you.

What Can You Do?

If you say this to yourself, and you have to write on the job, stop saying it.

Also ask yourself this: Do you hate to talk? If you think of writing as talking on paper—and this book will show you how to do that—you stop hating it. But first, stop repeating that phrase to yourself.

It may also be useful to identify what you specifically dislike about writing:

◆ Is it because it's not usually a social activity but rather one you do alone? If so, be sure that you get input from others on a writing task whenever you can.

◆ Is it working with words? If you dislike working with words, you definitely must make every effort to write the way you would talk. (I discuss how in Chapter 7.)

◆ Do you dislike computers and keyboards? Face it: You need computer skills in today's workplace. You can get training. With the *tutorials*, tips, and help facilities in today's word-processing software, you can learn to write a good memo without spending hours at the computer. Also, you can always do your first draft with pen and paper, but I don't recommend this. It's much more efficient to get used to composing on the computer.

◆ Does deadline pressure drive you nuts? You'll benefit from managing your writing time more efficiently, as you'll see in Chapter 5.

My goal is not to get you to love writing (although that'd be nice), but rather to minimize your pain if you dislike writing and have to do it.

FYI

Tutorials are interactive lessons that come with software that show you how to use the basic, and sometimes more advanced, features of the software. You can complete a lesson in most tutorials in less than half an hour. Although many people avoid tutorials, going through them can save you hours of figuring it out on your own or developing your own "work-around" methods of performing an operation.

Problem: "I Was Never Good in English"

Many people's writing troubles began in school, which is reasonable. What kid wants a big book report or a huge paper on Brazil hanging over his head for five weeks? And when you didn't get good grades on these projects, it hurt.

Also, a lot of people have been traumatized by teachers who marked them off for word usage, spelling, and punctuation—even when they knew the subject matter. This doesn't make them feel good about writing and can create a life-long lack of confidence.

What Can You Do?

Realize that if you weren't good in English it doesn't have to ruin your business writing. Many of the rules you learned in school can bend, even break, with no loss of power, sometimes with a gain. Business writing doesn't have to follow every point that the well-meaning Miss Grundys of the world tried to drill into us.

Also, practice helps a lot. So can a dictionary and a writing guide like this one.

Problem: "I Have No Time"

Like anything else, writing takes time. I often wonder whether people realize that in many jobs writing is as important as meetings and budgets. We make time for important things.

Not having time can come from waiting too long to get started. If you have trouble with writing, you may procrastinate on writing projects, even short memos. (Writing can, however, go much more quickly for you. Taking the three-step approach you will learn in Chapter 4 will make writing easier and faster for you.)

What Can You Do?

If it's part of your job, make writing a priority, because it gets things done. If you are genuinely pressed for time (aren't we all?), there are ways to make time to write:

- ◆ Try to use the shortest form of communication that will do the job. Don't write a long memo when a short one will do, or a hard-copy document when an e-mail will do, or an e-mail when a phone call or voice mail will do.
- ◆ Carve out blocks of time for writing. Schedule it the way you would a meeting or a sales call. These blocks can be as short as half an hour. Most people feel they need hours to write, which is one reason they never find the time.
- ◆ Break up the writing of long, important memos into sub-tasks. For example, gather information in one step, do an outline in another sitting, write a first draft in another, then edit the draft in a final step.
- ◆ If you can close your office door, or at least tell people not to disturb you and let voice-mail answer the phone, do it.
- ◆ If all else fails, use time before or after hours for writing. Many people do this because they're on the firing line all day. If there's just no other way, it's worth it until you get to where you can easily pump out correspondence.

Tricks of the Trade

If English is your second language, you face a special situation. Spend extra time planning what you will write, and keep your sentences and paragraphs short. In fact, this is good advice for most business writers. Also, see Chapter 27 for some pointers.

Pitfalls

If you try to avoid writing on the job, or you discount its importance, you may hurt your chances for advancement. In most organizations, to reach or move beyond a middle management position you must display solid verbal and written communication skills. Many business people see such skills as a sign of education and even intelligence.

Problem: "I Have No 'Style'"

Many people feel that they need to sound like a cross between William Shakespeare and Danielle Steel when they write a memo. They feel they're supposed to sound smart or lofty or commanding or like someone they aren't.

What Can You Do?

Stop worrying. In business, it is *your* personal style as a professional doing your job that is supposed to come through in your writing. I'll talk more about this in Chapter 11. The more self-conscious you are about your writing style, the worse your writing will be. This problem goes away if you think less about your style and more about your subject and your readers.

Problem: "I Don't Write Well and Others Do It Better"

Many people compare their writing to others', and it doesn't do them any good.

What Can You Do?

You may not be the best judge of your writing skills. I've met many people who do not write nearly as badly as they believe they do. Anyway, you don't have to be A Great Writer to write great business correspondence. You merely have to make sure that you include the "Characteristics of Greatness."

When you see others write better than you think you could, look closely at the memo or e-mail. Analyze it. See how they do it. What kind of an opening do they use? How do they ask for action or help? How do they use specifics and examples to support their point? How do they leave the door open for follow-up?

Don't be shy about going to writers you think do a good job, complimenting them, and asking for pointers. Most people are happy to share and to talk about something they know and do well.

> **Pitfalls**
>
> Don't avoid or ignore criticism of your writing. Many people do just that because it can be hard to listen to. But criticism from people who know good writing can be your most valuable tool for improving.

Assessing Your Business Writing Skills

Now it's time for you to get a better idea of your business writing ability. Please answer the following questions as honestly as you can:

	Often	Sometimes	Never
1. When I face a writing task, I get on with it instead of putting it off.	❏	❏	❏
2. I enjoy writing on the job.	❏	❏	❏
3. I write correspondence quickly and productively.	❏	❏	❏
4. Before writing a letter or memo, I make an outline.	❏	❏	❏
5. I go back and edit my letters, memos, and e-mails.	❏	❏	❏
6. I have been complimented on my business correspondence.	❏	❏	❏

	Often	Sometimes	Never
7. My writing gets results; people respond well to it.	❑	❑	❑
8. What I write is clear to readers.	❑	❑	❑
9. I have been given special writing tasks on the job.	❑	❑	❑
10. On the job, I've been asked to write for the signature of another.	❑	❑	❑

Give yourself a two for each "Often," a one for each "Sometimes," and a zero for each "Never." If you scored 12 or more, you are probably at least an average business writer. If you scored 11 or less, you need to work on several aspects of your business writing.

The first five questions have to do with how you handle the writing process. Low scores here may mean you simply lack the information you need about how to go about it. Or perhaps you don't go about it the way you know you should. You will benefit from following the three-part writing process I present in Part 2).

Questions six through ten focus on the results you are getting with your business writing, with the way it comes across to others. Low scores here mean that regardless of how you are going about it, your business writing could be better. You will benefit by focusing more on how you present your messages to readers, and by applying the material in Part 4.

Where We Go from Here

At this point, the key is to relax and know that you are not alone. Most people have trouble with specific business writing tasks from time to time. (I know I do.) Other people find almost all writing difficult.

Wherever you fit in, please understand that business writing is a skill, not an art, and that doing it well requires a bit of work as opposed to a lot of talent.

The Least You Need to Know

- Most people have problems with business writing from time to time.
- Even long-standing writing problems can be corrected quickly with the right information and some practice.
- Finding time to write, one of the most common problems, can be overcome by scheduling the task, arranging for privacy, and doing the writing over several sittings.
- When you see business correspondence that works, try to figure out why.
- Ask for help and constructive criticism; if someone on the job writes better than you do, he may be willing to help you.

Chapter 3

The Right Tool for the Writing Situation

In This Chapter

- The differences among types of business correspondence
- Using the "cc" on a letter or memo
- The pros and cons of e-mail
- Choosing the right type of written communication

Most people think that the way to write is to just start writing. But throughout this book, I'll stress that it really pays to *think* before you write. Think about your reader, your message, and the best tool for getting your point across.

This chapter looks at the major forms of written business communications and their uses, starting with letters and memos, and then going on to e-mail.

Letters: Professional, Yet Personal

A letter is typically set up on *letterhead*. It begins with a date, an inside address, and a salutation, then continues with the body of the letter, before finally displaying the closing, signature, and the name and title lines.

If you own a small business or freelance, you can set up your own letterhead with word-processing software. While this will not look as good as letterhead done by a printer (especially done in color by a printer), it will be acceptable.

A letter conveys a more personal touch than a memo. Although the language in a letter and a memo can be equally personal, a letter lends itself to a less official, more informal style of communication. You should usually use a letter when you write to someone outside your organization.

A letter typically seems more personal and directed only, or at least primarily, toward the reader. Thus it's usually best to write a letter when you intend to address only one person or you want to create that impression, for example in a direct-mail campaign.

FYI

Letterhead is stationery that has been preprinted with an individual's or organization's logo, name, address, telephone number, fax number, and often, e-mail address and the URL (universal resource locator, or "address") for the individual's or organization's website.

Sample 1 shows an example of a letter on "homemade" letterhead. Good word-processing software offers a wide variety of fonts (styles of type) in a range of sizes, as well as a library of *clip art*.

You can incorporate graphics and artwork into your business documents for use in letterhead, or occasionally to add visual interest—but be tasteful and don't overdo it. We'll discuss this more in Chapter 9.

Sample 1 has each of the four "Characteristics of Greatness" discussed in Chapter 1.

The Coffee Klatch
901 Washington St.
Dumont, NJ 07628

March 9, 2006

Mr. Ralph Jones
Director—Career Development Office
Dumont Community College
345 Deer Park Lane
Dumont, NJ 07628

The subject line tells the reader what this letter is about right away.

Subject: Request for Job Bank Listing

Dear Mr. Jones:

We are a local coffee-shop chain with five units in the Dumont area. I am writing to you because we are often seeking responsible young men and women to work part-time, and we would like to list open positions in your job bank.

Our rapid growth means that your students would have a good chance of finding employment with us. Our standards of service and policy of job rotation give young people a chance to learn how a business operates. Students also develop good work habits and can move to positions of greater responsibility, such as shift leader and assistant manager. We offer flexible hours and a starting salary of nine dollars an hour, with annual raise reviews.

I would be happy to meet with you at your convenience at your office or at one of our units.

I'll call you early next week to learn how the job bank works and to see if you would be interested in listing openings at The Coffee Klatch. Thank you for your consideration.

Sincerely,

Lou Brown

Lou Brown

President

FYI

Clip art is a predrawn graphic or piece of artwork available in a word-processing package, on a CD-ROM, or on an Internet-accessible database. Often the graphic or artwork is in color. (Of course, you need a color printer to get that onto paper.)

Sample 1: "Homemade" letterhead.

Memos: A Bit More Official

A memo (short for memorandum) typically has a special format, which may either be generic or specific to the organization. You can usually pull a generic format from your word-processing software's library of templates, or you can create your own template. Also consider using the memo templates on the CD-ROM that came with this book.

The appearance of a memo is more official than that of a letter. A memo lends itself to a more formal tone, but the language you use in a memo can be just as personal as in a letter. (We'll discuss language and tone in Chapter 11.)

The samples at the end of this section show three typical types of memos.

Two lines on the header of Sample 2 and Sample 3 may need explanation:

The "Re" line lets the reader know right off what the memo is about. ("Re" is pronounced "ray" or "ree" and is short for "regarding.") Instead of "Re," the word "Subject" is often used. In Sample 1, the same device immediately told the reader the focus of the letter. A "Re" or "Subject" line also helps the reader file the document.

CAUTION

Pitfalls

A memo often has no space for a signature, as there is on a letter. This means that anyone could create and distribute a memo in anyone else's name. This dishonesty occurs very rarely, but to be safe, many people sign their initials—or sometimes their first initial and last name or first name and last initial—near their typewritten name on the "From" line. This is a good habit to get into, but it only applies to memos distributed in hard copy and not as e-mail attachments.

Don't settle for a bland or vague subject line. Be as specific as you can without getting wordy. For instance, in Sample 2, the line "Request for a Meeting to Discuss Expense Controls" tells the reader much more than a line like "Expense Controls" or "Meeting Request."

The "cc" line lists other recipients of the memo. The term "cc" (often written in capital letters) is the abbreviation for "carbon copy." This term is left over from the days when people used carbon paper to make copies when typing the original. Today, you'll also hear the term "courtesy copy." A "cc" can also be placed at the end of a memo instead of before, but always goes at the end of a letter.

Another device you can use when you have more than four or five readers to be "cc'd" on a memo or letter is the distribution list. This is a list of people who will receive their own copy of the document. It usually appears at the bottom of a one-page memo or letter or on the last page of a longer document, and contains the first initial and last name of each person on the distribution. Sample 3, found at the end of this section, shows a distribution list following Sue McFarland's memo.

Tricks of the Trade

It is wise to keep a hard copy of any letter or memo that you think you'll have to refer to in the future. Don't rely on your computer or disks as your only filing system. Set up a filing system that works for you and use it for important correspondence. You want to be able to lay your hands on important documents quickly.

Using the "CC" to Get Action

The "cc" can be a powerful tool for getting action from your reader, but you must use it carefully.

Consider Sample 2. If P. Lowy, cc'd on the memo, is Jack Entrup's boss, Sue McFarland's strategy makes Jack realize that his boss (Lowy) knows that she has requested the meeting. This puts pressure on Jack. Depending on the personalities involved, Jack may believe this is a threat or just keeping Lowy up-to-date.

Now consider the version of this memo shown in Sample 3. Here Sue has a distribution list of seven people. Whatever the personalities, it's safe to assume that Jack will not appreciate this move on Sue's part: Seven people now know that Jack's expenses are running over budget. The memo makes Jack look bad to a lot of people. Sue may be at her wit's end with Jack or she may have gone too far here, or both.

A salutation (Dear So-and-So) should never go on a memo. This is another way that memos are less personal and more formal.

Because memos have no inside address and a more formal look, they are usually used inside an organization. You don't always use a memo internally and always use a letter outside, but it is the way to go in most cases.

Memos to the File: A Record-Keeping Tool

Memos to the file are memos that you write as a record of a conversation or event. These are for yourself and for others, such as those who will fill your position after you.

This memo is a particularly good method for keeping a record of problems. Typical uses would be to create a written record of a verbal reprimand or to record promises from a supplier. Such a memo can be very informal, as shown in Sample 4.

A memo to the file can go into your own hard-copy or digital folder, or into a file that your company maintains on a supplier or employee, or both. It serves as a record, a reminder, and a piece of evidence.

Memorandum

Date: March 9, 2006

To: Jack Entrup

From: Sue McFarland ≤.м.

Re: Request for a Meeting to Discuss Expense Controls

cc: P. Lowy

Since expenses in your department are running about 16 percent over budget, I would like to meet with you to discuss ways in which we can get them back under control.

The discussions we have had up to this point have been informative, but not terribly effective. I realize that your sales are also running above budget, and that is good news. But your sales are only 8 percent above budget while expenses are ahead by double that.

I'm sure you agree that we have to address this situation sooner rather than later. Control of expenses will make or break our division's performance for the year.

I'll call you on Friday to arrange a meeting for early next week.

Sample 2: Typical memo.

—— Sue gets Jack's attention by "cc-ing" (sending a copy of her letter) to Jack's boss.

Memorandum

Date: March 17, 2006

To: Jack Entrup

From: Sue McFarland ≤.м.

Re: Request for a Meeting to Discuss Expense Controls

cc: Distribution

Since expenses in your department are running about 16 percent over budget, I would like to meet with you and Peter to discuss ways in which we can get them back under control.

I'll call you on Friday to arrange a meeting for early next week.

Distribution:

P. Lowy R. Brinner

C. Probyn   K. Mulvaney

W. Carter   M. Montgomery

D. Wyss

Sample 3: Memo with distribution list.

—— A distribution list lets you "cc" more than two or three people.

Memo to the File (by Vivian Singer) vs

March 17, 2006

The repairman from Acme Copier Sales visited us again today and again claims to have fixed the copier in the east hallway. This is the third time in two weeks they have had to repair this machine.

I told the repairman, Fred Stybel, that next time we will demand a replacement machine. He told me (in a friendly way) that I would "have to take that up with the office."

I called Mandy Kemp at Acme (212-555-0800) and told her of our situation. I mentioned that it was unacceptable and that we would demand a new machine if another breakdown occurred. I stated that this many repairs is not okay for a machine that is only four months old and is used well below the usage it is rated for.

Mandy said that she would have to deal with this situation if and when it happens because she believes that the machine is now fixed for good.

We will see.

Sample 4: Memo to the file.

Always mention the next expected step when you're making a record of a problem.

E-mail All Over

Chapter 4 covers this newest and most widespread form of business correspondence in depth. You'll also find coverage of e-mail and how it can be used in various writing situations throughout Part 4.

For now, the key point is that e-mail is *not* always the best form of communication to use. This is particularly important to grasp if you joined the business world in the past few years, after e-mail came to dominate our written interactions. To understand why, let's examine the pros and cons of e-mail, first the good news, then the bad news.

On the upside:

- E-mail is easy, and sometimes even fun, to use.
- You can send the same message to dozens, hundreds, or even thousands of readers at the same time regardless of their location.
- You and your readers can save your message to disk or print it out and save it in a hard-copy file, or both.
- E-mail can often replace the telephone, and work better. For instance, you can deliver a message when you don't have time to chat, and you can present requests, announcements, and ideas without dealing with real-time feedback.

◆ *E-mail services* such as Hotmail, Yahoo, Google, and AOL offer tremendous flexibility for storing, forwarding, and replying to messages.

◆ You can attach Word or WordPerfect documents—or PDFs—to e-mails instead of using regular mail, interoffice mail, or a fax, all of which are slower and more cumbersome.

FYI

An **e-mail service** provides e-mail capabilities to users, often for free (that is, in exchange for exposing yourself to advertising). These services enable you to set up an e-mail address and to send, receive, forward, reply to, and store e-mails. Chapter 4 covers the key features offered by e-mail services.

FYI

A **PDF** (portable document format) is a document encased in a special type of file, developed by a company called Adobe. The document retains its original format and can be sent, stored, and read by users with various types of personal computers. To view a PDF file, you need an Adobe Acrobat Reader, which you can download free from Adobe's website (www.adobe.com). The reader will allow you to view PDF files, but not make any changes to them. To make changes to or create new PDF files, you must own the actual Adobe Acrobat software, not just the reader.

On the downside:

◆ In a large organization (or elsewhere), someone may be reading your incoming or outgoing e-mail, or both. Some companies treat employee e-mail as private, but others reserve the right to monitor it. Be aware of your employer's policy in this area.

◆ The written record provided by e-mail can come back to haunt you, as several indicted executives can attest.

◆ The ability to reach multiple users encourages some e-mailers to send needless "For Your Information" messages to everyone on their address list.

◆ E-mail has wrapped an endless chain of jokes, gag photos, and website recommendations around the globe. While I like a good giggle as much as the next guy, this "humor" can distract us from our jobs. Add political ax-grinding and other *spam* and you've got a lot of deleting to do.

FYI

Spam refers to unsolicited e-mail about products or services sent to large numbers of people. Spammers get your e-mail address from e-newsletters that sell it to them, from newsgroups or websites where you've posted it, or from programs that they use to send e-mail to generate addresses, such as rsmith@aol.com, rsmith1@aol.com, rsmith2@aol.com, and so on. If you open or reply to spam, you dramatically increase your chances of being sent more of it. Take advantage of spam filters and the "mark as junk" feature of your e-mail software. Spam filters screen out obvious junk mail as well as e-mail from any source you list as junk mail.

CAUTION **Pitfalls**

Even if you use the right address (one of the basics), your message may be delayed because a recipient's computer or network is down or because of high volume at their end. Most e-mail programs notify you of delayed delivery and continue to re-send it at intervals. But after a certain number of tries (or if the address is not valid), you're notified of delivery failure. Delays and failures are all too common, and you should check to see that important messages have reached the recipient.

E-mail in Action

Here are some examples of internal e-mail messages. These examples reflect the proper style and form as well as typical situations where e-mail beats a letter or memo.

To: All Department Heads

From: J. McNamara

Subject: Meeting on Capital Budgets

We need to meet regarding the capital budgets for next year. I expect that it'll take about three meetings for us to get numbers on the table and to then work things through to the final allocations.

I'd like to hold the first meeting on Oct. 15 or 16.

Would you please get back to me via e-mail by the close of business Friday (at the latest) regarding times on those days that are good for you?

Thanks,

Jim

To: All Consulting Personnel

From: C. Delise

Subject: Stop Servicing Amalgamated Industries

CC: J. Brion

Effective immediately, PLEASE STOP SERVICING Amalgamated Industries.

After three years as clients paying us an annual retainer, they dropped their contract as of the end of last month. Therefore they are not entitled to any more service. But word has not gotten around to all personnel at Amalgamated, since we keep getting calls from some people there.

I realize this may be awkward, since many of us have built up relationships with people at Amalgamated. But we clearly cannot service a company that is no longer a client. Please explain this to anyone who calls from there.

If any caller from Amalgamated wants to discuss this, please refer them to me at ext. 2333 or to John Brion at 2343.

Thanks in advance for your cooperation.

To:	M. Redding
From:	F. Pollack
Subject:	Thank You!
CC:	L. Cincotta

Mike,

Thank you for all your great work on the Lewiston project. As you know, this was a really big one for our group, and it was thanks to you that the project got out the door on time.

I, along with everyone in the Northeast district, truly appreciate and applaud your work.

Best regards,

Frances

These are examples of business situations in which e-mail can be highly effective. For reaching a group of people with a quick, informal request or directive, e-mail is the way to go.

You can also direct e-mail outside the organization, for example to freelancers or even clients, as in the following example:

To:	L. Ropier
From:	B. Blanchard
Subject:	Report Covers Still Not Delivered

Lisa,

You were going to have the final versions of the report covers delivered to me here at Consolidated yesterday. They never arrived.

Please get in touch with me ASAP. We need those covers!

(I left a voice mail for you this morning as well.)

Barbara

The Impact of an E-mail

I've come to believe that a letter or memo can often command more readers' attention simply because it's not e-mail. They can open, unfold, and hold a hard-copy document in their hands, and see an actual signature on it. That said, many people prefer e-mail to hard-copy documents. That's especially true in certain industries (high tech and publishing), demographics (young people), and applications (internal communications).

However, you can always send a letter or memo along as an e-mail attachment. The impact of the attachment will not exactly match that of an actual letter or memo. You give up the signature, color letterhead, and control of paper and print quality. Also, the reader can always choose to read the attachment on his screen rather than print it. In those cases, the attachment lacks the tangible look and feel of a hard-copy letter or memo. Yet the attachment will retain the formality and the formatting of a letter or memo.

Bear in mind that e-mails you send on the job, like everything else you do on the job, will reflect the care, knowledge, professionalism, and character that you put into your work. Your e-mails will leave an impression on your bosses, colleagues, employees, customers, suppliers, and anyone else you deal with on the job. You want that impression to be positive, right?

Tricks of the Trade

Consider placing a standard confidentiality notice at the end of your e-mail documents. Many professional firms in the legal, financial, consulting, and health-care industries do this. The confidentiality notice typically says something like this: "The information in this e-mail is strictly confidential and intended only for the designated recipient. If you received this e-mail in error, please delete it immediately."

While the notice provides no protection against anonymous misuse, it does inform the mistaken recipient of the message's confidentiality and may prompt people to discard it.

Handwritten Notes: Very Personal, Very Proper

The handwritten note is becoming a thing of the past, which is too bad. Handwritten notes provide the ultimate personal touch. Until fairly recently, notes were *the* networking tool. George H.W. Bush and Jackie Kennedy were both famous for sending handwritten notes to friends and contacts.

Although today's informality and busy pace—plus e-mail and all-purpose greeting cards—have cut into the use of notes, don't discount them. They may seem a bit formal, but they still strike the right—well, *note*—on many occasions.

Handwritten notes typically express congratulations (on a promotion, for example), thanks (for example, for a luncheon or dinner), or condolences. They can also be used to keep in touch or to announce personal or professional news.

Although they are not as widely used as in the past, nothing should stop you from writing a note if you want to. Just be personal and write from your feelings—but don't gush.

March 21, 2006

Dear Jean,

Thank you for the wonderful dinner this past Saturday. Your years of living in Rome have certainly paid off based on the chicken cacciatore you served. Steve and I truly enjoyed the evening and will remember it for years to come.

It's great to meet such nice people when you're new to a city. Thanks so much.

Best wishes,

Judy

A note like this takes minutes to write, but can leave a good impression that lasts a long time.

Handwritten note.

When to Use a Letter, Memo, or E-mail

In Part 4, you'll see many cases in which a traditional, hard-copy letter or memo will almost always work better than an e-mail. Such situations include sales letters, proposals to clients, collection letters, employee reprimands, letters seeking employment, rejection letters, and letters of recommendation. In some cases, however, you can attach a letter or memo to an e-mail, with good results.

We'll examine these situations case by case, but in general use a letter when you …

- write to someone outside of your organization and want to have a greater impact or command more attention.

- need to reach only a few people with the original and cc's (exception: direct mail).

- want to send a document that's more personal and a bit more formal than e-mail, whether you know the reader or not.

In general, use a memo when you …

- write to someone inside your company, and you have more information than you can comfortably convey in an e-mail.

- need to reach many people with copies of the document and want them to have or retain a hard-copy version (for example, of an announcement that they should post in their departments).

- want a formal, official look and style and, as in the case of a letter, believe a hard-copy document may have greater impact or command more attention.

Use e-mail when you …

♦ reply to an e-mail message (usually).

♦ want to send a written message by the quickest possible means or to multiple readers, or both.

♦ want a speedy reply or need to exchange a series of short, back-and-forth messages, for instance about a fast-breaking project.

♦ want to send a letter or memo as an attachment.

Avoid e-mail when you …

♦ want the formality and impact that only a hard-copy letter or memo can deliver.

♦ know that the reader prefers hard-copy for the type of message you're sending.

♦ don't want a written record of your message (use the phone or meet in person).

♦ don't want your message to be readily forwarded to others.

♦ have highly sensitive or confidential material to communicate.

The Least You Need to Know

♦ Letters tend to be more personal and geared toward communications outside the organization, while memos are more formal and geared toward internal communications.

♦ A memo to the file provides evidence of a verbal conversation and a record to which future employees dealing with the same situation can refer.

♦ Use e-mail when you reply to an e-mail, when speed is important, when the recipient prefers it, or when you want to send attachments quickly and cheaply.

♦ Avoid e-mail when you want the formality, impact, and permanence that only a letter or memo can provide, when you know that the reader prefers hard-copy, or when you have highly sensitive material to communicate.

♦ The "cc" can help you get action, but be sure to use it with sensitivity toward the people involved. Don't "cc" someone's boss or colleagues in an attempt to embarrass them into acting; it will almost certainly backfire.

E-mail Mastery

In This Chapter

- Key capabilities and features of e-mail
- Writing effective e-mail messages
- Striking the right tone in business e-mails
- A few words on emoticons

Rarely has a new technology so quickly become so much a part of our daily interaction as e-mail has. Did I say daily? Make that hourly. Most of us receive more e-mail than we would like. On top of that, we have to reply to and write at least several, and sometimes dozens, of e-mails a day.

In this chapter, you'll learn how to make your e-mail stand out in any in-box. Before we get to the writing, let's briefly tour the key features of most e-mail services.

E-mail Basics, Bells, and Whistles

E-mail has evolved from a simple text messaging system to a full-blown communication medium. Thanks to the efforts of tireless programmers, e-mail is user friendly and equipped with an ever-growing array of features, which include …

- **Mailboxes and folders:** An e-mail account gives you at least one mailbox for receiving mail, and the ability to create "folders" for storing various types of messages. Many users maintain multiple mailboxes for different uses—for instance, business and personal—often at different e-mail services.

- **Instant reply or forwarding capabilities:** E-mail programs enable you to address a reply to the sender or to the sender and all recipients of the original e-mail with a single click. A similar facility lets you forward the e-mail, along with a message of your own, to whomever you choose.

- **Attachment-sending capability:** One of the best features of e-mail is the ability to send Word or WordPerfect documents, PowerPoint presentations, Excel files, photographs, PDFs, and even audio and video files as attachments to e-mails. Expanded capacity provided by some e-mail programs, such as Microsoft's Hotmail, lets you send very large attachments, provided your recipient has the capacity to receive them.

- **Multiple typefaces and effects:** Some e-mail programs let you choose various sizes and styles of font, and create effects such as boldface or italics and bulleted lists.

- **Copy and paste capabilities:** You can generally copy the text of e-mails and paste them into Word or WordPerfect documents and store them as files in the word-processing program. Unfortunately, you will often find odd formatting in the text of the e-mail message when you transfer it to Word or WordPerfect. You can either ignore the formatting *tags* or go into the document and format it as you wish.

- **Signatures:** Many programs let you create one or more "signatures" and, with a click or two, place one at the end of your e-mail. You can include whatever information you want in your signature, but it should usually state your name, company, department, address, phone and fax numbers, and e-mail address.

FYI

Tags are symbols embedded in a document that indicate various font and paragraph formats, such as bold, italics, underscore, indentation, bullets, and so on. Usually, tags are invisible, but they sometimes become visible when a document is copied from one program to another. Tags are also used to indicate format in websites.

CAUTION Pitfalls

Be sure to get permission before sending someone a large attachment, such as one with graphics or animation. An e-mail with a large attachment will be returned to the sender if the recipient's mailbox doesn't have room for it. Even if there is enough room, your attachment may take up the remaining space and cause subsequent e-mails to be rejected. Some people don't like large attachments because they have to print them out at their end (using their time and toner). Moreover, many people simply don't open attachments from senders they don't know or recognize, because of the potential for viruses.

Why Bother to Write Good E-mails?

Perhaps you are one of the many e-mailers who have been happily tapping out messages as your thoughts occur to you. Unless you are a remarkably lucid thinker (and writer), you are probably adding to the miasma of messy messages that each of us must plow through every day.

What do I mean by messy messages? The following example illustrates.

Marie,

thanx for sending the report before it went to clients . . . . . i glanced at it &
it doesn't look like some of them couldn't find some things to object to . . .
but i MAY MAKE SOME EDITS BECAUSE SOME CLIENTS CAN BE SENSI-
TIVE . . . we R the experts and they no that but some don't read what we
write . . . they read what they think we wrote . . . ;-)

If U let me no when it goes out i'll do it B4 . . .

BTW howzit going on the telecom industry executive briefing????

Betzee

Sample 1: Example of a bad e-mail.

This kind of thing clogs e-mail boxes around the world. It's also why you
should take time to write e-mails carefully and clearly.

What's wrong with this e-mail? First, this "style" is very distracting to many
readers. When you omit capital letters at the start of sentences, use nonstandard punctuation, shout at readers in all caps, and cop your spelling from the
Artist Formerly Known as Prince, you detract from your message (that is, if
people can *understand* your message). Second, the writing itself is unclear. For
example, the statement "it doesn't look like some of them couldn't find some
things to object to" features a double negative ("doesn't" and "couldn't") and
takes way too long to figure out. Saying "some clients can be sensitive" is too
vague, and the closing question about an unrelated project is out of place in
this message. Third, the writer conveys no clear opinion of the report or any
real information about the scope of her anticipated edits. Finally, this is not
businesslike communication.

Some journalists and teachers see bad e-mail as yet another sign of the decline of
civilization. It may be, but my view is more tempered. Most of us accept that
language keeps changing. Indeed, one real strength of English is its readiness
to accept new expressions from foreign languages (latté, shish kabob, ad hoc,
avant-garde, status quo, machismo), subcultures (bummer, rip-off, wipeout,
camp, chill, fly, floss), and technical and professional *jargon* (online, offline,
interface, drive-by, perp, sound bite).

Bad e-mail may not mean the end of the world, *but* the goal of language—and
e-mail—is to communicate. For instance, the terms "3:30 p.m." and "57th Street
and Fifth Avenue" orient us toward time and place. Likewise standard grammar,
spelling, and punctuation orient us toward what a piece of writing means.
Abandon them, and you may leave your reader stranded.

The following is another type of bad e-mail, featuring a "telegraphic" style of
writing. Back in the day when people sent telegrams, they were charged by the
word. So they wrote clipped messages: "Glad you arrived safely stop Charlie
wants meeting on 23rd stop Wants no more delays stop If okay comma say so
and I'll confirm with Charlie end." Telegrams were in all caps and allowed no

FYI

Jargon refers to
words specific to a technical specialty (plumbing or
computing), a profession
(law or medicine), or a
pastime (surfing or being
cool). Jargon is usually col-
orful "shorthand" that
keeps outsiders from knowing what the in-group is
saying. In general, avoid
jargon in your business
writing.

punctuation, hence the words "stop," "comma," and "end." Some people, including some too young to know what a telegram is, write e-mail in a telegraphic style.

> John,
>
> Got your e-mail re mailing samples. It's right on. Except time frame. If before labor day miss vacation people, or else September rush . . . vacation people may be bad . . . split mailing???. . . let's talk.
>
> Donna

Sample 2: *Bad e-mail in "telegraphic" style.*

They had better talk, because if John can comprehend anything other than a need for him and Donna to talk, he deserves Man of the Year from the Society of Language Arts. The message is too disjointed and the sentences are incomplete. The telegraphic style often becomes the telepathic style, in which your reader would need the gift of telepathy to understand your message. Such e-mails, along with those like Sample 1, are excellent arguments for using full sentences, proper grammar, and standard punctuation in e-mails.

FYI

Unclear e-mail has reached epidemic proportions. On December 7, 2004, a *New York Times* article, "What Corporate America Cannot Build: A Sentence," decried the decline of business writing skills, particularly in e-mail. The article bemoaned the hours and dollars wasted by people parsing or following up on unclear, unpunctuated messages. It may take a bit longer to write a proper e-mail, but it saves time, effort, frustration, misunderstanding, and embarrassment for all concerned.

Yes, but Is E-mail Really *Writing?*

The answer is, "Yes, but ..." The principles of clear writing apply to e-mail, yet e-mail is, in fact, a hybrid medium. It's an electronic medium because messages are created, sent, and received electronically, on screens instead of on paper, but, thanks to printers, it's also a print medium.

So e-mails don't require the formality of a letter or memo, but they are still business writing. They must be clear and understandable, and appropriate in style and tone for the audience. They must also do the job, whether you are requesting action, suggesting a plan, lodging a complaint, or delivering an apology. So in that sense, e-mail is definitely writing and, like all writing, it must communicate effectively.

Five Steps to E-mail Excellence

Follow these five steps to make sure your e-mails excel:

1. Write an interesting and informative subject line.

2. Have a point and state it early.

3. Be brief.

4. Gear your style and tone to your readers.

5. Spell check, proofread, and make sure it's right.

Let's look closely at each step.

Choose Loyal Subjects

The subject line on your e-mail is the second thing that most readers see, after your e-mail address. That line, along with the address, will determine the priority your reader gives your message. When you want immediate attention, make your subject line as interesting as you can, but don't go overboard. Subject lines should be factual, rather than hype. (You can, of course, mark an e-mail as urgent, but with overuse the effect diminishes.)

Here are examples of dull subject lines that have been punched up:

A Snore	A Wake-up Call
Revenue projections	Revenue projections due Nov. 30
Tuesday's luncheon	Talking points for Tuesday's lunch
Jerry's idea	I'm not sure about Jerry's idea
New phone system	Problems with new phone system
Reference checks	Future reference checking procedure

People are drawn to subject lines that say something. Of course, if your reader expects your e-mail, she will probably open it even with a sleepy subject line. On the other hand, she might assume you're offering a bland comment and leave it for later.

Some people find a "lead" subject line useful (like the "lead" that starts a newspaper story). These subject lines are actually the start of the first sentence in the message. Then the sentence, and the message, continues in the body of the e-mail, as the following example shows:

To: Tom Gorman

From: Joan Maier

Subject: I can't meet this Friday but ...

... postponing until next week would be better anyway. Paul Brenner, our VP of marketing, will be back in the office on Monday, and he'll be free any afternoon next week. That way, the three of us can meet at the same time.

The best times for Paul and me would be Monday or Tuesday afternoon at 2:00 p.m. or later.

Please pick one of these afternoons if it works for you, and give me a time. If Monday and Tuesday are no good for you, give me a time for Thursday or Friday afternoon.

Thank you for your flexibility. We're excited about moving ahead on this project.

Regards,

Joan

Sample 3: *E-mail with a "lead" subject line.*

In Sample 3, Joan could have used a subject line like, "I can't meet Friday," then started with "Tom" or "Hi Tom," and then explained about Paul Brenner and so on, but this kind of subject line can pull the reader in quickly.

What's Your Point?

Sometimes your subject line may capture your whole point, but often it won't. In any case, you should state the point or purpose of your e-mail in the first sentence, or at least in the first paragraph, of the message. Look again at Sample 3; Joan stated her point in the first paragraph. Rambling around is bad enough in a hard-copy document. In an e-mail, it's even worse, because the recipient is probably trying to read it on a screen, which is more difficult for most of us.

Be Brief

Do you like reading e-mails with big words, long sentences, huge paragraphs, and endless text? Neither do your readers.

Tricks of the Trade

Most e-mail programs allow you to create your message in Word or Word-Perfect and then copy (or cut) and paste it into the space where you would compose the body of the e-mail. This is a good way to compose long e-mails (again, if you must) and to better control the format and fonts. Also, some e-mail programs lack spell check, which all word-processing software provides.

Style: Formal, Informal, or Friendly?

In all documents, but especially in e-mail, gear your style and tone to your readers. Why especially in e-mail? Several reasons. First, most people will probably see more e-mail from you than any other form of writing, and some may see only your e-mail. So they will judge your writing skills by your e-mails. Second, e-mail encourages most people to use a casual writing style, so guard against being too casual. Third, remember always to consider readers aside from the addressee who might see the message. Are you cc'ing anyone on the e-mail? Might the addressee forward it to his boss? Could someone forward it to an even broader distribution list, including people you don't know? In business, you really can't go wrong by putting your best, most professional, foot forward.

Below are three sample e-mails from Ted with different levels of formality. Sample 4 is formal, written to Ted's boss. Sample 5 is informal, written to his subordinate. Sample 6 is friendly, written to a colleague with whom Ted is friendly.

To: Jim Greer <jgreer@acmeindustries.com>

From: Ted Jameson <tjameson@acmeindustries.com>

Subject: Progress report on product development

Jim,

Things are moving ahead nicely on the product development effort that you assigned to Barry Harnos and me. This e-mail is the first of the weekly updates you asked me to send you on the project.

As you suggested, we are going to start with a survey of our customers to learn about the new products they would like to see. Barry and I are putting together alternative survey designs for your approval. The key variables are the number of customers we should survey, the form of the survey (mail, telephone, personal interviews, or a combination), the length of the questionnaire, and the cost of the research project.

We are nearly finished writing the questions for the survey, and I'll have a draft questionnaire for your review by next Friday. Also, Barry and I (and Jeanine Taylor and Ray Bancroft) will be meeting next week to discuss the pros, cons, and costs of the various survey methods.

Best regards,

Ted

Sample 4: *More formal e-mail (to the writer's boss).*

To: Jeanine Foster <jfoster@acmeindustries.com>

From: Ted Jameson <tjameson@acmeindustries.com>

Subject: Please prep for our lunch next week

Hi Jeanine,

Just a reminder about our lunch next Tuesday at 1:00 p.m. with Barry Harnos and Ray Bancroft. I'll come by your office at 12:30 and we can drive to the restaurant (So Sushi) together.

As we discussed this morning, for that meeting you should bring price quotes and time estimates from at least three different market research vendors for:

- mailing and tabulating the responses to 1,000, 2,000 and 3,000 surveys with 15 to 20 questions
- conducting and tabulating the responses to 100, 200, and 500 telephone interviews with 15 to 20 questions
- conducting and tabulating the responses to 100, 200, and 300 in-person interviews with 15 to 20 questions

You have the samples of the kinds of questions we'll be asking and the names of the two vendors we've used in the past.

If you have any questions or want help choosing market research vendors to approach, let me know and I'll lend a hand.

Thanks much,

Ted

Sample 5: *More informal e-mail (to a subordinate).*

Pitfalls _____

Bear in mind that an e-mail can stand as a written record of any plans, opinions, and commitments you present. All the recipient has to do is save the e-mail. You may feel that you're just putting forth ideas, while the recipient (your boss, for instance) believes it's a plan of action. So be clear and commit only to what you can do and to deadlines you know you can meet. Otherwise, after an unmet deadline, your boss may send your e-mail back to you with the question: "What happened on this???"

To: Anne Abbott <aabbott@acmeindustries.com>

From: Ted Jameson <tjameson@acmeindustries.com>

Subject: Looking forward to lunch next Thurs.

Lunch next Thursday at 1:00 p.m. at So Sushi sounds great.

I'll bring our new market research analyst, Jeanine Taylor, along. You haven't met her, but she recently joined us from Whitcom Financial Services. Jeanine and I will have some information and ideas on the product development research for Jim Boyle.

I'd like to cover the following questions at lunch:

- ◆ How are we going to create and field the surveys?
- ◆ Which customers do we want in the survey sample?
- ◆ Are we using mail or phone surveys or personal interviews, or some combination?
- ◆ Which product areas are the most promising?
- ◆ What's our time frame for completing the research and recommending pilot product development projects?

We're investigating the form and the cost of the survey at our end. Jim is expecting answers to these questions by the end of next week, and I'd appreciate any thoughts that you and Barry may have regarding them.

Thanks in advance for your help.

Best,

Ted

Sample 6: Friendly but businesslike e-mail (to a colleague).

Check Your Work

Hundreds of thousands, perhaps millions, of e-mails are sent every day without their authors editing, proofreading, or spell checking them. That's a glaring lack of quality control on work that always benefits from it.

The beauty of the written word—unlike words we speak at meetings, lunches, and happy hour—is that we can edit or erase anything bizarre, bogus, or blatantly banal. Why in the name of *Webster's Dictionary* would anyone pass up that chance?

You'll learn about editing in Chapter 8. For now just know that you want to make sure that you read every message over carefully and edit as necessary.

Emotional Rescue

In the first edition of this book, I warned against the use of emoticons in business messages. Back then (1997), almost all emoticons were "home-made," with the smile :-) and the wink ;-) and the frown :-(being the most popular.

I still feel these symbols are best left out of business communications. But I may be in the minority, because since then a new generation of emoticons has sprung up in websites, Microsoft products, and e-mail software. These include ☺ , ☹ , ☺ , and 💣 among many, many others. An entire electronic cottage industry now supplies cartoon, and even animated, emoticons for every taste and situation.

I must be L7 (that is, square) because clearly, many people enjoy using emoticons, including people who regularly send me business e-mails. Their point isn't lost on me. Many remarks can be easily misunderstood in e-mail, where you don't have the instant feedback you get in a phone call or personal conversation. So an emoticon can let someone know you're kidding (even if you're not), that you don't mean it (even if you do), that you like an idea (even if you don't), and so on. To me, however, one of the enjoyable challenges of writing is trying to say what you mean in a way that respects everyone's feelings and point of view.

I recommend using emoticons—and only nonanimated ones—sparingly, if at all, in business e-mails. Then again, you're reading a book by a guy who likes to avoid using exclamation marks, so it's your call.

Pitfalls

One of the most important, and most easily overlooked, items to check in your outgoing e-mail is the address. Whether you are keying in addresses or clicking them in from your address book, it's easy to goof or go wrong.

In one company I worked in, a woman who had been viewed as very professional erroneously sent an e-mail, during business hours, to dozens of co-workers about a lingerie party at her house next Thursday evening. It was innocent stuff, basically a Tupperware party to sell panties and peignoirs. She had obviously clicked on the wrong list in her address book. Do I have to mention that many of the recipients (not me, of course) cheerfully forwarded the message to their own address lists, along with their, ah, comments?

She survived, but I distinctly recall her crimson complexion in the days after that e-mail.

The Least You Need to Know

♦ E-mail is fast, efficient, accessible, and convenient, and allows rapid transmission of text or graphic attachments. However, it isn't completely private or reliable, and it encourages many people to write badly.

♦ While you can bend the rules of grammar and punctuation in e-mail, it is best generally to stick with standard usage in all written business communication. Also, be sure to edit and proofread all e-mails that you send—in hard copy, if they are longer than a few lines.

♦ You can and should vary the style and tone of your e-mails, depending on the audience. Be more formal with superiors, suppliers, and customers, less formal for most e-mails to employees and colleagues, and friendly when you have a more personal relationship.

♦ E-mail can encourage emotional responses, so never send an e-mail, or forward one with comments, when you are angry, frustrated, or insulted.

Writing is Easier Than You Think (So Please Relax)

Do you enjoy writing? Does writing "flow" for you? Have you ever experienced the creative energy of having your ideas and words moving effortlessly from your mind to the page? Or is writing a chore for you? Is it something that you try to avoid? Does the thought of having to write a letter or memo turn you off?

The way you answer these questions may have something to do with your approach to the writing process. If you find yourself muddling through, struggling over every other word, trying to puzzle out what you're really trying to say when you write, the problem may be the way you go about writing.

Writing shouldn't be a hassle—if you know how to go about it.

Chapter 5

Three Easy Steps to Eloquence

In This Chapter

- How the writing process really works
- The three steps to good writing
- How to budget your writing time
- Dealing with "writer's block"

Writing consists of three separate steps. Master these principles and you're already way ahead of the pack. They are:

1. Planning
2. Drafting
3. Editing

Notice I said "separate" steps. It's important to do these steps in sequence. Begin with a plan or an outline, then write a draft based on that plan or outline, and finally edit that draft.

It's okay to do the three steps all in one sitting, but it is *not* okay to combine them into one step. And don't try to omit the planning or editing step. That's what a lot of business writers do, and it's where most of their problems begin.

Let's take a look at each of these steps—separately.

Step One: Plan (Decide What to Say)

By a plan, I mean anything from a formal outline like the ones you were taught to do in school—you remember, with the Roman numerals and the letters of the alphabet and so on—to a set of bulleted points on a cocktail napkin (not recommended, but often used).

Your plan does not have to be elaborate. This isn't school, so you aren't going to have to show your outline to anyone. Do it to get your thoughts on paper in some logical order *before* you begin writing your actual letter or memo.

How Planning Helps You

If you have trouble getting started with your writing, coming up with a plan first helps a lot. In the plan, you don't have to worry about grammar, spelling, or the quality of your writing. You are just jotting down points to cover.

A plan also jump-starts the flow of your ideas and helps you get all those ideas together before you start to write. You can see from your outline whether you have covered all the points you need to cover. From your outline, you will know whether you have to talk with someone, visit a few websites, or do other research before you write.

A plan simply represents preparation. It's a matter of being organized and professional in your approach. Would a builder start constructing a house without a blueprint? It makes as little sense to begin writing without some kind of an outline.

Does an E-mail Need a Plan?

Judging by the e-mail that hits my mailbox, some e-mail definitely needs a plan. However, as noted in Chapter 4, e-mail has replaced the telephone in many situations. You might be e-mailing a colleague to confirm a lunch or to ask a quick question that has a simple answer. In those cases, you don't need a plan.

But if you're describing a complicated idea or project, or making a request that the reader might resist, then a few moments of planning will more than repay themselves. Vague, unclear, disorganized e-mail results from the "stream of consciousness" approach, also known as "the brain dump." E-mail encourages that kind of writing.

If you plan your e-mails, they will be clearer, crisper, and far more effective. Simply adapt the techniques and tips in this chapter and the three that follow to your e-mail messages. Bear in mind that in this context a "plan" can take only a minute or two and can consist of three or four bullets or headers that you will briefly expand upon.

Tricks of the Trade

When an e-mail would benefit from a plan, key in the main point you want to make and two to four related details or supporting points instead of composing the message itself. Those points become your plan. The simple act of just setting things up in that way will create a more orderly presentation of the ideas. You'll also often cover points that wouldn't have occurred to you if you hadn't taken a moment to organize your thoughts.

Step Two: Draft (Say It)

Many people think that writing consists of just one step: drafting. People who write without a plan often find writing difficult, slow, and unenjoyable. But when you work from a plan, you can write very quickly. In fact, you *should* write the draft very quickly.

If you write quickly, from a plan, you have a good chance of coming up with something fresh. For many people, writing fast, and the demand that it makes on their brain, boosts creativity.

Here's a key point: Write your draft without editing it. Most people try to edit the draft as they write it. They go back and make changes, and then they change it again. They fiddle around with the wording and even the punctuation. They put the comma in. They take the comma out. Instead, they should focus on content.

The quickest, most enjoyable (or, anyway, the least troublesome) way to write a letter or memo is to:

1. Have a plan to follow before you write.

2. Write without editing until you have a complete draft.

Just write it. Don't worry about grammar or spelling or punctuation. Don't judge how it looks or sounds while you're still writing it. Wait until you have something to edit before you start to edit.

Step Three: Edit (Improve the Way You Said It)

When you have a complete draft, pull out your red pen and get to work. During the editing process, you should fine-tune the wording, correct any grammar and spelling errors, and correct or insert punctuation.

You can even pretend to be a real editor, editing the work of someone else, if you like. Some people find this useful because it helps them look objectively at the piece.

The Benefits of Three Steps

This three-step process delivers four great benefits:

♦ Writing will become easier.

♦ Your writing style will improve.

♦ The content of your letters and memos will improve.

♦ Writing will become faster.

First, you'll find that writing becomes easier. Planning, drafting, and editing are three very different kinds of tasks, each one necessary for good writing. When you try to omit steps or do all three at once, you make writing more difficult.

Second, the style of your writing will improve as your eye improves. When you make editing a separate step at the back-end of the process, you can coolly assess your writing style and make improvements. You are also far more likely to catch *typos* and grammatical errors using this method.

Pitfalls

The spell-checking programs in today's word-processing software will catch most spelling errors. However, spell checks will not catch errors that are actually words ("form" when you meant "from"), nor will they flag punctuation errors.

Tricks of the Trade

When you organize your information in a separate step—for example, by covering "The Five W's and an H": who, what, when, where, why, and how—you improve your chances of seeing what's missing.

Third, planning ensures that the content of your document will be complete and organized. When they don't plan, writers often leave an important point (or two) out of letters and memos. They forget to include basic information, like the time or place of a meeting or the price of the equipment they are recommending.

Finally, writing becomes faster because you have an outline that tells you what to write and when to write it. Writing becomes an automatic response to having the plan in front of you and having to get the memo done.

Organized letters, memos, and e-mails are a natural by-product of doing a plan and an edit. In planning, you gather your material and figure out beforehand the order in which you'll present it. In editing, you catch any omission or repetition, or anything that's not in the right order.

Holding off on editing until the draft is finished also speeds up the process and helps you overcome that old devil, writer's block. That's the feeling even professional writers get sometimes that they just cannot write. The best cure for writer's block is to use the three-step approach.

> **FYI**
>
> **Typo** is short for typographical error. A typo can be a spelling error, misplaced or incorrect punctuation, or just about any small thing that got in the document by mistake.

> **Pitfalls**
>
> As with planning, e-mail benefits from editing. Even a simple e-mail confirming a lunch can get the time or day wrong. On the telephone, your listener can simply ask for clarification, but not with e-mail. There she has to reply via e-mail ("Didn't you really mean …?") and you have to reply to the reply. Life's too short. Editing—and only editing—can ensure that you get it right the first time.

Run Around the Block

As you probably know, your brain has two sides. The left side (or left brain) takes care of the rational, analytical, and judgmental functions your mind performs. This side of your brain is detail-oriented, objective, and step-by-step in its approach.

The right hemisphere takes care of intuitive, creative functions. The right side is oriented toward the big picture rather than details, is subjective rather than objective, and is simultaneous rather than step-by-step in its approach.

Editing requires a rational, analytical, judgmental mindset. The problems that many people have with writing—they write slowly, they think it's no good, they think others do it better, and so on—often stem from editing while they write.

They write a sentence, look at it, and start crossing it out. They agonize over every word. They keep telling themselves that they don't write well. No wonder they hate to write! They are combining two tasks that are so fundamentally different that they actually draw on separate parts of the brain.

Writer's block, mentioned above, is usually caused by excessive self-criticism. When television shows or movies want to portray a frustrated writer, they usually show him sitting in front of a typewriter, typing a few lines, reading them over, yanking out the page, crumpling it up, tossing it toward the wastebasket, and missing. Time passes and those balls of paper are now carpeting the floor. That writer has failed to separate the editing function from the drafting function. (On top of that, he's probably trying to write without a plan.)

Overall, there is no surer way to improve your writing than to adopt the plan-draft-edit approach. But some people resist this approach.

Overcoming Resistance to the Three-Step Process

Having spent some years as a writing instructor, I realize that most people don't like to plan. They would rather dive right in and start writing—and edit as they write.

When people resist the three-step approach, they usually say one of two things:

"I don't have time to plan."

Or:

"I like to get as close as possible to final form on my first shot."

Let's take that first statement. It doesn't hold up. The time you save by not planning will be the time you waste by muddling through. Planning makes writing go faster.

If you're like most people who adopt the three-step process, you'll find that you do spend more time planning than you did before. But you'll also find that you save even more time by writing the draft much more quickly than you could before. And you can do that because you not only have a plan, but you have stopped editing as you write.

The second statement, about getting as close as possible to final form on the first shot, is understandable. The computer encourages such thinking because it looks like final form on the screen and it's so easy to move text around. But while it may look like final form, it is anything but final.

Typically, people who want to rush right to the final form aren't writing very well. Getting it done and getting it done right can be two very different things. These writers usually spend a lot of time editing as they write, often without realizing how much time goes into that editing. Had that time gone into planning, the draft would have gone more quickly and the final product would have been better.

Tricks of the Trade

Over time you'll find yourself spending less time editing as the quality of your writing gradually improves. Trust me, it happens.

Budgeting Your Writing Time

I asked people in the hundreds of writing workshops I led to tell me how they allocated their writing time across the three steps.

I usually heard things like, "0 percent planning, 100 percent drafting, and 0 percent editing"; or "10 percent planning, 80 percent drafting, and 10 percent editing." A couple even said, "100 percent on planning and drafting and editing—all at once."

I'm here to ask you to allocate about one third of your writing time to each of the three steps. This means you should spend about *one third on planning, one third on drafting,* and *one third on editing.*

For most people, this will mean more planning and more editing (separate from the drafting) and a lot less time writing the draft.

Even if you have only one hour to spend on a writing task, you should budget your writing time roughly into thirds. When I worked in big companies (and sometimes even now), I often had to get letters or press releases out quickly, sometimes in just an hour. In those cases I would spend about 20 minutes getting my information organized, usually as a list of points to cover. A point could be one word, several words, or a full sentence. Then I would review the points, maybe add a few or delete a few, then number them and put them in order. My plan was complete.

Then I would spend about 15 or 20 minutes writing a fast draft. After I had a complete draft, I would spend the remaining time—20 to 25 minutes—editing the piece.

I found this much better than thrashing around for an hour, trying to get by without a plan or trying to draft and edit at the same time.

As Easy as One-Two-Three

Millions of writers have found the plan-draft-edit approach to be the best tool for making writing easier and more enjoyable. And that includes me. These three steps free your mind to do what it does best at each phase.

Remember:

1. Step One: Plan (Decide What to Say)
2. Step Two: Draft (Say It)
3. Step Three: Edit (Improve the Way You Said It)

The Least You Need to Know

- Business writing is a skill you can learn, not an inborn talent.
- Writing consists of three separate tasks: planning, drafting, and editing.
- E-mail messages about complicated situations or requests that people may resist require a bit of planning. Review even short e-mails for accuracy and clarity, and edit longer ones for accuracy, clarity, and style.
- Perform the steps of planning, drafting, and editing a document separately, even if you do them all in one sitting.
- Budget your time on a given writing task as follows: one third planning, one third drafting, and one third editing.

Chapter 6

Step One—Know Where You're Going and Who You're Taking with You

In This Chapter

- Defining your message
- Understanding your reader
- Getting started on the writing process
- Creating a useful plan quickly

Too many letters, memos, and e-mails use too many words to say too little. Common reasons for this include:

- Being unclear about the point of your document
- Trying to make too many points in one document
- Blurring your message because you think readers will find it unpleasant
- Wordy, unclear writing

I won't worry about that last point here; it's covered in Chapter 8. This chapter deals with the first three points, because a good plan should address them.

An Exercise in Pointlessness

For your memo to make a point, you have to have a point. Please read the following bad example, a memo from a subordinate to his boss, and decide what it is about.

To: Susan Larabee, Director of Marketing

From: Cliff Richards, Manager of Customer Service

Date: October 11, 2006

Re: Office Space

This memo throws too much at the reader too quickly.

Given that we have added five new people to our staff in the last quarter, some issues have come up about office space. Gene Michaels, a grade 17, was hired in August and was put in a cubicle. During the interview process, he had asked for a windowed office because he needs light in the winter time. He says that he was told by Jeff Gleason in Human Resources that he could be considered for one. But his grade is too low for him to rate an office, certainly one with a window. I think this could be a problem.

At the request of Facilities Management we doubled up Maria, who also joined us in August, with Cynthia in Cynthia's office. Cynthia isn't too happy about this. Shouldn't Maria be in a cubicle? We would have to add one and since Facilities says you really can't add just one, we would have to add two. Maria is a grade 17 also.

Everett, who just joined us last week, is in the windowless office just to the right of the entrance to the department. He says there is a burning, electrical smell in there sometimes. Charlie in Facilities Management thinks it's Everett's imagination. In general, I don't think Facilities has been very responsive to our office space problems.

Also, there is our relationship with the sales force. They seem to think that Customer Service is their private staff instead of Customer Service. They have us doing a lot of work that their people should be doing.

A poorly organized memo.

What's the Problem?

People write memos like this all the time. What's the purpose of this memo?

It is clearly not a recommendation. There are a couple of questions in the memo, but no clearly stated request. And if the purpose is to inform the reader (that's my guess), it needs to present its point far more crisply.

On top of this, the final paragraph has nothing to do with office space. This reflects the overall lack of focus in the memo.

A memo like Cliff's tells the reader that the writer is confused, frustrated, and not on top of things. This is not the image any of us wants to project.

This kind of memo stems from poor planning, or no planning. The writer *seems* to have a point, but we don't know what it is. Unfocused memos like this just throw a lot of facts at the reader. Presumably, the reader is supposed to figure it all out.

It's your job as the writer to figure it all out—and then present it to the reader. Cliff's memo displays a common fault: He appears to be trying to figure it all out on paper, in the memo.

That doesn't make a good memo. Cliff needs to figure it all out and *then* present the result to Susan—as a request or recommendation or as information. The best

Tricks of the Trade

You may find it useful to think of your letter or memo as a product. A product is a reflection on the person or company that made it. A product also has requirements: It has to serve its purpose, it has to be of good quality, and it has to sell. If the "customer" ignores the product, you have failed.

response that Cliff can hope for with this memo is a call from Susan asking what the heck is going on in his department.

To Make a Point, You Must Have a Point

Before writing, Cliff should have decided what main point he wanted to make to Susan. His point could have been to make Susan aware of office space problems, or perhaps he could have recommended a solution. That recommendation for action would be his point. Maybe Cliff should request a meeting with Susan and someone in Facilities Management. If so, that should be his point.

Whatever his point is, he should not be blurring it because he hates to deliver bad news or he can't get organized. Instead, he should decide on his point, present it, and support it with organized facts and opinion.

Sample 6-A shows a better way Cliff could have presented this entire issue.

Pitfalls

In general, don't use memos to make your problem your boss's problem—or anyone else's. Use your memos to request action or to recommend solutions.

To:	Susan Larabee, Director of Marketing
From:	Cliff Richards, Manager of Customer Service
Date:	October 11, 2006
Re:	The Need for Additional Office Space

Given that we have added five new people to our staff in the last quarter, we're now very short of office space. I am writing to recommend that you and I meet with Facilities Management to work out a solution, or at least to improve the situation.

Here are the key issues, along with the approach I'd like to take on each one:

◆ Gene Michaels was hired as a grade 17 in August. He was assigned to a cubicle, but wants a windowed office because he needs light in the winter. He says Jeff Gleason in HR told him when he interviewed with us that he could be considered for an office. Jeff did say this, but adds that he never promised Gene an office. I'd like to find a way to get Gene enough light without giving him an office.

◆ Maria joined us in August as a grade 17 and should be in a cubicle. Instead, we have her doubled up with Cynthia in Cynthia's office. I want to talk with Facilities about adding a cubicle for Maria.

◆ Finally, Everett, who just joined us last week, says there is an electrical, burning smell in his office. Charlie in Facilities thinks it's his imagination, but I smell it in there too. I'd like a more thorough investigation by Facilities.

I'm prepared to meet with Facilities alone on this, but I feel your backup would help me get these issues resolved faster. Please let me know if I can set up this meeting with Facilities and if you could attend it. Can we talk after you've reviewed this memo?

— This revised memo does a good job of "setting up" the writer's problem.

— Cliff makes good use of bullets.

Sample 6-A: *A well-organized memo.*

Tricks of the Trade

Even some light research into facts that the reader will want verified or supported with sources will help you be a better writer, and a more competent professional. There's nothing like having your facts straight.

Except for the recommendation to meet with Facilities Management, the content is similar, but the approach is quite different.

- The second memo is organized and focused. It has a point, states the point clearly, and supports that point. Also, notice there is no mention of the sales force issue, which doesn't belong in this memo.

- It considers the reader's needs. The reader wants to know what is being requested or recommended. That is now clear.

- The writer did some research up front (verifying what Jeff told Gene, finding that there is an odor in Everett's office) and mentions that to Susan. In planning you must anticipate the reader's questions ("Is there a smell in there or not?") and answer them.

The entire approach in this second memo makes Cliff appear on top of things. Cliff did some research, laid out the problems, presented solutions, and asked for help.

Reader Analysis

To write a memo like the second one, you have to consider the reader and her needs. Meeting the reader's needs is the surest way to get your own met. After you have your point defined in your mind, ask yourself:

- Who is my reader?
- What does the reader know—and need to know—about the subject?
- What do I want the reader to do?

Consider the position of the reader. Do you report to the reader? Does the reader know you? Trust you? Is the reader basically interested in your point? Will he be supportive of your potential solution?

The answers to these questions will help you know what to write in your memo.

How Can I Help the Reader?

If the reader knows you, cares about the subject, and will be supportive of your point, you have a relatively straightforward task.

If you don't know the reader or think she might not be supportive, you have work to do. You must establish your credibility on paper. You must show the reader what she gains from the solution, or how the greater good would be served. You must give the reader enough information to go on.

How to Establish Credibility

Here are two of the highest compliments you will hear in business:

- "You really do your homework."
- "You're very organized."

When you hear these it means that you're on top of the situation, rather than the situation being on top of you. It means that others like the way you handle yourself in your correspondence. Until you are a famous CEO, "doing your homework" and "being organized" represent the surest ways to establish your credibility.

Do Your Homework

"Doing your homework" means researching a situation before writing about it. This may mean making some phone calls or meeting with people. It may mean a visit to a few websites or even to a library. It may mean a research project—for example, a survey of suppliers, customers, or employees. Or it may simply mean reading some files to update yourself on "the story so far."

Unless you know everything about the topic, research is the first step in planning. Even if you know a lot about the topic, having more information can raise your credibility. If you have research to back up what you say—if customers say it, if suppliers say it, if the *Wall Street Journal* says it—your credibility increases. And you have "done your homework."

Tricks of the Trade

One way to gather information to support your point is to conduct some quick and dirty primary research. (Primary research involves going to actual respondents; secondary research involves going to print and online resources.) Four or five phone calls or e-mail messages to fellow employees, customers, or even suppliers usually yield opinions, examples, or areas of concern that would be impossible to get any other way.

When you do quick and dirty research on the phone, write out your questions beforehand. Create a brief explanation of why you're calling, plus three to five questions on the subject. Write down the answers in the respondent's words. A quote or two from another source often makes a memo memorable.

When you use e-mail, you can cut-and-paste exact quotes into your documents, which is as effective as it is easy.

A word of caution: Make sure you have the authority to make these calls or send these e-mails. For example, in many companies salespeople get very upset when their accounts are called without their knowing about it. If in doubt, get clearance to make this kind of contact.

Getting and Organizing Your Ideas

After you've got your point, analyzed your reader, and done any necessary research, planning a letter or memo requires two final steps:

1. Generating ideas for your letter or memo
2. Organizing your ideas into an outline

Generating Ideas

In business writing, you often write to motivate others to follow your suggestions, implement your plans, and support your positions. This means that writing a memo often requires more than simply having a point, knowing your reader, and doing some research. It means that you may have to dig more deeply and, using your message and research as raw material, come up with a creative approach to the situation.

Today, it often takes true creativity to excel in business. Devising new strategies, solving old problems, and meeting competitive challenges require fresh thinking. Therefore, when your writing covers strategic issues, thorny problems, or competitive challenges, you should take another step before the actual writing in order to generate ideas that reinforce your message and move the business forward. Those kinds of ideas are what you ideally want to present to the reader.

How do you get these kinds of ideas?

Although ideas can hit you any time—as you shower, on your commute, while you exercise—there is a technique for generating ideas. A way exists to prompt your mind to come up with ideas. The technique is called *brainstorming*, and it can be a very useful tool in business writing.

The Brainstorming Technique

Brainstorming is traditionally a group exercise for generating ideas, but you can get good results doing it alone. In a brainstorming session, a group—usually four to eight people—spends as little as ten minutes or as long as an hour coming up with as many ideas as they can on a topic. Typical examples of a topic for brainstorming include:

- How can we grow faster?
- What is the best way to introduce our new product?
- How can we attract better job applicants?
- How can we increase productivity?

Brainstorming works best if you limit the session to one topic and push as hard as you can on that topic. Almost any open-ended question—that is, one you cannot answer "yes" or "no" to—can work as a topic. Also, you don't have to use a question. For example, the topic could be "ways of addressing our office space problems."

There are only two rules in a brainstorming session:

1. Everyone should mention any idea that comes into his head.

2. No one is allowed to criticize another's idea.

Both of these rules help the creative right side of your brain bypass the judgmental left side. Being judgmental kills creativity. Brainstorming overcomes judgment, and also produces a lot of ideas because one idea will generate another idea the way one firecracker in a string sets off the next.

In brainstorming, the goal is quantity of ideas, not quality. The more ideas you come up with, the better chance you have of coming up with some that are truly new and creative, or with a *breakthrough idea*.

FYI

A **breakthrough idea** represents a totally new way of looking at a situation. It's a new solution or point of view.

Creating a Brainstorm

Although brainstorming began as a group exercise, I suggest you try it by yourself when you plan a letter or memo.

After you've defined your topic and done any necessary research, ask yourself a question and write down as many ideas as you can. Do this as quickly as you can. The faster you go, the better your chances of bypassing that judgmental left brain.

Here's an exercise that will show you how this works.

Try It Now!

Pick a topic from your own work life. For example, you may have to write a memo or put a request in writing. Or you can choose a new topic such as "Why I should be promoted" or "Why I should receive a raise."

If you're not employed, your topic could be "Why I should be hired as a So-and-So at Such-and-Such Company."

If you have your own business, your topic could be "Why should new customers do business with me?" Once you have a topic, follow these instructions:

Allow yourself 10 to 15 minutes for this exercise, and …

◆ Write your topic at the top of a page or computer screen.

◆ Jot down or type as many ideas as you can on the topic; also jot down those that seem unrelated.

◆ Use up the entire time, even if you feel you're running out of ideas.

You should use all 15 minutes, because in the first few minutes you'll tend to come up with standard ideas. Then, after you "hit a wall," you may get a burst of genuine creativity.

Again, don't judge any idea. Write them all down. Writing down any idea that you get signals your brain (both sides of it!) that you are open to ideas.

Question Yourself

Another way to generate ideas is to ask yourself a series of questions, then answer them. The "Five W's and an H" traditionally used by professional journalists is one ready-made set of questions you can use: *Who? What? When? Where? Why? How?* Always ask "How?" in a business situation: "How long will this take? How much money should we budget for this?"

You can also create your own questions. Try asking yourself the questions your reader might ask. For instance:

- Is this costing us money?
- Are customers or employees being affected?
- Are there legal issues involved?
- What's been tried to solve the problem?
- What outside resources can we tap?

Getting Organized

After you have your ideas, it's time to judge them and organize an outline. Follow these steps:

1. See which ideas you can omit and which ones go together. If you have a lot of ideas, start with a fresh page for this step. If you have just a few ideas, you can group them by number or symbol. For example, put a "1" next to the ideas that go together, a "2" next to those for the next group, and so on; or use one asterisk, two asterisks, and so on.

2. Write descriptive headings for the groups of ideas that go together. You don't have to use the headings, or all of the ideas, in the final memo, so if you're in doubt, leave the idea in. In this step, you are creating the outline.

3. Look over the sequence of the ideas in the outline. Are the common ideas grouped together? Do the thoughts flow logically? Can anything be eliminated? What effect will the order in which you present the ideas have on the reader?

Your outline should look something like the one in Sample 6-B.

Topic: How Do We Solve Our Office Space Problems?

Opening: Introduce Topic

- ◆ Describe the overall problem
- ◆ Mention how serious it is

First Problem:

- ◆ Describe the problem
- ◆ Add to description
- ◆ Who is affected
- ◆ Costs and effects

Second Problem:

- ◆ Describe the problem
- ◆ Add to description
- ◆ Who is affected
- ◆ Costs and effects

Third Problem:

- ◆ Describe the problem
- ◆ Add to description
- ◆ Who is affected
- ◆ Costs and effects

Closing:

- ◆ Ask for action
- ◆ Mention follow-up
- ◆ Mention time frame

Sample 6-B: Outline or plan for memo in Sample 6-A.

Sequencing: First the Good News, Then the Bad News

Have you noticed that letters with bad news rarely begin with the bad news? For example, early-stage collection letters usually start out by noting that, "You have been a valued customer for years, and we want to continue that relationship."

Meanwhile, letters with good news—or at least what the sender wants you to think is good news—tend to let you know that right off. For example, "Congratulations, you have won a free test drive of the new Roadblaster Dream Machine!"

What's at work here?

Frankly, what's at work is management of the reader. Nobody likes bad news. So if the reader would see the point of your memo as bad news ("We will be doing away with casual Fridays from now on"), you should sequence the message so that the bad news comes later. Build up to it and help the reader understand the situation in context, but don't blur the message or take forever to get to the point.

If you have good news ("We are on our way to record profits this year and every employee will share in this success"), you should lead off with it. That way, you grab the reader's attention.

I'll explore sequencing more in Part 4 when I turn to specific types of letters and memos.

The Least You Need to Know

- You need a plan if you're going to write clear, focused letters and memos (and, often, even e-mails).
- To make a point, you have to *have* a point, so first decide what your major point will be.
- Analyze your readers: What is your relationship? What do they know about the topic? Will they resist your message?
- Brainstorming can help you get lots of ideas quickly. Remember to generate as many ideas as possible, and hold off on criticism or evaluation until later.
- Questioning yourself can help you generate useful ideas, particularly if you take the reader's point of view.
- The sequence of the ideas in your memo will affect the reader. Remember, you want the reader to read and keep reading, and to take the recommended action.

Chapter 7

Step Two—Get Those Fingers Moving

In This Chapter

- How to make a draft out of your plan
- How to sound like yourself
- Putting the reader in the picture
- The secret to writing quickly

How do you use your outline? If you can't read a blueprint, you can't build a house. This chapter will look at how to use the plan you created in step one of the writing process.

This chapter is about what most of us think of as writing: putting our thoughts into sentences and paragraphs. If you have ever had trouble doing that, you'll notice a big difference when you follow a plan.

How Do I Follow a Plan?

Once you have a plan, you have answered some major questions:

- What's my point?
- Who is my reader?
- What am I going to write about?
- In what order am I going to write about it?

So … start writing!

That's right, start writing. But "How?" you ask.

FYI

A **topic sentence** is the first sentence of a paragraph. It tells the reader what the paragraph is about.

Here's how: Take the first point on your outline and write that idea down in a sentence. That sentence is the *topic sentence* of your first paragraph. Develop the idea in that paragraph. Then move on to the next idea in the next paragraph.

One Idea per Paragraph

For topic sentences to work, you must write about only one idea per paragraph. Think of the paragraph as the building block of the document.

Many writers create problems for themselves (and their readers) by trying to get one sentence, one paragraph, or one document to do too much. So they write long sentences that no one can understand. They write long paragraphs with too many different ideas. And they try to make three, four, or more big points in one memo. You're lucky if the reader can absorb one big point per memo.

Tricks of the Trade

If you have trouble writing after you have an outline, ask yourself why. Do you believe in what you're writing? Do you need more information or research? Are you intimidated by the reader(s)? Do you have the organizational authority and responsibility to write what you're writing?

You may need to dig more deeply into the topic, get to know your readers better, or see if someone else can write the memo. Writing takes confidence. If it's lacking, find out why and, if possible and appropriate, build that confidence.

The Topic of Topic Sentences

Sample 7-A, a letter asking for a job interview, shows how topic sentences work.

Notice that the first and last paragraphs are only one sentence long. I put those in on purpose because I've met many people who believe that you can't write a one-sentence paragraph. You can. They are not at all improper, and they can be very effective.

Now let's look at the three middle paragraphs. Each of these paragraphs has only one topic, and that topic is stated in the topic sentence.

- The topic of the second paragraph is the reason for Lee's interest in working for Rincon.
- The topic of the third paragraph is Lee's sporting-goods sales experience.
- The topic of the fourth paragraph is Lee's interest in interviewing with Mr. Conway for a sales position.

Kevin Conway
President
Rincon Surfboards
999 Ocean Way
Redondo Beach, CA 09887

Dear Mr. Conway:

I am writing to tell you of my desire to work as a salesperson for Rincon Surfboards.

My interest in working with Rincon grew out of my experiences with your product. I am a three-time champion of the South Atlantic division of the International Surfriders Association. I rode a Rincon to each of those championships. I also won the Waimea Invitational in 2004 on a Rincon. I've tried other boards, but they don't ride like my Rincons (I own three of your boards).

More important, I offer a record of success in sporting-goods sales. As the enclosed resumé shows, I have successfully sold light boats and windsurfing gear to distributors throughout the South Atlantic region. Over the past three years, I have met or beat my sales targets in all but one month, and that was when Hurricane Ichabod hit the Carolinas.

I'd like to set up a meeting soon to interview with you for a sales position. I'll be in Southern California for the first two weeks of next month and would like to meet with you during my visit. Knowing that you're busy, I won't waste your time. As a surfing enthusiast, a believer in Rincon boards, and a successful salesperson, I feel I have a lot to offer your company.

I will call you next week to see about arranging a meeting, and I thank you for your consideration.

Sincerely,

Lee Shaw

Lee Shaw

— Strong topic sentences help you—and the reader—stay focused.

Sample 7-A: Letter (with good topic sentences) requesting a job interview.

What's So Terrific About Topic Sentences?

Topic sentences keep you on track while you're writing and they keep readers on track while they're reading. They keep you on track because if you limit each paragraph to one topic, you know what to put in and what to leave out of that paragraph. The reader stays on track because the ideas are logically presented.

As you write each paragraph, write down a topic sentence, then write sentences that develop that topic. These sentences will usually build on the ideas in your plan, but it's also okay to add new ideas.

Building Paragraphs, Sentence by Sentence

Before you know it, you're writing. You may have heard the old joke, "How do you eat an elephant?" Answer: "One bite at a time." You write a letter or memo (or a book) one sentence at a time. (Okay, actually it's one *word* at a time, but let's keep this manageable.)

How do you write all these sentences? I suggest that you write the way that you talk. This means that you shouldn't think about how it sounds but instead about what you're saying. Just say it. On paper. Look at the point in your plan, and write about it the way you would talk about it.

Think of writing as talking to yourself or to your reader as the words appear on the screen or paper. This technique is especially important if you have trouble writing. In business writing, you should strive to express your ideas clearly and concisely while sounding like yourself. You do it on the phone every day. There isn't one reason that you can't do it on the keyboard—provided you think of writing as talking.

Right now, I am not physically in the room with you and the ideas I'm expressing were put on paper months or years ago, but I am still talking to you. That is the mindset that I've developed as a professional writer. That is the mindset that you should develop. If you can talk, you can write great business letters and memos.

Tricks of the Trade

The better your plan and the more carefully you follow it, the better your draft will be. It will still need some editing, but usually for style and presentation rather than content.

Keep Writing

Remember the rule: Don't edit as you draft. Editing as you draft will slow you down—maybe to a standstill. You don't want a case of writer's block, do you? Then keep writing.

What if, as you are writing, you think of a better way to say something? What if you think of a better word? Shouldn't you go back and make the change right then and there?

No! Just keep writing. Before you know it, you'll have a finished draft. Believe me, if the change is worth making—and, very often, it is—you'll remember what the change was when you edit the piece.

A Few Words on Sentence Length

While you shouldn't worry about it at this point, I'll say a brief word here about sentence length. After all, the draft stage is when you have to write complete sentences.

Many memos lack clarity because the sentences are just too long. When a sentence is too long, it's tough for the writer to control and hard for the reader to understand. I'm not saying that all of your sentences should be short. You want variety and your reader does too, so aim for a mix of long and short sentences in most paragraphs.

Tricks of the Trade

Use longer sentences to convey information and to set readers up with the background they'll need to understand your point. Use shorter sentences to make the point. For example:

"During the past three years, we've tried many ways of selling the Supremo Widget, including direct mail, telemarketing, in-person calls, trade shows, and independent distributors. Nothing has worked. We simply can't sell it."

"What could be clearer? The product is a loser."

How Long Is Too Long?

There are some general guidelines on sentence length. Your *average* sentence should be in the range of 15 to 20 words. Your *maximum* sentence length should be about 30 words.

Notice that I'm not saying that all of your sentences should be 15 to 20 words. The average for all the sentences in a given letter or memo should be in that range. Nor am I saying that you should never write a sentence longer than 30 words. But if you do, be careful. A really long sentence is hard for you and the reader to keep track of, and it will raise your average. Then you have to balance things out with shorter sentences.

By the way, the reader won't notice the length of your sentences if you handle sentence length well. If you don't handle it well, bad things happen.

What happens? Short sentences sound choppy. Choppy writing irritates readers. They see it. They hear it. They become aware of it. It draws their attention to the writing. Then they lose track of the ideas. You'd be irritated if I kept writing like this. Right? I'll stop. Honest.

On the other hand, long sentences tend to wear your readers out as they try in vain to follow your train of thought and the development of your ideas and the content of your message way back from the beginning of the sentence, trying to see it through to the end without any kind of a break for them to catch their breath. If you put enough long sentences together, you will probably not irritate your readers, but you will put them to sleep, provided they keep reading, which most of them will not be able to do with their eyes closed.

Variety. That's what you want in sentence length.

What About Paragraph Length?

The basic rule for length—variety—is also true for paragraphs. Too many short ones create a choppy effect and make your memos look like pages of bulleted points. On the other hand, too many long paragraphs scare readers off with huge blocks of text. It looks like too much to read.

Paragraph Length Guidelines

In a typed letter or memo, you generally want paragraphs from a line or two long up to a maximum of about six lines or so. If you write a paragraph of more than six lines, you run two risks:

- The reader may get lost or bored with all that text.
- You may create a paragraph with more than one topic.

Notice that bullets, which you see used throughout this book, are a good way to make several points neatly. (I'll discuss them in Chapter 9.)

Remember, these are *guidelines*. I'm not saying that you should never write a paragraph longer than six typed lines. I'm saying that if you do, you should be very careful to keep the material under control.

CAUTION **Pitfalls** _____

When gauging paragraph length, think of readers viewing the document on their computer screens, especially with e-mail. Most of us find reading on a screen harder and more tiring than on paper. (Savvy website designers figured this out years ago.)

Yet many writers create e-mails and even websites with huge paragraphs. Some writers don't realize how much the space between paragraphs does for readers. Others just say, "People can print it out if they want." Well, sure, but A) Why make them do that when they are already reading it? and B) Unless readers take the further trouble of reformatting it, they'll still face huge blocks of text.

Short paragraphs help the cause.

Putting the Reader in the Picture

Readers of business letters, memos, and e-mails are always asking themselves, "What has this got to do with me? What, if anything, am I supposed to do because of this document or message?"

To engage the reader, put him in the picture. Essentially, there are two ways to do this:

1. Tell the reader what the material has to do with him.
2. Address the reader directly by using the words "you" and "your."

In Chapter 6, I discussed telling the reader what the material has to do with him. This means you have to tell the reader what you're requesting or recommending he do. If you are just conveying information, tell him that.

Focusing on the reader when you analyze your audience with questions like "What does my reader know?" helps you place the material in the reader's frame of reference.

Say "You"

Using the words "you," "I," "your," "mine," "we," and "ours" is also key in creating the personal style of writing preferred in business today. And the chief words here are "you" and "your."

Look back at Lee Shaw's letter requesting the surfboard sales job. She uses the word "you" right in the first sentence: "I am writing to tell you of my desire ..." She goes on to say, "I'd like to set up a meeting soon to interview with you for a sales position ..." and so on. Lee's closing sentence mentions "you" twice and "your" once.

People respond to this because it sounds to their inner ear as if you are talking to them. This is "writing the way you would talk." It's not a way of tricking the reader, but a way of placing the reader front-and-center. You are addressing the reader; why not address him directly?

The notion of being indirect or constantly using the *editorial we* is outmoded. There is nothing wrong with using this, but don't overuse it and don't be afraid to say "I," which is more personal and usually sounds more convincing. It is also somewhat outmoded to use the word "one"—as in "If one were to understand the situation, surely one would support me."

You'll find the "you approach" is used all the time in direct mail for one simple reason: It works.

> **FYI**
> The **editorial we** refers to use of the word "we" even when you are really one person doing the writing. In an organization, "we" can be used to create a sense of teamwork, but don't use it to sound official when you mean "I."

"Well, Jim ..."

Using the reader's name in the body of the letter is generally not a great idea. This is often done in direct mail (for example, "Like most writers, Mr. Gorman, you need to stay informed. That's why we're bringing you this special offer."). I'm not impressed with the personal touch of my name inserted by computer into direct-mail pieces. However, this must be working, because direct-mail houses regularly test copy strategies and drop the ones that don't pull in orders. (However, I'm seeing it less often over the past few years.)

I feel that in a business letter or memo, direct use of the reader's name is not useful unless you know the person well and it is part of your style. ("Jim, I know your people are already going flat-out, but our growth depends on your help.") Otherwise, it can sound forced or phony.

The key is to think about the reader and "talk" to him. Tell that other human being, person to person, what's on your mind.

The Least You Need to Know

- To follow your plan, take an idea from your outline and write it down as a topic sentence. Then develop the idea in a paragraph, describing that idea and building on it sentence by sentence.

- Keep each paragraph to one idea.

- In a draft, you can write sentences of any length. But get in the habit of keeping your average sentence length to about 15 to 20 words and your maximum to about 30 words.

- A paragraph can be as short as one line. In a letter or memo, keep the longest paragraphs to about six lines of type. Be especially careful to avoid large paragraphs in e-mails or other text people read on computer screens.

- Use "you" to put the reader in the picture. This means using the words "you," "your," and "yours," as well as "I," "my," "we," and "ours."

- Get in the habit of "talking to the reader."

Chapter 8

Step Three—Fast Fixes and Quick Repairs

In This Chapter

- ◆ What to do first
- ◆ How to identify problems in a document or message
- ◆ Eliminating wordiness and bothersome phrases
- ◆ Fixing what needs fixing, quickly

Congratulations! You have a draft. But now what? What kind of shape is it in? Will it take forever to get the letter or memo into final form?

No, it won't. Not with the fast fixes you'll learn in this chapter.

Leave It Alone

The first thing that you should do to a letter or memo you've written is nothing. That's right, nothing. Leave it alone. Get some distance on it. Don't look at it or even think about it for a while.

How long "a while" is depends on the letter's length and importance. It also depends on how you work and how long you have to get it out the door. If the memo is long and important, it would be good to give it more, rather than less, time to sit. For a short, routine letter or memo, you can get enough distance if you simply turn to another activity for a few minutes—make phone calls, visit a co-worker, or go for a walk. Leaving a letter or memo, particularly a long one, alone overnight is best, because the next morning you can see it with really fresh eyes.

For an e-mail of reasonable length, the time it takes to print may—along with seeing it on paper rather than on the screen—give you the distance you need in order to look at it objectively.

The amount of distance you need also depends on how quickly you can shift mental gears. However, unless you get some distance from whatever you write, you stand a good chance of missing the things you are supposed to see and fix.

> **CAUTION Pitfalls**
>
> If you ever write a letter, memo, or e-mail while you are angry or frustrated, definitely get overnight distance on it. In fact, a couple of days' distance and a chat with someone about it may be in order. Many a career has been scuttled because someone sent out in writing what they should not even have said.
>
> Once you've written and sent your letter or hit the send button, it's too late. When it comes to writing, cool reasoning from a set of facts will get you much further than anger or sarcasm.

Whether you have five minutes or several days, get distance before you edit. Otherwise, what you've written will tend to sound okay to you. Why wouldn't it? After all, it's the product of your own mind, and that's the mind you're going to use to do the editing.

So first, give your draft a rest.

Finding What Needs Fixing

As you edit a letter or memo, what should you be looking for? The major enemies to beware of are:

- Poor organization of the material
- Vagueness and lack of clarity
- Wordiness and gobbledygook

With these three things in mind, please take a look at the following example.

To: Mary Camden, Chief Operating Officer

From: Stan Spencer, Vice President—Sales & Marketing

Date: October 15, 2006

Subject: Our Year-to-Date Sales

I feel that I must bring to your attention the fact that our level of sales for this year is falling well below our objective for the year. This memo will convey the dimensions of the problems and issues that we face and some recommendations for improving the situation.

Our employee turnover in the sales area has been out of whack. Out of six regional managers, two are new this year and two others have less than three years of experience with our company. This might be okay in the software business, but it is not in consumer-packaged goods. On top of that, we have three openings in the sales ranks that have gone unfilled for the better part of the year. These problems seem to all be due to the fact that we have had a new compensation package for salespeople since the start of the year. Since then we have had trouble keeping and attracting talented salespeople.

Then there is the productivity of the remaining sales staff. The new sales call reporting system, which is based on laptop computers, is not giving us the kind of performance we expected to get. A number of salespeople have said they want to stop using the system because they spend more time fooling with the computer and the call reporting system than they do making sales calls. This is bad for morale, to say the least.

This year we are not going to be able to meet our sales targets and the company may as well admit this now instead of later when we can't do anything at all. We also have to get our new salespeople up to speed and we may as well forget about the new call system unless we can improve the user-friendliness of the system. The compensation system is a mess and can only be fixed if we go back to something like the old system that we gave up due to the fact that the commissions got to be so high. At least people were selling then though. I'll keep you updated. Meanwhile, I thought these problems should be brought to your attention.

This memo runs on and on, making the writer sound like he's not on top of things.

Sample 1: Example of a draft requiring a thorough edit.

Now, there's nothing wrong with this if it's a draft. But writing like this needs a thorough edit.

He Used a Plan—What Happened?

Stan did use a plan that looked like this:

      Paragraph 1.   Tell Mary why I'm writing

                        Sales are below objectives

                        Make her aware of problems and recommendations

Paragraph 2.	Turnover in sales department
	Specifics about people
	Cause: New compensation system
Paragraph 3.	Sales call reporting system hurting productivity and morale
	Salespeople don't like it
Paragraph 4.	Recommendations
	Get salespeople up to speed
	Forget new call system unless …
	Get back to old compensation system

Stan pretty much followed his plan, but now he has to edit this draft, first by looking for the three things I mentioned that usually need fixing:

- Poor organization of the material
- Vagueness and lack of clarity
- Wordiness and gobbledygook

Fixing Poor Organization

Overall, the memo is not too badly organized, since Stan had a plan. But it could be better. For example, the third paragraph opens with a topic sentence about productivity, when it is actually about the laptop-based call reporting system. It's true that productivity is a related issue, but Stan should mention the system in the topic sentence. ("The new laptop-based call reporting system has cut salesforce productivity.")

When you find poor organization of the material in your letter or memo, do three things:

Review your outline: Did you follow it? If you did, was the sequence correct? Don't go back and fix the outline and start over unless your memo is hopeless and you can see no other fix.

Check your topic sentences: Did you use topic sentences? Could they be improved? (That's Stan's problem in the third paragraph.)

Omit material unrelated to the message: Is each sentence in each paragraph related to the topic sentence? What can you omit without sacrificing clarity?

Fixing Vagueness and Lack of Clarity

Vagueness and lack of clarity often result from a poor choice of words, poor organization, or saying too little about the subject.

Stan's memo certainly includes vague language. For example, the *slang* phrase "out of whack" tells the reader little. "Out of whack" just means "bad." In this case "quite high" would be more precise.

FYI

Slang words are neither Standard English nor vulgarisms (for example, curse words). Slang usually consists of new words (such as "bummer" from the hippies), or old words used for new meanings (such as "bogus" to mean "disagreeable" rather than "phony," its actual Standard English meaning).

You'll find more vague language in the last paragraph. Look at the phrase "up to speed," another example of slang. Does Stan mean fully trained? Does he mean more productive? Does he mean selling enough to make budget?

We will discuss language and slang in Chapter 11. For now, know that precise Standard English words convey more meaning—and sound more professional— than slang. The term *Standard English* refers to the established, uniform, most widely accepted form of the language. This includes the accepted standards of spelling, punctuation, and word definition.

Fixing Wordiness

Fixing wordiness, a process called streamlining, represents the essential skill in editing. Even well-organized writing in proper English will be unclear and tough to read if it is too wordy or riddled with *gobbledygook*.

FYI
Gobbledygook is stuffy, pretentious writing. This often results from the writer trying to sound formal or official.

The fastest way to streamline a draft is to shorten just about everything. Take long paragraphs and make them shorter or break them into two or even three paragraphs. Break long sentences into shorter ones; replace long words with shorter ones. Get rid of every word you can without losing clarity or changing the meaning.

Take a look at the simple job of streamlining I did on the following page. Compare the marked-up version of Stan Spencer's letter with the final version of these two paragraphs. The underscored text is new.

Streamlined version of Stan's memo (first two paragraphs):

I feel that I must bring to your attention the fact that our level of <u>Our</u> sales for this year ~~is~~ <u>are</u> falling well below our objective ~~for the year~~. This memo <u>describes</u> ~~will convey to you~~ the ~~dimensions of the problems and~~ issues ~~that~~ we face and <u>includes</u> ~~some~~ recommendations for improving the situation.

Our employee turnover in ~~the~~ sales ~~area~~ has been <u>quite high</u> ~~of whack~~ for most of this year. Out of six regional managers, two are new this year and two others have less than three years ~~of experience~~ with our company. ~~This might be OK in the software business, but it is not in consumer packaged goods. On top of that, we~~ <u>We also</u> have three openings ~~in the sales ranks~~ that have gone unfilled for <u>most</u> ~~the better part~~ of the year. ~~These problems seem to all be due to the fact that we have had a~~ <u>Our high turnover began when we started the</u> new compensation package for salespeople <u>at</u> ~~since~~ the start of the year. Since then we have had trouble keeping and attracting talented salespeople.

Final version of Stan's first two paragraphs:

Our sales for this year are falling well below our objective. This memo describes the issues we face and includes recommendations for improving the situation.

Our employee turnover in sales was quite high for most of this year. Out of six regional managers, two are new this year and two others have less than three years with our company. We also have three openings that have gone unfilled for most of the year, while another three people are new this year. Our high turnover began when we started the new compensation package for salespeople at the start of the year. Since then we have had trouble keeping and attracting talented salespeople.

Once you have addressed the major organizational problems, clarified any vagueness, and omitted wordiness, you can work on style, punctuation, and some fine points—all of which I cover in Part 3. There I also cover grammar issues in business writing, which get a chapter of their own. The next chapter looks at issues of format.

Put Your Writing on a Diet

Punctuation is covered in Chapter 10, and style in Chapter 11. In this chapter on editing, I focus on getting rid of wordiness because it's the biggest problem in business writing.

Here are three additional techniques for cutting down on wordiness. These, too, fall under the general heading of streamlining:

◆ Cutting down bothersome phrases

◆ Eliminating redundancy

◆ Compressing modifying statements

Cut Down on Bothersome Phrases

A number of useless, old-fashioned, bothersome phrases have crept into business writing. Omit them or shorten them when they creep into yours:

Bothersome Phrase	Instead Try
due to the fact that	due to, because
a number of	several, some
each and every	each *or* every (but not both)
it has come to our attention	we've noticed (or omit)
it is important to note that	note that (or omit)
in the event that	if
please feel free to	please
at this point in time	now

Eliminate Redundancy

Redundancy is meaningless repetition—for example, "We drew some round circles." Some redundancy comes from carelessness, some from bad verbal habits. Eliminate it whenever you see it. It's so obvious in the following examples that I don't even have to show you the fixes.

- Final conclusion
- Brief summary
- Present status
- Past history
- Plans for the future
- First and foremost
- Possible risks
- True facts

Compress Modifying Statements

Watch out for the words "that," "which," "who," and "when," because they rarely show up in a sentence alone. They usually trail several words behind them. Often you can compress them into a single word, a combination word, or a single modifier. Take a look at the following examples.

Before:

In snowy weather, employees who stay late should use the east door when they leave the building.

After:

In snowy weather, employees staying late should leave by the east door.

Before:

Accounts that are under $500, which amount to about 15 percent of all our accounts, are those on which we lose money.

After:

We lose money on accounts under $500—about 15 percent of our accounts.

Editing the Easy Way

Here are five steps to doing a quick edit on just about any letter or memo.

- **Check for organization.** There should be a beginning that mentions the purpose, a middle that logically presents the material, and an ending that provides a true closing (instead of just stopping, like certain foreign films).
- **Check for completeness.** Is information missing? If so, can you get hold of it? If you can't, can you get by without it?

- **Make long sentences shorter.** Get the average sentence length into the 15- to 20-word range. Limit sentences to 30 words. Include a variety of sentence lengths.

- **Make long paragraphs shorter.** Aim for a mix of paragraph lengths, with none longer than six typed lines or so.

- **Eliminate all unnecessary words.** Get rid of every word that you can without sacrificing clarity. Omit bothersome phrases and redundancy and compress modifying statements whenever you can.

If you do all of this, you'll have an acceptable final letter or memo. Of course, you want to go beyond acceptable and on to greatness. That's what the rest of this book is about.

The Least You Need to Know

- Even if you use a plan, you will need to edit your draft.

- The first step in editing is to get some distance on the piece. On long, complex letters and memos, and on anything you write when you are angry or frustrated, try to get overnight distance. Print out e-mails longer than a few lines, and edit them in hard copy.

- Check for organization and completeness first. There is little sense in editing sentences and words if you still have to rearrange or add material.

- Wordiness is a major problem in business writing. Streamline your sentences by eliminating every word you can without changing the meaning or sacrificing clarity.

Chapter 9

What About Format?

In This Chapter

◆ Using format to get readers' attention
◆ How to use specific formatting tools
◆ When to use exhibits and attachments
◆ Overformatting and how to avoid it

Let's say you're sitting at your desk going through the stack of letters and memos in your in-box. Or you're opening e-mails from various sources. You're scanning them, trying to decide what to read, what to get into, what to act upon, and what to leave for later. You notice that some of these documents turn you off just by their appearance. Just looking at them tells you that you don't want to read them. Others seem to get your attention and pull you in. You're reading them before you know it.

What's at work in these documents? What is it that turns you off or draws you in even before you read a word?

Mostly it's the *format* of the document. That's the subject of this chapter.

Great First Impressions

Please take a look at Samples 1 and 2 on the following pages. Don't read them. Just look at them and see how you react upon first seeing them.

To: Jayne Campbell, Director of Human Resources

From: Scotty Weston, President, Acme Office Equipment

Date: November 12, 2006

Re: **Communication Issues**

We have to improve the quality of the communications in this company. I would like you to take the lead in this effort in your role as head of Human Resources. Customers regularly complain that they cannot understand the documentation we send out with our products and then that when they call for support, they cannot understand the explanation we give them over the phone. On more than one occasion I have heard complaints that our people seem confused themselves about our products.

Internally, at a recent round of informal breakfasts with employees, the issue of clear communication came up repeatedly. People said that they are not clear about our corporate strategy, about our position in the market, or even about who they report to at times.

We need to take a long look at our needs in this area and then do something. I suggest that we first systematically assess our needs, which might mean taking a survey, and then address those needs, which might mean training. There may also be some simple measures that we can take right away to improve things, such as making sure that the customer support people have been oriented to the products and that they have product samples in front of them as they take calls from customers.

Please give this some thought and present a plan for management's review and approval by the end of the year. While funds are tight as usual, I assure you that we can free up money to address this problem, and that you will have my complete support in correcting this situation.

Sample 1: A poorly formatted document ("before").

To: Jayne Campbell, Director of Human Resources

From: Scotty Weston, President, Acme Office Equipment

Date: November 12, 2006

Re: **Request for a Plan on Communication Problems**

We have to improve the quality of the communications in this company. I would like you to take the lead in this effort in your role as head of Human Resources.

Background: Who Is Affected?

Both our customers and employees are being affected.

CUSTOMERS:

Customers *regularly* complain that they cannot understand the documentation we send out with our products. Then, when they call for support, they cannot understand the explanation we give them over the phone. I've heard several complaints that our people seem confused about our products.

EMPLOYEES:

At a recent round of informal employee breakfasts, the issue of clear communication came up *repeatedly*. People said that they are not clear about our corporate strategy, about our position in the market, or even about whom they report to at times.

Potential Solutions: Assessment and Training

We need to take a long look at our needs in this area and then do something. I suggest that we:

- First assess our needs, which might mean taking a survey.
- Address those needs, which might mean training.

There may also be some simple measures that we can take right away to improve things. For example, we could make sure that the customer support people have been oriented to the products and have product samples in front of them as they take calls from customers.

Action Requested and Time Frame

Please give this some thought and present a plan for management's review and approval by the end of the year.

Statement of Support

While funds are tight as usual, I assure you that we can free up money to address this problem. Also, you will have my complete support in correcting this situation.

Sample 2: A well-formatted document ("after").

Which one would you rather read?

Most people would rather read Sample 2. Although I did break up a few sentences that were too long, the main difference between the two memos is in format.

Formatting Tools That Work

What formatting tools have been applied in the second memo? There are several:

Tricks of the Trade

The most popular fonts for business letters and memos are Times New Roman and, to a lesser extent, Courier, and for faxes, Arial. For e-mail, Arial and Verdana are the preferred fonts. Stick with these and you'll be fine.

- **A longer, more specific subject line in boldface type.** That kind of subject line grabs the reader's attention more than the blandly worded one in regular (nonbold) type in the first version.

- **A short first paragraph that states the purpose of the memo.** Remember, readers want to know quickly what the memo means to them.

- **Headlines in boldface type.** Notice that these headlines are descriptive. Instead of just saying "Background," the heading poses a question. Questions, either as headlines or in the text, tend to engage the reader. (What do you think?)

- **Subheads in regular type, underlined.** Subheads are not really necessary in a memo this short, but I wanted you to see how they work. They break up text further and add white space.

- **Bullets.** Bullets also break up the text and highlight important material.

- **White space.** White space invites the reader into the memo because the document looks—and *is*—easier to read.

- **Italics.** The words "regularly" and "repeatedly" are in italics for emphasis. Scotty wants to get across the seriousness of the problem.

Tricks of the Trade

As a rule, stick with 12-point type as your usual font size: It's the generally accepted standard. It's also easy for people to read. (The term "font" refers both to a style of type and a size of type.) 11-point type is acceptable at times, but it's harder for many people to read. If your company uses 11-point, use it internally, but use 12-point for external communications.

10-point type is too small for most people to read comfortably. It also puts far too many words on the page. Anything larger than 12-point looks too large and uses too much space.

Blocks of text turn readers off. It just looks like too much to read. A memo that looks like it's going to take a lot of work to read will lose the battle for reader attention. In contrast, one that looks airy and open, with short sentences, short paragraphs, headlines, bullets, and white space, will probably get immediate attention.

Remember, though: Don't go overboard! Sample 2 is about as far as you should go with format on a memo. Even this level would be a bit too much for a letter.

CAUTION **Pitfalls** _____

Don't go wild with format. You may be tempted to use all the fonts and effects that Word and WordPerfect offer—such as italics, underscoring, double underscoring, boldface, and boxes—all at once. Please don't.

Use these effects sparingly. Format and effects should never draw attention to themselves.

How Long Is Too Long?

Most people would rather read short memos than long ones. Knowing this, many writers try to keep their letters and memos to one page. For years, several large U.S. companies told employees, "If you can't put it on one page, you don't understand it." (The opposite, unfortunately, is not always true.) This often led writers to use narrow margins, long paragraphs, and small type so they could fit more onto the one page. This, of course, creates the dense, block-of-text look that turns readers off.

You are much better off going to two pages and presenting a more inviting, easier-to-read document.

Most business letters and memos should not go beyond two pages. Three- or four-page letters or memos are not absolutely banned, but they should be the exception. Relatively few issues in business demand such a long treatment. Much longer than two pages and you are really writing a *report*, which is outside the scope of this book (although the three-step process and many other principles in this book also work well for reports).

If you always write three- and four-page letters and memos (or have a reputation around your organization for writing them), put your writing on a diet. Either you're getting into overkill—writing beyond what you should to cover the issue—or you're in the habit of covering too many issues in one document.

Try to limit a letter or memo to one issue. Covering too many issues in one memo can confuse readers or make you sound unfocused or as if you're complaining. While one issue may have a number of areas, it's best to decide which area is the most important and focus on that. If you have several closely related issues, decide what the overall issue is and address that.

Regarding e-mail length, I've heard some business writing coaches advise against writing a message that requires the reader to scroll down. I disagree. Although I've wished that certain people who e-mail would follow that rule, I think it goes too far. Most of us are used to scrolling and we all do it when reading e-mail, particularly when we're looking at a trail of e-mails that's been forwarded to us. Yet if the reader must scroll through five or more paragraphs, especially long paragraphs, it's wise to consider attaching a memo in Word or WordPerfect.

FYI _____

A **report** is usually a summary, or the summary plus the details, of an investigation, analysis, survey, or other research. The style and the approach to the material is more formal and less personal than that of a letter or memo.

A report can run from 3 to 5 pages up to several volumes of more than 100 pages.

How to Shorten Long Memos

After you've done your editing, if your memo is too long (more than three or four pages), you can do one of three things:

♦ Write a short report instead.

♦ Write a separate memo (or two) for the secondary issues.

♦ Use exhibits to move material out of the memo itself.

Of these strategies, the first two are self-explanatory, but let's look at ways of using exhibits. (Exhibits are also called "attachments," as in Attachment "A," Attachment "B," and so on; I use the term exhibit exclusively here to avoid confusion with e-mail attachments.)

Using Exhibits

Suppose your memo has financial or technical details that take several paragraphs or a couple of pages to explain. Or you may have background information, such as a page of quotes from survey respondents or the summary of a study or other research. If you included this information, you would have a four- or five-page memo.

In these cases, attach an exhibit to your letter or memo and simply refer the reader to it. For example, let's say that you have detailed sales projections for the next three years for several sales regions, plus some footnotes, and you don't want everything in the memo. Just add these figures and footnotes as exhibits. That's what's been done in the example on the following page.

Then, in the body of the memo, direct the reader to the exhibits with a sentence such as, "Please see Exhibits A, B, and C for detailed sales projections."

You can also use exhibits for text material. Suppose you have a lot of technical details on some equipment you are requesting for your department. You can add an exhibit with the title "Equipment Specifications" or "Technical Note on Equipment Requirements" and put those details there.

An exhibit is a great way to show that you have done your homework thoroughly. Those who want or need to study the details can do so; those who do not can ignore them. But everyone will see that you did your homework.

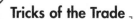

Tricks of the Trade

One way to provide detailed information to readers is not to include it with the memo, but to add a sentence such as, "If you would like the complete details of this analysis, please call me and I'll send them to you." Readers who want the details can get them; others won't be burdened with the paper. (This also saves wear and tear on your copier!)

Exhibit "A"

Sales Projections by District, Eastern Region

(in millions of U.S. dollars, 2007–2009)

	2007	**2008**	**2009**
New England *	5.4	6.4	7.8
Mid-Atlantic **	9.8	11.8	13.0
South Atlantic ***	7.8	8.2	8.8
TOTAL	23.0	26.4	29.6

* ME, VT, NH, MA, RI, CT

** NY, NJ, PA, OH, MD, DE, DC

*** VA, WV, NC, SC, FL, GA, AL, TN, KY

An attachment to a memo.

Other Formatting Tools

So far we've covered the basic formatting tools—boldface and italic type, under-lining, bullets, and white space. We haven't talked about clip art or the more exotic fonts. My advice is to use these rarely except in your letterhead, as dis-cussed in Chapter 3. In a business context, it's best to stay away from anything "cute," and that includes clip art and fancy type in the body of your document.

Charts

In practice, *charts* are seldom used in the body of a letter or memo, but inserting one or even two can occasionally be useful if they summarize data that supports your point dramatically. Be sure that any chart you present is accurate and properly labeled.

Charts can quickly present a visual story that you would need many words to tell if you were trying to describe the relationship among the numbers in a table. Types of charts include bar charts, pie charts, and line charts.

Charts are most commonly used as attachments to memos and reports. If you write reports, you should learn a bit about how to create charts. A *spreadsheet* like Microsoft Excel enables you to create charts in black and white or color from data you insert into the tables in the spreadsheet. Then you simply "cut and paste" the chart into your document in the word-processing program. Alternatively, and if you use a lot of charts in your work, presentation software like Microsoft PowerPoint enables you to create charts and easily insert them into text documents.

Including a small chart in a memo can be quite effective. Just be sure that it dramatically supports your point. Otherwise, it will look as if you are showing off. The following example shows a properly labeled bar chart.

FYI A **chart** or **graph** pictures the relationship between two or more sets of data; for example, sales and time periods, interest rates and loan vol-ume, or prices and profits.

FYI A **spreadsheet** consists of columns and rows that form "cells" into which you can place data, text, or formulas based on values in other cells. Presentation software provides tools for creating bar, pie, line, and other standard charts to use as exhibits in a text document or slide presentation.

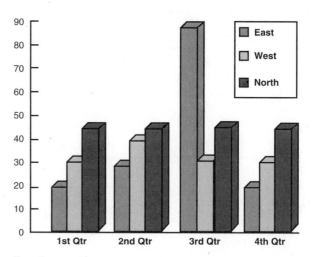

Quarterly Sales by District
(2006, in millions of U.S. dollars)

Bar chart.

Boxes and Callouts

Boxes call attention to information. With Word or WordPerfect, you can readily place a box around material to set it off or highlight it. Direct mail pieces or sales letters offer an opportunity to use boxes because you are trying desperately to get and hold attention and to highlight a real "grabber." A *callout* is a bit of text, either boxed or not, that points out or explains a point in the text itself. For example:

<u>Call Us Now!</u>

If you call our toll-free number (1-800-555-1234) to order your sample within 48 hours, we will include a voucher for a *20 percent discount* off your first purchase. Please act now!

In fact, the book you have in your hands shows you (I hope) how effective boxes can be when you have to present lots of information of different types.

The Least You Need to Know

♦ Large blocks of text turn readers off. Use formatting tools to create open and airy documents.

♦ The major formatting tools include a specific subject line in boldface type, a short first paragraph stating the memo's purpose, descriptive headlines and subheads, bulleted points, white space, underscoring, and italics.

♦ Limit your use of formatting tools in e-mail messages, unless you know that your reader uses the same e-mail software. Otherwise, quotation marks, exclamation points, and other punctuation will appear as symbols, while effects such as bold and italic type won't appear at all.

♦ Unless you decide to write a report, divide long memos into short ones, use exhibits, or do both.

♦ Formatting should support your point and make things easy for your reader.

♦ Use these tools sparingly and tastefully or they will draw attention to themselves and lose their effect.

Chapter 10

Where the %&@# Do the Commas Go?

In This Chapter

- ◆ A quick, straightforward guide to proper punctuation
- ◆ How to use—and not use—punctuation to make your point
- ◆ Going beyond the comma and the period to enliven your writing

Do you really have to think about all those commas, colons, dots, and dashes?

Fortunately, no. You just have to know a few simple guidelines regarding the major forms of punctuation. If you can handle that (and I *know* you can), you can use punctuation to boost the power of your message.

What's It All About?

Punctuation marks are a set of signs and signals, the kind you see when you're driving down a street. Punctuation tells you when to pause, when to stop, what's ahead, and where you've been. Picture the chaos on our roads if there were no signs or signals. (It's bad enough as it is!)

Can you imagine what trying to read would be like if there were no punctuation?

Punctuation helps you control the relationship between all those words you write. It also helps the reader understand what you're saying. Punctuation is essential to clear writing.

What Will People Think?

Consider this: In most organizations, many people know proper punctuation. If you don't, you look bad. If, on the other hand, you know proper punctuation, you and your correspondence look great.

Incidentally, you don't have to think much about punctuation while you're writing your draft (and not at all while you're planning). In fact, if you think about it while you're writing the draft, try to ignore it during that step.

Now let's take a quick tour of the major punctuation marks and see how to use them. For each type of punctuation, I'll give you a brief comment and then a few guidelines and examples. (I won't bother you with periods and question marks, which you already know about.)

Comma, Comma, Comma

The comma tells the reader to pause. As a writer, you should think of the comma as a tool for joining and separating words within sentences.

1. Use a comma to link two separate ideas that go together.

    Mark is probably the best manager we have, and that's saying a lot.

    Our sales are rising quickly, which means that our profits will soon rise too.

2. Use commas to separate extra information from essential information.

    Our company, which was founded in 1910, will soon celebrate its centennial anniversary.

    John McCormick, the president of our company, has hired a team of consultants.

3. Use commas to separate the items in a series.

    Marie, Jacques, Steve, and Diane joined us recently from our Canadian subsidiary.

    Increasing our sales, lowering our costs, or shrinking our business represent our only options.

4. Use a comma (or two) to separate an introductory or qualifying word from the rest of a sentence.

    Ideally, we should see rising exports in the next several years.

    The main issue, however, is how to increase investment in our region.

Tricks of the Trade

You can either put in the final comma before the word "and" or "or" in a series, or leave it out. Many people feel this final comma (properly known as the "serial comma") adds clarity; others see it as a bit old-fashioned. Either way is correct.

With commas, don't go crazy trying to remember rules. Instead, get a feel for where the commas go by reading your sentences aloud. Then put a comma where you would pause.

You can learn to use a lot of punctuation, not just commas, by ear. Your sense of how your writing sounds tells you a lot, if you let it. The best way to get the rhythm of your writing is by reading it aloud to yourself.

Colons: When Should You Use Them?

The colon indicates a longer pause. It says to the reader, "and here it is" or "here they come."

1. Use a colon before a list.

    We need the following items at the presentation: a projector, a stand, a screen, and a pointer.

2. Use a colon to introduce a major point or conclusion.

    The bottom line is this: We won the battle for market share.

    Only one person could possibly close this deal: Harry Jenkins.

If the item following the colon is a complete sentence, capitalize the first letter; otherwise, leave it lowercase.

Don't Fear the Semicolon; Instead, Learn to Use It

The semicolon mystifies business writers more than any other form of punctuation; therefore, most try to avoid using it. It's really quite simple.

1. Use a semicolon instead of a conjunction, such as "and" or "or," to link two equally important ideas.

    The company will buy more equipment next year; the new machinery will double our capacity.

    Asian management practices often find their way to North America; North American marketing ideas move quickly to Asia.

2. Use a semicolon before "however," "therefore," "moreover," "in addition," and other *transition words* and phrases that link two sentences.

    We need to raise prices; however, that is sure to lower our sales.

    Many of our workers want early retirement; given this, the layoff will be fairly painless.

FYI

Transition words are words that create special links between ideas. For example, they may indicate contrast (*however, nevertheless*), similarity (*likewise, similarly*), or order (*first, second, third*).

The Apostrophe's Uses

Many business writers are needlessly confused by the apostrophe. It's a relatively straightforward form of punctuation.

1. Use the apostrophe in contractions to indicate missing letters.

    I'll get back to you with an answer soon. (I'll = I will)

    The new copier can't handle the volume we were told it would. (can't = cannot)

    Using contractions in business letters and memos is now widely accepted. It adds a personal touch, because it sounds as if you're talking directly to the reader.

CAUTION Pitfalls

Writers often confuse different words that sound alike. Two common pairs are *its* and *it's* and *your* and *you're.*

"Its" is the possessive form of "it," as in, "This company has lost its bearings."

"It's" is the contraction for "it is," as in, "It's sure to rain this Saturday."

"Your" is the possessive form of "you," as in, "Mark your answers clearly."

"You're" is the contraction for "you are," as in, "You're sure to be satisfied with our service."

Be very careful with these kinds of words when you're editing.

2. Use the apostrophe to indicate possession.

Mary's analytical skills have improved during the review period.

The software's warranty will remain in effect.

 Pitfalls

Forming possessives for words that are plural or end in "s" can be tricky.

Correct:

My boss's office was professionally decorated.

Our bosses' offices were professionally decorated.

Incorrect:

My bosses office was professionally decorated.

Our bosses's offices were professionally decorated.

I Say, "Learn How to Use Quotation Marks."

Quotation marks serve three basic functions in business letters and memos.

1. Use quotation marks to indicate something said or written by someone else.

One survey respondent said, "You guys are miles ahead of the pack."

According to The New York Times, *personal-computer sales "will rise dramatically next year," and that's our forecast too.*

2. Use quotation marks to clarify a word or term that should stand apart.

When you click on "Help," a menu will drop down.

Please send a sample to everyone who chose "Very Interested" in response to question four.

3. Use quotation marks to indicate irony or humor.

The government's "tax breaks" never put money in our pockets.

Some employee "socializing" breaks up marriages.

Pitfalls

Be careful when using quotation marks to indicate irony or humor. It can easily get out of hand if used too often. Also, use discretion and common sense. For example, don't refer to your Chief Executive Officer as "Chief Executive Officer."

Also, periods go inside quotation marks, while semicolons and colons go outside. Otherwise, keep the punctuation marks with the text that they are part of.

Example: *The customer said, "Your employees are the most poorly trained I've ever seen." Then Jim said, "Why do you say that?"*

The Hyphen Is a First-Rate Helper

The hyphen adds clarity by helping readers know what words go together.

1. Use a hyphen to tell readers what words go together, if there is any ambiguity.

A strong marketing effort must be our first-line defense.

Fat-burning snacks are selling very well.

2. Use a hyphen in certain combination words when they are *modifiers* and not when they are *nouns* or verbs.

   We expect strong fourth-quarter sales. (modifier)

   We expect sales in the fourth quarter to remain strong. (noun)

   Follow-up steps will include more meetings and more memos. (modifier)

   I will follow up with all participants in this project. (verb)

3. Use a hyphen when you break a word at the end of a line of type.

   We've lost customers whenever we've lost sight of the fun-damentals in our business.

Dashes—How Dashing!

The dash is underused in business letters and memos. While overusing it would be worse, the dash—if used properly—can boost the power of your message. Don't use the dash (—) and the hyphen (-) interchangeably. The dash is longer and is used differently from the hyphen.

1. Use a dash instead of a colon (but not before a list) when you want to emphasize a point.

   Those who opposed our new strategy were correct—we lost business.

   We now know what we should have known all along— our price increase won't stick.

2. Use two dashes to set off a point that you want to emphasize within a sentence.

   To fight the toughest of government agencies—the IRS—was lunacy.

   Homebuyers who want low interest rates—and who doesn't?—will love our new plan.

CAUTION **Pitfalls**

Don't use the dash too often, but rather only when you have a point you really want to emphasize. Never use it more than twice (that is, more than two sets) in one letter or memo.

Parentheses Work Together (and Travel in Pairs)

In my experience, writers either don't use parentheses at all or they use them too often. This punctuation has its uses but shouldn't be overused. If you overuse parentheses, your readers will think you're always qualifying what you say or constantly adding little asides.

1. Use parentheses to set off extra material that you want to gently emphasize.

   Experienced people (and Karen is one of them) know that you need a plan before you act.

2. Use parentheses to set off directions to the reader.

   Our budget calls for a 12 percent reduction in paper costs (see Attachment "C").

   This memo summarizes our strategy for next year. (If you want complete details, please call me at extension 947.)

CAUTION **Pitfalls**

Put the period or other punctuation that goes at the end of a sentence outside the final parenthesis, as in the first example shown in 2, unless the entire sentence is in parentheses, as in the second example.

Wow! The Exclamation Mark

I believe that the exclamation mark (also known as exclamation point) should rarely, if ever, be used in a business letter or memo. Unless handled properly, it seems cute or juvenile or like something out of a gushy article in the company newspaper.

1. Avoid the exclamation mark in most letters and memos. It's better to find the right word or words to create the excitement you're trying to convey with the exclamation mark.

   Instead of: *Our sales have increased by 45 percent in the past year!*

   Try: *Our sales have bounced up a dramatic 45 percent this year.*

2. Use the exclamation mark only in special situations. Two situations in which I'd use the exclamation mark are in memos for certain announcements and in sales letters, and then mainly because readers expect it.

   The holidays are here! That means it's time for our Toys-for-Tots drive.

   You can cut your employee benefits costs by up to 30 percent!

The Least You Need to Know

- As with format, your reader and your message should guide you in punctuation. Don't use punctuation to get cute or to show off. (I do some of that in this book—but this is a book. Use the sample letters and memos in this book and on the CD-ROM as models, not the text!)

- Be careful in formatting e-mail, because your readers' systems may be different and items such as dashes, quotation marks, and exclamation points can show up in the message at their end as distracting symbols.

- Get used to the colon and semicolon; they can help you link ideas without using another word.

- Don't overuse any form of punctuation, even commas. Be especially careful not to overuse dashes and parentheses, and use the exclamation mark rarely.

- You can quickly get to a point where you can do most punctuation by ear. Train your ear by reading your letters and memos aloud to yourself for a while.

Part  Polishing Your Correspondence

To bring your correspondence to truly professional levels requires one final bit of polish. With that final polish, you present yourself and your ideas to your readers in exactly the right way. That comes down to style. Sometimes you'll want to be formal and a bit impersonal. Other times you'll want to be informal and make strong personal connections. At all times, you'll want to avoid being either stuffy, on the one hand, or, on the other, breezy or unprofessional. There are easy ways to achieve the right style.

In these three easy chapters, you'll learn how to add that final polish that marks you as a professional. Your readers will thank you, and your letters, memos, and e-mails will be welcome wherever they go.

Put Your Personality into Your Writing

In This Chapter

- ◆ Understanding writing style
- ◆ Choosing the right style for each document
- ◆ Structuring sentences for maximum impact
- ◆ How to adjust your writing style

Part 2 showed you how to get your ideas down on paper and into a document. This chapter is about how to make your writing really stand out. It's about how you present your personality in writing—and how much of your personality you present. This in turn depends on your audience, and on the kind of correspondence you're writing.

One thing is certain: You can't always use the same style and still write great letters and memos. So let's talk about how to be stylish.

What Is Style?

Style refers to the *way* in which something is done—as opposed to that something's content or substance. We all get dressed, but we dress in different styles. Many athletes who play the same sport, even the same position, have very different styles of play. Motion pictures are shot by exposing strips of film to light at 24 frames per second, but directors shoot movies in many different styles.

In writing, style centers on how much of your personality you show along with the material. Consider the following two memos, which both have very similar content.

To: Michael DeCamp

From: Jonas Erstadt

Re: Marketing Needs Task Force

You have been chosen as a member of the Marketing Needs Task Force. The task force will hold its first meeting on the first Thursday of next month and will meet on the first Thursday of each month thereafter until the end of the year. The goals of the task force are to assess the strengths and weaknesses of our current marketing operation in light of our customer base, the market place, and our product line.

You have been designated as the representative from the Technology Department in order to bring the perspective of that area to the marketing challenges we face as a company.

Please report to Room 714 at 9:00 a.m. on the first Thursday of the month for the initial meeting of the task force.

To: Michael DeCamp

From: Jonas Erstadt

Re: Marketing Needs Task Force

Congratulations. You've been chosen as a member of the Marketing Needs Task Force. We'll be meeting on the first Thursday of every month, from next month to the end of the year. Our goal is to assess the company's strengths and weaknesses in marketing, given our customers, markets, and products.

You'll be the task force's Technology Department representative. We need the perspective you can bring to the group.

Our first meeting will be in Room 714 at 9:00 a.m. on the first Thursday of next month. I look forward to working with you.

The style of the second memo is much more personal, isn't it? It's more personal because the writer talks more directly to the reader. He addresses the reader in a more personal way. He talks to the reader as a person instead of presenting the information in a way that maintains distance. Style is about how much of your personality you present along with the material.

Shouldn't We Write Just the Way We Talk?

I did say that we should write the way we talk, and it's still great advice. Many business writers have trouble writing because they feel they should sound like professors from Oxford, resulting in an overly formal, stuffy way of writing. It's much better to sound like yourself on paper—but how *much* of yourself you should present along with the content is another story.

Here, as in other aspects of writing, it comes down to the subject and the reader. Going back to the two sample memos used earlier, you might adopt the more formal style of the first memo if you didn't know the reader, especially if you were in a senior position to him. However, if you know the reader and expect to work closely with him on the project, the style of the second memo would be better.

Your choice of style also depends on how formal the company is, which can vary among the functions within an organization. If you are a manager, you're going to run into many writing situations that call for a formal, impersonal approach. Delivering a written reprimand is a good example. You are focused only on the employee's behavior and how it must change. You're not trying to be personal; in fact, you want to maintain distance from the material you must deliver. There is a risk that the employee will fail to improve and will become an ex-employee. Under the circumstances, a personal approach would not be appropriate.

Tricks of the Trade

Every organization has its own style. You can learn about a company's style by looking at its website, product literature, and the documents the employees write.

Choosing the Right Style

As with how you dress, it's useful to think of writing style according to how formal or informal you should be for the occasion.

A formal style is best when you are focused exclusively on the material. Manuals, textbooks, and academic journals are good examples of a formal style; so are police, medical, and insurance reports. All have in common the goal of presenting material as objectively as possible.

An informal style is best when you're relating to the reader as a person as well as relating the material to the reader. For instance, when you want to get attention, generate enthusiasm, or win cooperation, you should use an informal style. Formal writing, no matter how eloquent, creates too much distance between writer and reader to forge much of a relationship—and in most (but not all) correspondence, you are trying to forge relationships. Business writing should be clear, direct, and interesting to the reader.

Pitfalls

You can get into trouble by choosing the wrong writing style. If you are overly formal, you may appear awkward or cold. If you are too informal, you might seem immature. The correct writing style will put you in the best light.

Here is a range of writing styles:

Stuffy ↔ Formal ↔ Personal ↔ Informal ↔ Casual

Business writing should never be stuffy or overly formal. On the other hand, it should never be too casual or chatty, either, except perhaps in e-mail messages to people you know and regularly communicate with by e-mail.

In most letters and memos, you should strive for a personal style. Just "talk to the reader" in a matter-of-fact way about the material. Address the reader directly about common goals, what you're trying to accomplish, and what you need from him. A style in the personal-to-informal range is the one to use for most letters and memos to someone you know inside or outside the organization.

You can be informal and even casual in certain announcements; for example, one about the division's softball league or the company picnic. Other kinds of announcements, especially difficult ones like announcements of layoffs, require a more formal style to distance the writer from the unpleasant facts. Reprimands and letters of termination call for a formal style.

Sales letters should be in a personal style, but the style of a proposal should be more formal. That's because a proposal is more in the nature of a contract (a legally binding agreement) than a sales letter.

Business letters you write for personal reasons should take a personal tone. These include most thank-you letters and written apologies. Letters of rejection, however, should be in a fairly formal (but not totally impersonal) style, reflecting that you are not rejecting the reader—only his proposal or request.

Cover letters and other letters to potential employees or clients should have a personal but not casual style.

Let's Get Stylish

So how do you approach the issue of style? Whenever you sit down to write, three factors will shape what you create:

- ◆ Your approach to the material
- ◆ How you address the reader
- ◆ Word choice and sentence structure

Let's look at each of these separately.

Your Approach to the Material

Your approach to the material has to do with your mindset. The more objective your view of the material, the more formal your writing about it will be. By an "objective" view, I mean you're not personally involved. The more personally involved you are with the material, the more personal your writing about it will be.

A scientist writing up the results of an experiment must use an impersonal, formal style, even if he has devoted three years of his life to the experiment. He must at least appear to be personally uninvolved and to have an objective view of the material. Yet that same scientist writing a love letter had better be personally involved and put some emotion into it, or his ladylove might feel she's part of a failed experiment.

Compare these two paragraphs:

Regarding the prices of our products, respondents to our recent survey were negative: One third of them stated that if they could buy from another supplier, they would.

Clearly we are making enemies with our high prices. Many customers can't stand it. An astonishing one third of the respondents to our recent survey would leave us if they could only find another supplier.

Tricks of the Trade

There will be times in business when you might not feel objective but have to adopt that posture—fake it, to use the technical term—in order to get your point across. There is nothing wrong with that.

Isn't the first paragraph more objective? It presents the material and lets it speak for itself. The writer's approach in the second paragraph is not objective. In fact, that writer goes well beyond the material to state that the company is making enemies, the customers can't stand the high prices, and that the one third is "astonishing." She may be right, but she's not objective.

Either approach to the material can work, but which one you should use depends on the situation. If you were trying to simply report the survey results, you would use the approach in the first paragraph. If you were trying to persuade someone that the company's prices are too high, you might be better off with the second approach.

The key is to be conscious of your approach to the material, and to use the right one.

How You Address the Reader

As I wrote in Chapter 7, the more you use the words "we," "I," "me," "you," "us," and "ours," the more personal your writing will sound. Those pronouns are a big part of our daily conversations because they enable us to relate to others. To drop them from our writing when we are supposed to sound personal doesn't make sense.

By the same token, it stands to reason that if you want a more formal approach, you'll want to minimize your use of such words, especially the word "you." Instead of "we," use the term "the company" or "our organization" or the company name. If you're referring to your department, say "the department" or, if they report to you, "my people." Instead of "our goals" say "the company's goals" or "the department's goals."

Another issue is how directly you address the reader. Which sentence strikes you as more personal?

> *In the future, employees should park in the south section of the lot unless there is snow on the ground.*

> *In the future, please park in the south section of the lot unless there is snow on the ground.*

Most people would say that the second sentence is more personal. The writer is directing the comment to the reader and asking the reader to do something ("please park") rather than stating a more objective fact ("employees should park"). The second sentence has more impact, doesn't it?

Word Choice and Sentence Structure

Business letters and memos should be written in Standard English. However, Standard English allows for a wide range of styles.

Pitfalls

E-mail is inherently a more informal and personal medium than hard-copy correspondence. Therefore, in general, if you must be formal—for instance, when you write a reprimand or a collection letter—use a hard-copy document or attach a Word or WordPerfect file to the e-mail.

Within Standard English, watch out for those 25-cent words, the *polysyllables*. The more of them you use, the more formal your writing will sound. It can quickly make your work sound stuffy, as in the following example:

> *We need to facilitate the implementation of this plan immediately or maintenance of the company's revenue position will be impossible.*

...which can be translated as:

> *We must act on this plan right now or we will lose sales.*

It's best to minimize your use of certain formal-sounding phrases if you want your writing to sound personal. Otherwise, there's the danger that your writing will take on an overly formal, even pompous style. Here's a list of some overly formal phrases, along with some good substitutes:

FYI

Polysyllabic words, or polysyllables, are words that have more than three syllables.

Too Formal	Substitute
Enclosed please find	I've enclosed
In view of this	Given this
In the amount of	For
In connection with	Regarding, about
Due to the fact that	Because
At this point in time	Currently, now
I am prepared to	I can, I will
If you deem it acceptable	If you agree
Please don't hesitate to call	Please call

Use the phrases in the left column *only* when you're trying to sound very formal or even a bit stuffy (for example, if you're writing to someone who is stuffy, and you think it might help). Otherwise, stay with the phrases in the right column.

To make your writing even less formal, use more casual words. While some colloquial words will often work well in business writing, avoid slang, hip talk, street talk, and, of course, profanity.

Tricks of the Trade

While it's good to sound like yourself on paper, it can be better at times to match your style to your reader. If you write informally to someone who is very formal or if you write formally to someone who is very informal, you may hurt your case. Most people like to deal with people who are like themselves. It helps to write in the way that's most comfortable for your reader.

Here's an example of a very casual note.

> Dear Jim,
>
> Thanks a million for helping out by staying late last night. I heard you were here until the wee hours. Sorry I had to leave for the airport. I owe you one.
>
> Regards,
>
> Bob

In most situations, something this casual would be more appropriate for a hand-written note or an e-mail than for a typed letter of thanks. Bob has also used *clichés*, which are best avoided. They lack originality, can sound flippant, and can bore the reader.

> **FYI**
>
> A **cliché** is a phrase that has been used so often that it has become stale. Once a phrase becomes a cliché, it's almost useless to a writer who is looking for fresh ways to say things.
>
> Here are just a few examples of clichés: "dead in the water," "growing like a weed," "cleaned their clocks," "low hanging fruit," and "at the end of the day." You can probably think of dozens of others.

Sentence structure is another way to adjust your style. I'm not talking about sentence length, a topic I covered in Chapter 6. This is about putting a sentence together.

Using Active Voice

Earlier in this chapter, I pointed out the advantages of directness in business writing. One way of being direct is to use the active *voice ("as Jim said at the staff meeting …")* rather than the passive voice *("as was said at the staff meeting …")*. The passive voice creates an impersonal style of writing. It does help the writer and reader to stay objective about the material, but that, too, can be overdone.

The subject of a sentence is the word that the sentence says something about. The subject usually appears at the beginning of the sentence. The predicate (that is, the verb) describes the action or state of being of the subject.

For example, in the sentence "Jim sells cars," "Jim" is the subject and "sells" is the predicate (and, by the way, "cars" is the object). "Jim sells cars" is active voice. "Cars are sold by Jim" is passive voice.

> **FYI**
>
> **Voice** refers to the relationship between the subject of the sentence (a noun) and the predicate (a verb). In active voice, the subject is doing the action described by the verb. In passive voice, the subject receives the action described by the verb. A noun is a person, place, or thing. A verb describes an action.

Here are some examples of sentences in passive voice:

Next year's goals will be announced on November 15th.

This plan should be changed as soon as possible.

Sales were made by everyone at the trade show except Mike.

Our old equipment is being auctioned by Louie the Liquidator.

Memos should be written clearly and concisely.

Compared with active voice, passive voice makes it more difficult to know who is doing what, which can make the writing unclear. Passive voice also requires some form of the verb "to be" ("should *be* changed," "*were* made," "will *be* announced," "is *being* auctioned," and so on); thus it requires at least one more word than active voice. Finally, passive voice makes it harder to pin down responsibility.

The responsibility issue is one of the principal reasons people overuse passive voice in business writing. Many people don't like to identify who is doing what when they write. It makes them feel uncomfortable. As a consequence, however, they sacrifice clarity.

For example, suppose a boss writes a memo to her five employees saying, "The storage area should be cleaned up by Friday at 5:00 p.m." Each employee can think, "I'm glad she doesn't mean me!" It would be much better to say, "Steve and Mary should clean up the storage area by Friday at 5:00 p.m." That way, someone is clearly responsible for the task. Or she could write, "I would like all of you to clean up the storage area by Friday at 5:00 p.m." That at least holds them all responsible for the task.

Changing Passive Voice to Active Voice

Because sentence structure is a matter for step three in the writing process—the editing phase—there's nothing wrong with using, or even overusing, the passive voice in your draft. But when you edit your draft and want to improve your writing style and make it more personal, you'll want to change most passive-voice sentences to active voice.

Here's how to do that:

1. **Locate the passive voice.** Do this by asking yourself, "Is the subject of the sentence doing, or receiving, the action of the verb?"

   Next year's goals will be announced on November 15th.

   The subject is *goals* and the verb is *will be announced*. The subject is receiving the action of the verb (the goals are *being* announced).

2. **Find or supply the "actor"—the one who receives the action.** Sometimes the actor is part of the sentence, as in the earlier "Louie the Liquidator" example, but often you have to supply the actor, as in the "goals" example.

   Let's say the actor here, the person doing the action, is the president.

3. **Put the actor in front of the action and rearrange the sentence as needed.** Generally, once you put the actor in front of the action, the active voice sentence falls into place.

The president will announce next year's goals on November 15th.

Here's how to change the other sample sentences above to active voice:

Passive voice: *Sales were made by everyone at the trade show except Mike.*

Active voice: *Everyone made sales at the trade show except Mike. Or, Everyone except Mike made sales at the trade show.*

Passive voice: *Our old equipment is being purchased by Louie the Liquidator.*

Active voice: *Louie the Liquidator is purchasing our old equipment.*

Passive voice: *Memos should be written clearly and concisely.*

Active voice: *Write your memos clearly and concisely.*

Notice that there is no actor in the last sentence. Yet it is still active voice. How can that be? Because in this form the subject is referred to as "you, understood," which means that "you" is the subject without being mentioned. So that last sentence is understood to mean, "You (the reader of this memo), write your memos clearly and concisely."

Any direct order such as "Stop smoking," "Keep your hands off the subway doors," and "File your taxes early" has as its subject "you, understood."

When to Use Passive Voice

Most (about 65–80 percent) of the sentences in your business writing should be in active voice. However, you should use passive voice in the following instances:

◆ To occasionally vary your sentence structure and give the reader a change from active voice.

◆ When you can't (or don't want to) identify the actor who performs the action: *"Our chairman's car was broken into yesterday and his briefcase was stolen."*

◆ When you want to shift the emphasis a bit or because passive voice is the accepted way of making such statements. (But don't make this an excuse for overusing passive voice.) For example: *"This report was prepared by Larocca & Lambert Inc., an international consulting firm."*

Be sure you know the difference between active and passive voice and consciously choose which form to use. The more you use active voice, the clearer, livelier, and stronger your writing style will be.

CAUTION **Pitfalls**

Don't confuse *voice* with *tense*. Voice refers to the relationship between the subject and the predicate. Tense has to do with time. The tense of a verb tells you when the action did or does or will occur.

Don't Be Tone-Deaf

Let's turn briefly to the issue of tone. Tone is related to, but separate from, style. While style has to do with the way the writer approaches and presents the content, tone has to do with the writer's *attitude* toward the subject and toward the reader.

Tone really refers more to an emotional state. A writer's tone can be serious or humorous, gentle or angry, open or sarcastic, friendly or hostile, enthusiastic or skeptical.

The best tone to take in most letters and memos is a positive, professional, supportive one. You may at times be tempted to take a negative, sarcastic, or even angry tone. Don't. It's a bad idea.

You can check that your tone is businesslike and positive by allowing your spouse, or a friend outside the business, to read the memo and tell you what he thinks. If they say something like "It sounds strong to me," or "You aren't pulling any punches," you should probably tone it down (as the saying goes).

The Least You Need to Know

- Gear your writing style to the content, goals, and readers of the piece you're writing.

- Most business letters and memos should be written in a personal style, but some, such as reprimands, call for the distance of a more formal approach.

- E-mail lends itself to an informal, personal style, so when you want to be formal in e-mail, use hard-copy correspondence or attach hard-copy documents.

- You can adjust your writing style by adjusting your approach to the material, the way you address the reader, and your word choice and sentence structure.

- By using the active voice—having the subject of the sentence performing the action of the verb—your writing will be more personal, direct, and clear.

- Strive for a positive, supportive, friendly tone in business letters; avoid negativity.

Chapter 12

Nail Down the Basics

In This Chapter

- Why it's important to avoid grammar mistakes
- The basic parts of speech
- How to avoid (or at least fix) the most common grammatical errors
- Avoiding confusion on commonly confused words

Okay, this is it. Grammar. English usage. Rules! I'm afraid there's no alternative. We have to deal with it sooner or later. But I'll make this as painless as possible and keep the rules to a minimum.

In this chapter, you'll learn about the most common errors in grammar and usage, how to avoid them—and how to fix them if you can't avoid them.

Grammar Matters

Let's face it—there is no way that a letter or memo can be called great, or even good, if it's riddled with grammatical errors. And I do mean riddled. Such mistakes can make your writing seem like a riddle to the reader, even if it's clear to you.

Just because you have always said or written something a certain way doesn't mean it is correct. If your *grammar* is incorrect, it reflects poorly on you, even if your readers can figure out what you mean. Incorrect grammar is the mark of an uneducated person, and most businesspeople value education. It's really that simple.

I'm not saying that a lack of education makes you a bad person. It doesn't even mean you aren't intelligent. For various reasons, many intelligent people have not had much education. Meanwhile, many cheaters and liars have had wonderful educations and cheat and lie in perfect English. Still, mastery of written and spoken English will help your career and enable you to express your ideas and feelings in any situation. There's no reason for you to go through life without that ability.

So if you slept through English class, or if you were awake but thinking of other things, here's a chance to get a grip on the basics.

The Parts of Speech

To a professional writer, words are tools. A writer has to use the right tool for the job at hand, just like a mechanic or carpenter. Writers have to know their tools, just as mechanics and carpenters have to know theirs.

The writer's tools, the words in the English language, are classified into the "parts of speech." Each part of speech has a different function. The following table gives you a quick rundown of the parts of speech, their functions, and some examples of each.

The Parts of Speech

Part of Speech	Function	Examples
Noun	Names a person, place, or thing	*man, city, building*
Pronoun	Substitutes for a noun	*he, that, which*
Verb	States an action or condition	*run, swim, is*
Adjective	Modifies nouns	*fast, good*
Adverb	Modifies verbs	*quickly, well*
Conjunction	Creates links	*and, but, or*
Preposition	Creates links with phrases	*by, for, at, in, with*
Interjection	Signifies exclamation	*Oh, Egad, Wow*
Article	Identifies a noun	*the, a, an*

A few more items:

Adjectives and adverbs are also called *modifiers.*

A *proper noun* is capitalized and names a particular person, place, or thing, such as John (person), Paris (city), or the Empire State Building (thing).

There are a variety of pronouns. These include *personal pronouns*, such as "he," "she," "you," "I," and "we," which substitute for nouns; *relative pronouns*, such as "who," "which," and "that," which substitute for nouns and create modifying phrases; and *reflexive pronouns*, such as "myself," "herself," and "themselves," which refer to the subject of a sentence.

A *phrase* is a group of words that (usually) acts as a modifier. For example, in the sentence "He was the best salesperson in the company," the phrase "in the company" is a phrase modifying "salesperson." Actually, it is also a *prepositional phrase*, because it begins with the preposition "in."

Some examples of the uses of various parts of speech in sentences follow:

He and I got into the office early today.

Noun: office

Verb: got

Pronouns: he, I

Preposition: into

Conjunction: and

Adverbs: early, today

Article: the

Good managers demand and get the best work from every employee.

Nouns: managers, work, employee

Verbs: demand, get

Adjectives: good, best, every

Preposition: from

Conjunction: and

Article: the

You can be a good writer without knowing the parts of speech, but knowing them helps. It's also helpful for me to be able to refer to the various kinds of words by their names when I'm focusing on grammatical errors, as I'll be doing for the next several sections.

Fixing the Most Common Errors

Here's a summary of the most common grammatical and usage errors business writers make:

◆ Dangling modifiers

◆ Lack of parallelism

◆ Faulty comparison

◆ Unclear pronoun reference

◆ Incorrect pronoun case

Dangling Modifiers

A dangling modifier is a modifying word or phrase that is misplaced in the sentence. The result is a lack of clarity, sometimes with humorous results. Here are some examples of dangling modifiers:

Scalded with coffee, the machine injured several employees. (The machine was not scalded; the employees were.)

Happy at last, the plane finally got clearance to take off. (The plane can't be happy; who was?)

To fix dangling modifiers, rearrange the sentence and add or omit words as necessary to get the modifying phrase next to the word or words that it is modifying:

The machine injured several employees, who were scalded with coffee.

We were happy at last when the plane finally got clearance to take off.

Lack of Parallelism

Parallelism refers to the practice of presenting a series of words or phrases in the same way. Lack of parallelism can make your writing harder to read and understand, as in the following sentences:

Mary has everything needed for success in market research, including asking good questions, the ability to listen, analytical skills, and handles herself with poise.

The key challenges facing the European Union now are:

- *Unemployment*
- *Achieving competitiveness*
- *New member-nations*
- *A unified defense strategy*

To create parallelism, decide what form of word you want to begin a list with and stick with it. The list can be either within a sentence or in a bulleted list. Don't switch around—if you want to use "-ing" endings, use "-ing" endings; if you want to use articles, use articles; if you want to use nouns, use nouns:

Mary has everything needed for success in market research, including the ability to ask good questions, listen to others, analyze results, and handle herself with poise.

The key challenges facing the European Union now are:

- *Lowering unemployment*
- *Increasing competitiveness*
- *Absorbing new member-nations*
- *Establishing a unified defense strategy*

Faulty Comparison

Be sure that the words on the page compare exactly the things that you want to compare, which is not the case in these sentences:

The economy of California is bigger than Sweden.

Harry's business acumen is better than most experienced entrepreneurs.

To fix faulty comparison, add language and punctuation that clarifies the comparison:

> *The economy of California is bigger than Sweden's.*

> *Harry's business acumen is better than that of most experienced entrepreneurs.*

Unclear Pronoun Reference

Pronoun reference is clear when the reader knows what a pronoun refers to. The references are not clear in these sentences:

> *International trade will greatly expand the size of the world economy. It is growing by more than 5 percent a year.*

> *Kathy helped Louise with the analysis for this project, but she wrote most of it.*

To fix unclear pronoun reference, add language and rearrange the sentences to make the reference clear, or use nouns instead of the unclear pronouns:

> *International trade, which is growing by more than 5 percent a year, will greatly expand the size of the world economy.*

> *Kathy helped Louise with the analysis for this project, but Louise wrote most of it.*

Incorrect Pronoun Case

The term *case* refers to the form of the pronoun you should use in the situation. You use *subjective case* (such as "I," "we," "he," "she," or "they") when the pronoun is the subject of the sentence. You use *possessive case* (such as "mine," "ours," "his," "hers," or "their") to indicate possession. And you use *objective case* when the pronoun is the object in a sentence or in a prepositional phrase.

The following sentences are all examples of incorrect case:

> *Between you and I, we can easily make our sales goals for next year.*

> *Her and I are going to fly on Friday to the London conference.*

> *Jim has a much better attendance record than me.*

To fix incorrect pronoun case, use the correct case for the situation:

> *Between you and me, we can easily make our sales goals for next year.* (Hint: "Between you and I" is a common mistake. The key here is the word "between." "Between" is a preposition and needs to be followed by an objective-case pronoun like "me," "him," "her," or "them.")

> If this sounds too confusing, try taking away the "you and." Would you say "between I," as in "the man stepped between I and the TV screen"? No, you wouldn't, you'd say "between me." So "between you and me" is the correct choice.

She and I are going to fly on Friday to the London conference. (Hint: This one's even easier. Leave out "and I" and see how the sentence sounds without it. You wouldn't say "Her is going to fly on Friday," but rather "She is going to fly on Friday.")

Jim has a much better attendance record than I. (Hint: You're really saying "Jim has a much better attendance record than I do." You would not say "than me do," would you?)

Common Mistakes in Word Usage

Certain words in English are inherently confusing. They either sound the same but have different meanings (like "affect" and "effect") or the have similar, but nonetheless different, meanings (like "continual" and "continuous").

Here is a list of these easily confused words, along with their actual meanings and examples of their correct usage.

Affect and Effect

The verb *affect* means to influence or to change in some way. The verb *effect* means to cause or to bring about.

> *Economic conditions will not affect our business.*
>
> *This plan should effect an increase in sales.*

The noun *affect* (stress on the first syllable) is a technical term meaning behavior or demeanor. The noun *effect* means a change or result.

> *The employee's affect was inappropriate given the situation.*
>
> *Lower morale was the main effect of the cutback.*

All, Each

All is a collective noun that takes a plural verb. *Each* is singular.

> *All are invited to attend Jim's farewell party.*
>
> *Each is to donate five dollars for Jim's gift.*

As

Be careful when you use the word "as" because it can mean many different things, including "since," "while," "because," and "at that time" (for example, "as of last Friday …").

> Change: *We made the sale as Peter talked about sports with the prospect.*
>
> To: *We made the sale while Peter talked about sports with the prospect.*
>
> Or: *We made the sale because Peter talked about sports with the prospect.*

As Such

The phrase "as such" often sounds awkward and is frequently overused. It's best to omit it or use other words.

> Change: *We expect a bad winter. As such, we should arrange for snow removal.*
>
> To: *Given that we expect a bad winter, we should arrange for snow removal.*

Assure, Ensure, Insure

Assure, ensure, and *insure* all mean "to make certain" or "to make secure." However, you *assure* another person of something. *Ensure* and *insure* can be used interchangeably, except when you mean to insure the financial value of something with an insurance policy.

> *He assured me that the check was in the mail.*
>
> *This new capacity will ensure (or insure) that we can meet increased demand.*
>
> *This policy will insure your building and equipment for $250,000.*

Bad, Badly

Bad is an adjective and should be used to define nouns (a bad cold, a bad job), and after verbs such as "feel" and "look." *Badly* is an adverb and therefore defines verbs.

> *It is natural to feel bad about being fired.*
>
> *A poorly maintained machine will perform badly.*

Can and May

The verb *can* means "to be able to." The verb *may* indicates probability.

> *Marty can sell anything.*
>
> *Marty may sell his beach house this autumn.*

Cannot

The word *cannot* is one word. It should never be spelled "can not."

Continual and Continuous

Continual refers to something that happens repeatedly or intermittently. *Continuous* means uninterrupted.

> *The watchdog barks continually, whether or not there are intruders.*
>
> *This machine produces a continuous sheet of steel.*

Center Around

The expression *center around* actually doesn't make sense, since the center of something cannot be around something else. Instead of "around," use the word "on" or "upon."

> *Our concerns center upon his competence.*

Compare with, Compare to

Use *compare with* when you are comparing things that are similar to one another, and *compare to* when comparing fundamentally different things.

> *Comparing the Porsche with the Miata will tell us a lot about sports cars.*
>
> *Compared to the horse and carriage, any car represents advanced technology.*

Complement, Compliment

A *complement* is something that makes something complete or the number it takes to make something complete. (Hint: Think of the "e" in complete and the "e" in *complement*). A *compliment* is a favorable remark. Similarly, *complementary* means completing a task or filling a lack, while *complimentary* means favorable or free of charge.

> *With two more jurors, we will have the complement of 12.*
>
> *His boss gave him the sincerest compliment of all—a bonus.*
>
> *Irene will bring complementary skills to the department.*
>
> *Everyone likes to get a complimentary introduction.*

Data

Data is the plural of the Latin word *datum*, meaning a single unit of information. While formal usage would call for data to be treated as plural, it is acceptable in business writing for it to take either a singular or plural verb. If, however, the data is a single group of information, it's more correct to use a singular verb, as in the first example below.

> *The data is ready for you to pick up whenever you're ready.*
>
> *The economic data are contradictory at turning points in the business cycle.* (But "data is" would also be acceptable.)

e.g. and i.e.

The abbreviation *e.g.* stands for *exempli gratia*, which means "for example" in Latin. (Many people take it to mean "example given.") The abbreviation *i.e.* is from the Latin *id est*, meaning "that is." It's best to simply use the English words, since many people confuse these two abbreviations.

Change: *Government agencies, e.g., the DOD and CIA, often do business with companies.*

To: *Government agencies, for example, the DOD and CIA, often do business with companies.*

Or: *Government agencies, such as the DOD and CIA, often do business with companies.*

Change: *Our goal for next year, i.e., a doubling of sales, is simply impossible.*

To: *Our goal for next year, that is, a doubling of sales, is simply impossible.*

Or: *Our goal for next year, a doubling of sales, is simply impossible.*

Etc.

The abbreviation *etc.* means *et cetera*, which is Latin for "and others." *Etc.* is often overused in business writing and can at times create the impression that you're too lazy to mention the others or that there really aren't any others. It is often best to use the terms "such as" or "for example" and then mention several specifics. Also, it is incorrect to use *etc.* with "such as" or "for example" because it is redundant.

Change: *The person we seek needs sales skills, such as the ability to cold call, close, etc.*

To: *The person we seek needs sales skills, such as the ability to cold call and close.*

Fewer, Less

Use *fewer* for things that can be counted individually and use *less* for things that cannot.

This new line of snacks has less fat and fewer calories.

Former, Latter

Use the word *former* to refer to the first of two items mentioned and *latter* to refer to the last of two. When more than two items are mentioned, use words like "first" or "last of these" to be clear.

We have a chairman and a president. The former is responsible for overall strategy; the latter is in charge of day-to-day operations.

We need new products, new systems, and new ideas, the last of these being the most important.

Good, Well

Good is an adjective and *well* is an adverb.

> *She has good skills and she uses them well.*
>
> *He's got a good job and he's doing it very well.*

Imply, Infer

You *imply* something when you hint at it or indicate it. You *infer* something when you figure it out based on some evidence.

> *The boss was indirect, but he implied that a layoff could be coming.*
>
> *Since we have no plans to hire and we're losing money, I infer that a layoff is coming.*

Its, It's

Be very careful of these two. They are often confused. *Its* is the possessive form of the pronoun "it." *It's* is the *contraction* for "it is."

> *It's going to be a bumpy ride in the next recession.*
>
> *The machine was pushed beyond its capacity.*

FYI

A **contraction** is a combination of two words, with an apostrophe to mark the letter or letters that were left out. Examples include "don't," "can't," "it's," "doesn't," "that's," and "what's."

Lay, Lie

Lay means to put or place something somewhere. *Lie* means to recline.

> *If the stack of material is too heavy, lay it on the nearest desk.*
>
> *Any employee who feels dizzy should lie down.*

Numbers

The rule of thumb in business writing is to spell out the numbers one through ten and use numerals for those over ten. If a numeral over ten appears at the beginning of a sentence, either spell it out or reword the sentence so that it's not at the beginning. Page numbers should always be written as numerals.

> *As you'll see on page 5 of the report, we have approval to add four new employees, which will bring our total staff to 12.*

Principal, Principle

The noun *principal* means a person with position or authority, most specifically in an educational institution or a business. Principal also refers to a sum of money in a loan or fund.

We negotiate only with principals, not with agents or brokers.

We calculate the interest on this loan on the original principal.

The noun *principle* means a law or doctrine.

The principle of delegation is central to the art of management.

The adjective *principal* means the most important.

Poor performance was the principal reason for his termination.

The adjective *principled* (or *unprincipled*) means based on (or lacking) a principle or principles.

Principled behavior calls for fairness in all terminations.

Reason Is Because

The expression *the reason is because* is redundant. Either use the *reason is that* or the word *because*.

Change: *If costs are down, the reason is because inflation is low.*

To: *If costs are down, the reason is low inflation.*

Or: *If costs are down, it's because of low inflation.*

Regards, Regard

The word *regards* means "best wishes," while *regard* means "about" or "having to do with." People often use *regards* when they mean *regard*. However, *regard* can also mean "esteem."

Give my regards to everyone at the company.

I'm writing in regard to your most recent delivery to us.

I've always had high regard for Mike's management skills.

Time

The correct way to write *a.m.* and *p.m.* is with lowercase letters and periods.

Our office hours are from 9:00 a.m. to 5:30 p.m.

Their, They're

Don't confuse *their* and *they're*. The former is the possessive of "they," while the latter is the contraction for "they are."

They're bound to forget their umbrellas once the rain stops.

Very

Many people overuse the word *very* in their business writing. You're usually better off omitting it or finding a better adjective or adverb.

> Change: *Sales rose very quickly last month.*
>
> To: *Sales rose sharply last month.*
>
> Or: *Sales skyrocketed last month.*

Your, You're

Your is the possessive form of "you." *You're* is the contraction for "you are."

> *You're sure to find your new Maximillion Copier to be a superior value.*

Avoiding Jargon and Buzzwords

Try to stay away from *jargon* and *buzzwords* in your writing. Jargon can be hard to avoid, and used sparingly, it won't do much harm, provided your readers understand it. If you overuse it, however, your work will sound like technical writing instead of business writing.

FYI

Jargon is technical or specialized language, like "bandwidth" and "firewall" from technology and "securitized" or "leverage" from finance. Jargon is fine when experts are talking to experts.

Buzzwords are specialized, often pompous-sounding words that come into temporary favor in business, such as "paradigm," "right-sizing," "customer-centric," and "mission-critical." Buzzwords can become tiresome or dated fairly quickly.

Buzzwords often sound silly or overwrought on paper. In most cases, there is really no substitute for good, solid Standard English in your business writing, and you certainly can never go wrong with it.

The Least You Need to Know

- Grammar is the set of rules that describes the way a language is used. These rules ensure that the language makes sense.
- Correct grammar is the mark of an educated person. Most of the people who will play a role in your success in business will know if you speak and write correct English, and they will judge you at least partially on that basis.
- Words are a writer's tools; the more you know about those tools and how to use them, the better a writer you will be.
- Get to know the mistakes you tend to make and be on the lookout for them.

Pitfalls

There are many spelling and usage errors that spell-checking programs in word-processing software will not catch. Good examples include "from" and "form," "by" and "buy," "it's" and "its," "your" and "you're," and "their" and "they're." There's no substitute for careful proofreading.

Chapter 13

How It Looks Is How You Look

In This Chapter

- ◆ What it takes to create professional-looking documents
- ◆ What readers expect when it comes to appearance
- ◆ How to format letters and memos properly

This chapter is about cosmetics, not content. It's about how your letters and memos look, not how they read. In business there are professional ways of presenting words on paper, and then there are other ways.

Having worked so hard to make the content of your correspondence as good as possible, you owe it to yourself (and to your readers) to make it look good also. This chapter will show you how.

Neatness Counts

First impressions are lasting impressions, and first impressions are usually visual. This applies to people, places, and things. How a person is dressed, how a yard is kept, and how food looks on the plate all affect us before we talk with the person, enter the house, or taste the meal.

Similarly, how your memo looks when the reader first sets eyes on it will affect him. If it's messy or improperly formatted, the reader may still read it (but maybe not). If the material is compelling enough, the reader may even overcome that first impression (but maybe not).

The Professional Look

There are four basic elements to a professional-looking document:

- ◆ Flawless error correction
- ◆ Proper format
- ◆ Customary layout of extra information
- ◆ Proper letterhead and stationery

Getting Rid of ~~Missteaks~~ Mistakes

Given computer technology, readers' tolerance for errors has approached zero. They expect perfection. Many readers find spelling errors particularly irksome. Their first thought upon spying one is usually, "Couldn't they even run this through the spell check? How lazy can you get?" Always, always, always use the spell check feature in your word-processing software.

If you're not writing on a personal computer, you are placing yourself at a huge disadvantage when it comes to your personal productivity. This is true whether you're just starting your career or you're a seasoned senior executive who may be "keyboard shy." There is really no excuse for anyone in an organization—or working in a home-based business—to be writing on a typewriter or longhand.

Don't think that you have to spend big bucks on a computer. Because the technology changes so fast and companies are always upgrading to new machines, there's a healthy secondhand market for PCs. Be sure, however, that the machine can meet your need for Internet access.

Whether you use a computer or not, your readers will have almost no tolerance for errors, typos, or misspellings. A computer will make your writing life much easier, but you will still have to proofread carefully, preferably more than once and after you have gotten some distance on the piece.

Choosing the Right Format

In this section, I show you formats by indicating what goes where, rather than giving you actual sample letters and memos. The samples in the other chapters and on the CD-ROM are properly formatted. There are some variations, however, that you'll see in this chapter.

On the pages that follow are the basic formats for letters: The first two are for letterhead, and the second for situations when you need an inside address for your location. Remember, though, with many of today's word-processing packages, it's easy to create your own letterhead—with a graphic, if you like.

Sample 13-A shows the format for a letter on letterhead.

Given the informality of business in the United States (in contrast to Europe and Asia), it's often acceptable to use a first name simply on the basis of having spoken with the person on the phone. If you don't know the person, however, use "Mr." or "Mrs." or "Ms." plus the last name.

It's always best to write to a specific individual, but if you don't have a name of a person, use "Dear Sir:" or "Dear Sir or Madam:" rather than the somewhat old-fashioned "Gentlemen:" which may be considered gender-biased.

Note that nonindented paragraphs, rather than indented paragraphs, are considered standard today. That's one change from 30 or 40 years ago, when you would often see indented paragraphs.

Note also that these paragraphs have a *ragged* right margin as opposed to a *justified* right margin. Sample 13-B shows the same letter with a justified right margin.

Tricks of the Trade

In the salutation, "Dear" plus the first name, followed by a colon, is acceptable in a business letter, if you are writing to someone you know. E-mail salutations usually do away with "Dear" in favor of "Hi" or "Hello" and the recipient's first name, or just the greeting, or the first name.

FYI

The right margin of the text in a document can be **justified**, that is, lined up so that each line of text ends in the same place on the page, or **ragged** so that the end points of the lines vary. The term *justified* or *right justified* refers to a justified right margin, while *ragged right* refers to a right margin that is not justified.

Your Company Name
Company Street Address
City, State Zip
Telephone Number Fax Number
www.urlgoeshere.com

Date

Mr./Ms. First Name, Middle Initial, Last Name

Title

Company Name

Street Address Floor or Suite (if applicable)

City, State Zip

Dear Mr./Ms./Mrs. Last Name:

First paragraph First paragraph First paragraph First paragraph First paragraph First paragraph First paragraph First paragraph First paragraph First paragraph First paragraph First paragraph First paragraph First paragraph First paragraph First paragraph First paragraph.

Second paragraph Second paragraph Second paragraph Second paragraph Second paragraph Second paragraph Second paragraph Second paragraph Second paragraph Second paragraph.

Third paragraph Third paragraph.

Fourth paragraph Fourth paragraph Fourth paragraph Fourth paragraph Fourth paragraph Fourth paragraph Fourth paragraph.

Sincerely,

Your First Name, Middle Initial, Last Name

Your Title

> A ragged right margin is less dense and intimidating than a justified one.

Sample 13-A: Format for a letter on letterhead.

Company Name
Company Street Address
City, State Zip
Telephone Number Fax Number
www.urlgoeshere.com

Date

Mr./Ms./Mrs. First Name, Middle Initial, Last Name

Job Title

Company Name

Street Address Floor or Suite (if applicable)

City, State Zip

Dear Mr./Ms. Last Name:

First paragraph First paragraph First paragraph First paragraph First paragraph First paragraph First paragraph First paragraph First paragraph First paragraph First paragraph First paragraph First paragraph First paragraph First paragraph First paragraph First paragraph.

Second paragraph Second paragraph Second paragraph Second paragraph Second paragraph Second paragraph Second paragraph Second paragraph Second paragraph Second paragraph.

Third paragraph Third paragraph Third paragraph Third paragraph Third paragraph Third paragraph Third paragraph Third paragraph Third paragraph Third paragraph Third paragraph Third paragraph Third paragraph Third paragraph Third paragraph Third paragraph Third paragraph Third paragraph Third paragraph Third paragraph.

Fourth paragraph Fourth paragraph Fourth paragraph Fourth paragraph Fourth paragraph Fourth paragraph Fourth paragraph.

Sincerely,

Your First Name, Middle Initial, Last Name

Your Title

A justified right margin creates a more formal block-of-text format.

⊚ *Sample 13-B:* *Letter on letterhead—justified.*

Whether you use ragged or justified right margins is largely a matter of personal taste, subject to the custom in your organization. I prefer ragged right and I believe most readers do. I also see it far more often. The ragged right margin creates more white space and a less "boxy" and more inviting look.

If you do use justified right margins, use a proportional font (such as Times New Roman) rather than a nonproportional font (such as Courier). A proportional font automatically adjusts the spacing between the letters in a word so that there are no gaping spaces between the words in a line. A nonproportional (monospaced) font can't make this adjustment, so you wind up with some large spaces between the words when you use a justified right margin.

The spacing between words is not an issue with a ragged right margin, which is another good reason to use ragged right margins in your letters and memos.

Accepted Closings

Besides "Sincerely," the accepted closings for a business letter include "Very truly yours," "Yours very truly," "Yours truly," and "Very truly" all of which are considered more formal than "Sincerely" (which I prefer and most often use). "Cordially" is still more informal. "Regards" and "Best wishes" can be used for a personal touch when you have a personal as well as business relationship with the reader and the subject matter is somewhat personal.

Sample 13-C on the following page shows a letter formatted without letterhead. (This kind of letter is sometimes called a personal business letter to distinguish it from a business letter, which goes on letterhead.)

Your Street Address

City, State Zip

Date

Mr./Ms./Mrs. First Name, Middle Initial, Last Name

Title

Company Name

Street Address

Floor or Suite (if applicable)

City, State Zip

Dear Mr./Ms. Last Name:

First paragraph First paragraph First paragraph First paragraph First paragraph First paragraph First paragraph First paragraph First paragraph graph First paragraph First paragraph First paragraph.

Second paragraph Second paragraph Second paragraph Second paragraph Second paragraph Second paragraph Second paragraph Second paragraph Second paragraph Second paragraph.

Third paragraph Third paragraph Third paragraph Third paragraph Third paragraph Third paragraph Third paragraph Third paragraph Third paragraph Third paragraph Third paragraph Third paragraph Third paragraph

Fourth paragraph Fourth paragraph Fourth paragraph Fourth paragraph Fourth paragraph Fourth paragraph Fourth paragraph.

Sincerely,

Your First Name, Middle Initial, Last Name

Your Title

Be sure to align the closing ——— with your address at the top of the page.

◎ *Sample 13-C: Personal business letter (no letterhead).*

You would use this format if you were writing to a company from your home. But even so, with a computer it would be easy to create personal letterhead, as in the following example:

John Smith
33 East 33 Street
New York, New York 10022
(212)-999-9999

Personal letterhead created on a computer.

Just as computers have created the standard of zero errors and no cover-ups or erasures, the reasonable standard has become some form of letterhead done on a computer. From the practical standpoint, this makes the inside address positioned to the right (as in Sample 3) obsolete. However, I include it here because it is acceptable, and—who knows?—someday you may find yourself without access to a computer and the need to write to a business from your home.

Sample 13-D shows a format for a memo that has a justified right margin.

To:	First Name, Initial, Last Name, Title
From:	Your First Name, Initial, Last Name, Title
Date:	Month, Date, Year
Subject:	The Subject of the Memo
cc:	First Initial, Last Name (of each person who will get a copy)

First paragraph First paragraph First paragraph First paragraph First paragraph First paragraph First paragraph First paragraph First paragraph First paragraph First paragraph First paragraph First paragraph.

Second paragraph Second paragraph Second paragraph Second paragraph Second paragraph Second paragraph Second paragraph Second paragraph Second paragraph Second paragraph.

Third paragraph Third paragraph Third paragraph Third paragraph Third paragraph Third paragraph Third paragraph Third paragraph Third paragraph Third paragraph Third paragraph Third paragraph Third paragraph Third paragraph Third paragraph Third paragraph Third paragraph.

Fourth paragraph Fourth paragraph Fourth paragraph Fourth paragraph Fourth paragraph Fourth paragraph.

◎ **Sample 13-D:** *Format for a memo.*

Page Numbers for Letters and Memos

If your letter or memo is longer than one page, you should number each page at the top right corner, beginning on page 2, as shown in the following example:

First Initial and Last Name of Recipient　　　　　　**Page 2**
Month, Date, Year

In practice, this would read:

J. Jones　　　　　　**Page 2**
Nov. 12, 2006

and:

J. Jones　　　　　　**Page 3**
Nov. 12, 2006

… and so on.

After this material at the top of each page, skip two lines before starting the text.

Page numbers are important because you *do not staple* the pages of a letter together. Page numbers also help the reader not only to keep the document in order, but also to discuss it on the phone more easily with you or with anyone else who gets a copy ("On page 3 it says that …").

On a memo, page numbers can be placed either at the top of the page as they would be for a letter or at the bottom of the page, either centered or in the lower right-hand corner.

Marginal Thinking

The standard size for paper in the United States is 8½ by 11 inches. Do not use legal-size paper, which is 8½ by 14 inches, for business correspondence.

Proper margins for a letter or a memo are from 1¼ to 1½ inches on the right and left sides.

Letterhead can begin from ½ inch to 1¼ inches from the top of the page. This also applies to any other typing at the top of a page, such as the page number lines, but not to the text itself, which should be 1¼ inches from the top or two lines below the page number lines.

The "To" and "From" lines for a memo should begin from 1 to 1¼ inches from the top.

The bottom margin should be from 1 to 1½ inches.

In practice, most of us who work with word-processing software on a personal computer use the default settings for margins, which on most packages are 1¼ inches on all four sides. The *default setting* on a computer is the setting that the program automatically uses unless you manually override it.

Customary Layout of Extra Information

Often in a business letter, several lines below the closing, signature, name, and title of the sender, you'll see two sets of initials, separated by a slash, at the left-hand margin, for example:

Sincerely,

Thomas F. Gorman
President
TFG/mcm

This means that the document is from Thomas F. Gorman and that his secretary, Mary Celia McCaffrey, did the typing. This is formal practice for a secretary, and I include it for that reason.

If you are enclosing an attachment or additional information with a letter, it is customary to note that fact after the closing, signature, name, and title, as follows:

Sincerely,

Thomas F. Gorman
President
Attachment
TFG/mcm

or:

Sincerely,

Thomas F. Gorman
President
Enclosure
TFG/mcm

Finally, as noted in Chapter 3, you will often need to use a "cc" or distribution list to send out multiple copies of your document. Here's where the "cc" or distribution list would go in a business letter:

Sincerely,

Thomas F. Gorman
President
cc: J. Smith
     M. Doe
Attachment
TFG/mcm

or:

Sincerely,

Thomas F. Gorman
President
Distribution:
J. Smith
M. Doe
H. Hathaway
B. Rubin
Attachment
TFG/mcm

If the attachment or enclosure is integral to the letter, you would include it for those on the "cc" or distribution list as well. If it's not integral, it would be acceptable for those people to receive just the letter.

For memos, the information about the "cc" and distribution lists, the secretary, and the attachments and enclosures would be presented the same way, at the end of the memo after the text of the memo itself (since there are no signature, name, and title lines at the end of a memo), with one potential variation. As noted in Chapter 3, if they're not too long, you can put the "cc" or distribution list at the top of the memo; for example:

To:	First Name, Initial, Last Name, Title
From:	Your First Name, Initial, Last Name, Title
Date:	Month, Date, Year
Subject:	The Subject of the Memo
cc:	First Initial, Last Name (of each person who will get a copy)

or:

To:	First Name, Initial, Last Name, Title
From:	Your First Name, Initial, Last Name, Title
Date:	Month, Date, Year
Subject:	The Subject of the Memo
Distribution:	J. Smith
	M. Doe
	H. Hathaway
	B. Rubin

If a "cc" or distribution list is long, it should go at the end of the memo.

Letterhead and Stationery

The business world seems to be in a state of flux regarding standards for paper and stationery. Many people used to believe that paper and envelopes with a heavy feel, substantial *rag content*, and engraved letterhead were needed to create an impression of "class" and wealth. Again, however, the personal computer is changing things.

The weight of paper refers to the number of pounds that a ream (500 sheets) weighs. In general, the heavier the weight of the paper, the heavier and "nicer" the feel in your hands—and the greater the cost. Standard paper for a laser printer is usually 20-pound paper, while higher-quality paper can go as high as 60 or 80 pounds.

FYI

Rag content refers to the amount of rag (usually cotton) in paper. Good-quality paper usually has at least 25 percent rag or cotton. In general, the more rag or cotton in paper, the higher its quality and price.

Most businesses, even small home-based ones, are producing their letters and memos on computer printers. The requirements of the technology have become more important than notions of what looks "classy." When you're doing mailings with computer-generated labels, the envelope that the label goes on becomes something of a side issue. After all, the label is going to look rather cheesy no matter how nice an envelope it's on, won't it?

On the other hand, really flimsy paper and envelopes will not look good. Since most paper is white and most print is black, the use of color and graphics in letterhead has become more of a mark of quality than the heavy, ivory-colored paper that banks and law firms used to favor.

If you are a freelancer or have your own business, you can prepare letterhead on your word processor. However, depending on your business, your budget, and the way you sell, it's often worth it to invest in professionally produced letterhead, envelopes, and business cards. Adding a color (beyond black) will cost you a bit more, but will make your material stand out, especially if you have a nice logo.

Your local copy shop can work within various price ranges. They can also usually refer you to a freelance designer. Ask the designer for samples of work and take the time to develop a common understanding of your goals and price range. Although you can get by without a designer, a good one can help your letters get noticed. Just don't go overboard.

Remember, when you write letters longer than one page, your subsequent pages must match your letterhead. I have received letters in which the letterhead is gray, tan, or off-white and pages 2 and 3 pure white. This looks bad and is not acceptable.

When you have letterhead prepared by a print shop, you have two choices. Either have your letterhead done on standard white paper of the same weight that you will use in your printer, or buy a large enough supply of the nonstandard paper (whatever the color and weight) so that you won't run out before you run out of letterhead.

Practically speaking, you're probably better off putting your letterhead on standard white paper that matches what you use in your printer. First, it is always available; second, if you try to buy paper through printers, they'll often tell you they're not in the paper business and to order direct from the supplier, which can take time and be a hassle; and third, white paper produces the highest contrast against black ink and makes for easier reading than colored paper.

Print Quality

Before *ink-jet printers* and *laser printers* became affordable, *dot matrix printers* were widely used. However, dot matrix printers deliver poor print quality. Today, good ink-jet printers and laser printers are the standard for business letters and memos. Laser represents the true state of the art, but a good ink-jet delivers almost equally good results.

Of course, if you still type your letters, make sure your ribbon is in good shape.

FYI

Ink-jet printers create letters by shooting ink onto the page. **Laser printers** burn the letter onto the page. **Dot matrix printers** apply the ink with tiny pins grouped in the shape of the letter.

Ink-jet and laser printers both produce acceptable print quality. Dot matrix printers generally do not, because the pins do not produce clean lines at the edges of the letter.

The Least You Need to Know

◆ It's worth the extra effort to make sure that your documents look professionally prepared.

◆ Proper format is key to the appearance of a letter or memo. Put things where they belong or readers will think about your weird format, instead of about your message.

◆ Always use proper margins and never crowd words onto the page to save space. If your text doesn't fit on one page, either edit it to fit or add another page.

◆ The standards for the appearance of business documents today are driven by, and have been incorporated into, personal computer technology. If you have any significant amount of business writing to do, you should probably be doing it on a computer.

Part 4

Letters, Memos, and E-mail for Every Situation

Do you get the feeling that there's an unlimited number of business situations calling for a letter, memo, or e-mail? Well, as a matter of fact, it's true. But things are simpler than they look. To prove it, I've grouped these situations and the kinds of writing that they demand into some basic categories. The specific written correspondence you'll learn about in this part will cover over 90 percent of the writing situations that you'll come across in business.

You will find many outlines and samples that you can use as models. Take these samples as starting points. Improve them. Make them your own. Strive always to develop your own style and to sound like yourself. After all, that's where the fun comes in.

Chapter 14

Requests for Action That Get People to Act

In This Chapter

- ◆ Effective approaches to making requests
- ◆ Distinguishing between simple requests and complex requests
- ◆ Making the case for your request
- ◆ Using threats and consequences in the right way

The majority of business correspondence requests that someone take some form action. When you write a cover letter for your resumé, a sales letter, or a proposal, you are requesting action. But to narrow things down a bit, this chapter covers memos in which you are asking people to do something that they more or less have to do.

Usually, the person does what you ask because of his role in the organization. He may work for you. If not, the requested action may simply be part of his job. Of course, that does not guarantee that he will do what you ask and do it when and how you want it done. So this chapter shows how to write memos that get cooperation.

What Do You Want Done?

First, establish what you want done. In the planning stages of your memo, you must be very specific about this in your mind and in your outline. Readers will interpret your request according to their own *frame of reference*, which could very well be different from yours.

FYI

A person's **frame of reference** is the way that person sees things. For example, a hunter sees a forest as a sporting paradise; a logger sees the lumber he can sell; an environmentalist sees a need for conservation. Each viewpoint comes from that person's frame of reference.

Exactly how specific you need to be depends mostly on the reader. With some readers, including those who lack experience or expertise, you must be very specific. For example, if you ask an experienced painter to paint an office, he knows that he must first prepare the surface. An amateur may have to be told this.

How specific you need to be also depends on the complexity of the action requested and how fussy you are. If you're requesting that the cafeteria bring a cold lunch tray to a conference room, that may be all you have to say. If you expect shrimp salad and cold poached salmon, and instead get ham and cheese on rye, you should be more specific.

In general, the more specifics you include, the better. In most organizations, too little communication, not too much, is the problem.

E-mailing Requests

You probably use e-mail for most requests for information or action from coworkers and subordinates. The outline, samples, and guidelines in this chapter will help you make those requests more effectively. In fact, they apply directly to e-mail requests.

As usual with e-mail, take extra care to be clear and to strike a businesslike tone. A slapdash e-mail may not be taken as seriously, and it's quite likely to be unclear. If the request is complex or highly detailed, consider attaching a memo in a Word or WordPerfect file.

If you want information back from the reader in a form other than e-mail, for instance, as an attached Word, WordPerfect, Excel, or PDF file, mention that. Also, if the deadline is more than a week away, ask for e-mailed progress reports. Set up a *tickler file* to remind you when those reports are due, and if you don't receive them on time, send an e-mail the next day reminding the reader to keep you updated.

We'll look at samples of requests via e-mail later in this chapter, after we cover the basic outline and memos.

FYI

A **tickler file** is a way of reminding yourself that you must do something, or expect something from someone, on or by a certain date. An entry in your calendar may be enough to remind you, but many business people insert proactive reminders in the calendars of their personal digital assistants, computers, or hard-copy files.

Simple Requests

By a simple request I mean one that your reader should be fairly receptive to as well as one that's straightforward. It may be a request for action or a request for information—that is, a request for the reader to give you information. In these simple cases, doing the requested action is generally part of the reader's job and complying with the request should not present many difficulties. Sample 14-A is an outline for a simple request.

Paragraph #1:

◆ Lead with the general request.

◆ Note the deadline or timeframe.

◆ Mention the overall reason for the request.

Paragraph #2:

◆ Present the details of your request.

◆ Be clear about the way you want the job done.

Paragraph #3:

◆ Thank the reader for her help.

Sample 14-A: Outline for a simple request.

You can also add a follow-up step if you feel it would be useful, as shown in Sample 14-B, a simple request for action.

Sample 14-C is a request for information.

Notice how both samples use formatting to highlight the action requested. Headlines are used to good advantage in the first memo, while the second uses bullets. Notice that these bullets are actually small boxes that the reader can use to check the items off as he gathers them. Many word-processing packages enable you to customize bullets in this way. (But don't get too fancy or cute.)

Any time there is a date, time, and place where the reader must be physically, highlight that information. Ways of doing this are shown in Samples 14-B and 14-C.

> **Pitfalls**
>
> Be sure to make requests for information very specific. Information can be configured and delivered in many ways, and you can easily get weekly figures when you wanted monthly figures or an e-mail when you wanted a hard-copy report. Consider how easy or difficult the information may be to access or develop, and if possible adjust your deadline or time frame accordingly.

To: Louis Brillate, Manager of Food & Beverage Services

From: Alice Gerald, Director of Operations

Re: Request for Luncheon on February 12th

I'm writing to request lunch for eight to be delivered to an upcoming all-day meeting. Here are the details:

Day and Date: Thursday, February 12th

Time: 12:30 p.m.

Place: Second Floor Conference Room
(Room 217)

—— Alice uses a format that helps readers find the most important information quickly.

Desired Menu:

Since this will be a working lunch, I believe cold sandwiches would be best. A buffet-style layout would allow each person to make their own sandwich. Please furnish silverware rather than plastic disposables since the attendees are senior people.

Given the time of year, we would also like a hot soup (your choice). We can serve the soup ourselves from a heated tureen.

Soft drinks, tea, and regular and decaf coffee, plus your choice of dessert, will round out the meal.

Cost Center:

You should charge this luncheon to cost center #313.

I'll give you a call on the 11th to confirm these arrangements. Thanks in advance for helping to make this meeting a success.

Sample 14-B: Memo for a simple request for action.

To:	Jim Millerchip, Director—Sales
From:	Paul Kasade, Vice President—Marketing
Re:	Request for Detailed Sales Figures

I would appreciate your giving me the following sales data for <u>this year through the month of June</u>, by Friday, July 24th, for the upcoming management meeting in Aspen:

- ❑ Monthly total sales figures
- ❑ Monthly sales figures by product
- ❑ Monthly sales figures by sales district
- ❑ Quarterly total sales figures
- ❑ Quarterly sales figures by product
- ❑ Quarterly sales figures by sales district

Please include your comments on specific sales figures that are plus or minus 10% off the original projections prepared last November. These comments should explain each 10% variance separately.

<u>Note</u>: Please send the figures to me as an e-mail attachment in an Excel spreadsheet.

Thanks for your assistance. These numbers plus your comments will help me prepare for this important meeting.

Sample 14-C: Memo requesting information.

Underscoring, bullets, and white space make Paul's memo more readable.

To: All Employees

From: Kristen Katz, Manager of Employee Benefits

Re: Mandatory Attendance at Health Benefits Meeting

Effective January 1st, the company will change some provisions of the employee health plan. We will be holding meetings to inform employees of these changes and of choices you will have to make by December 1st. Attendance at one of these meetings is <u>mandatory</u>.

Meeting Schedule

The schedule of these meetings is as follows:

For employees whose last names begin with the letters A–M:

>   **Day and Date:** <u>Tuesday,</u> October 12th
>
>   **Time:**   9:30–10:30 a.m.
>
>   **Place:**   Tenth Floor Auditorium

For employees whose last names begin with the letters N–Z:

>   **Day and Date:** <u>Thursday</u>, October 14th
>
>   **Time:**   9:30–10:30 a.m.
>
>   **Place:**   Tenth Floor Auditorium

Thank you in advance for your attendance.

——— Kristen uses formatting tools to present potentially confusing information clearly.

Sample 14-D: Request to attend a mandatory meeting.

Too often writers bury the information about the time and place of a meeting somewhere in their third paragraph. The format of Sample 14-D ensures that the reader can't miss that important information.

Sample 14-D was written by someone in authority addressing many people whom she does not know personally. As a result, the tone is less personal than it would have been if she'd been addressing her subordinates. The authoritative tone suggests that the writer has probably seen poor attendance at these meetings, or that the company is legally required to hold them. This explains the commanding style of this simple request.

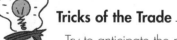

Tricks of the Trade —————————

Try to anticipate the mistakes readers might make, for example, confusing days of the week (Tuesday and Thursday) or times (a.m. and p.m.), and use formatting, such as the underlining in Sample 14-D, to highlight differences. Try also to anticipate stumbling blocks, such as people wanting to switch, trying to do things another way, or lobbying for an extended deadline. Defuse these issues in the memo if at all possible, by raising them and addressing them.

Requests via E-mail

Samples 14-E and 14-F show requests via e-mail.

Each sample reflects a good instance for using e-mail for a simple request. E-mails can also work well for more complex requests, as long as they are clear and well structured. Sample 14-E presents a request from one colleague to another to attend a lunch with a new hire. Sample 14-F is a request from a manager to a subordinate that asks for comments on expense figures attached to the e-mail as an Excel file.

From: William Bannon <wmbannon@americannetworking.com>

To: Mary Parks <maryparks@americannetworking.com>

CC: <alfeeny@americannetworking.com>, <jaynefleming@ americannetworking.com>

Subject: Can you attend a lunch on 6-17?

Hi Mary,

Would you please join me and Al Feeny (who runs telemarketing), for lunch with Jayne Fleming at the Palm on Tuesday, June 17?

You may recall that I introduced Jayne to you this past Monday, which was her first day with my group (and with the company). Jayne will be calling on mid-size companies in the southwest region. So I'd like her to know what goes on in Customer Service, and you would clearly be the best person to tell her.

It would be useful for Jayne to hear about the kinds of problems customers most often bring to your group, and how you go about resolving them. By June 17, Jayne will have been over our service contracts, and she'll probably have some questions about the levels of service customers purchase.

Al will be filling Jayne in on Telemarketing's activities and how his group generates leads and gets them to our salespeople.

If the 17th doesn't work for you, let me know and give me some alternative dates.

Thanks much.

Best regards,

Bill

Sample 14-E: E-mail request to attend a lunch.

From: Marv Golumberg <marving@unitedinsurance.com>

To: Terry Mo <terrym@unitedinsurance.com>

Subject: Please comment on the attached accounts by the 5th

Terry,

I know you're busy, but I just got a call from Lew Lipman in finance. He wants to sit down with me next Monday to review our year-to-date operating expenses, and I need your help to prepare for the meeting.

The attached Excel file shows the line-by-line gross amounts we've spent this year in all 18 major expense categories. Would you please comment, in the last column of the Excel table (labeled "Comments"), on the overages? (Warning: overages occurred on all but three accounts.)

The comment should state the major reason we've overspent. When possible, cite dollar amounts. For instance, I know that we blew the training budget when we absorbed Gary's group. So put in the dollars we spent training them, and a text note about our group absorbing that group.

In cases where you can only cite a verbal reason, do so. But whenever possible, show the actual major expense or expenses that blew the budget.

Thanks a million for your help on this. I know this is short notice, but as I said, I just got the call from Lew myself, and you're the one who knows these numbers the best.

Marv

◎ *Sample 14-F: E-mail request to comment on attachment.*

Note the level of detail in each of these e-mails. The messages are short, yet they clearly describe the action requested, give the reasons for the requests, and provide details so the readers will (in Sample 14-E) be prepared for the lunch and (in Sample 14-F) supply the proper commentary in the proper space.

Note also that the e-mails use correct grammar and punctuation, but also employ a personal style and take a businesslike, but collegial, tone.

Complex Requests

More complex requests may involve more complex tasks. Perhaps you need to request something that the reader does not necessarily have to do, or you're following up on earlier requests. Such situations demand that you exercise persuasiveness and establish follow-up strategies.

How to Be Persuasive

Being persuasive does not mean pleading. It means making a case for your request. What does your case rest on? Unless you are the reader's boss, if your only rationale is that you really, really, really want the person to comply with your request, you need to support your case with specific reasons.

CAUTION Pitfalls

Most people keep track of favors. If you're always asking Joe for help but never help him, try to get favors flowing in his direction. Offer to help Joe, connect him to someone who can help him, or just buy him lunch or send flowers or candy to his department after he does you a favor. Thank-you notes help, too. Don't get the reputation of always taking, never giving.

Good communicators try to identify mutual goals. Even if your request will benefit only you or your department, you can play upon the fact that people like to appear helpful. By making a request, you give your reader—let's call him Joe—an opportunity to be helpful—and perhaps run up a "credit balance" with you. If you've helped Joe in the past or can help him in the future, he'll have a reason to help you now.

Another tactic is to appeal to Joe's higher instincts by pointing out how his help will benefit the entire organization. Most people want to be "team players," and helping others is part of playing on a team.

Sample 14-G, a memo from the head of the mailroom to the company's managers, shows persuasive writing.

To: All Managers and Administrative Personnel

From: Henry Clavin, Manager, Mailing & Shipping Services

By summarizing the memo's ———— **Re:** The Need for Cost-Center Codes on Outgoing Mail
message, this subject line
saves the busy reader time.

Please be sure that your <u>cost-center code</u> is written in the upper right-hand corner on all outgoing mail. We have recently received many pieces of mail without cost centers on them.

While I understand that everyone is busy, we in Mailing & Shipping Services are also busy. The volume we handle does not allow us to put cost-center codes on outgoing mail. When we do have to put cost-center codes on outgoing mail, it slows up both that mail and delivery of everyone's incoming mail.

If you do not know your cost-center code, you can get it from the Finance and Accounting department website (www.abccorp.com/internal/financeaccounting/costcentercodes) or by calling me at ext. 653 or Mary Beth Morris at ext. 311 in Accounting.

Thank you in advance for your cooperation.

cc: M. E. Morris

Sample 14-G: Memo that uses persuasion.

Note how the writer acknowledges that everyone is pressed for time. That helps create common ground. The point that everyone's mail is delayed when the mailroom has to look up cost center codes will not be lost on those who do put their codes on their outgoing mail, only to have their mail slowed up by those who don't. That puts peer pressure on those who don't use cost-center codes.

Finally, notice that Henry offers help in case some readers do not know their cost-center codes.

Using Threats and Consequences

Depending on the situation, it can be useful to include a threat or consequence in the memo. Reserve this strategy for the second or third request, if the first or second one doesn't get results. Sample 14-H shows the second request on the cost-center issue.

Read Sample 14-H carefully. It demonstrates how to use a threat or, more politely, a consequence properly. It also shows how to use format—in this case, underscoring and italics—to highlight key information. Note the use of "Second Request" in the subject line.

Note also that Harry has obtained a vice president's approval before making this threat. If you are ever in doubt about your authority or about the practicality of a consequence, be sure to check it out with someone above you.

CAUTION

Pitfalls

Be very careful with threats. Never use them in first requests unless you have a good reason. Always try to make them sound like consequences, not threats. Be sure you can follow through on the threat, that it is practical, and that you have the authority to make it and to enforce the consequence.

To: All Managers and Administrative Personnel

From: Henry Clavin, Manager, Mailing & Shipping Services

Re: Second Request: Please Use Cost-Center Codes on Outgoing Mail

As a follow-up to my earlier memo, I repeat: Please be sure that your cost-center code is on all outgoing mail. While almost all outgoing mail now comes to us with cost-center codes, there are still exceptions.

Please note: As of the first of next month, any outgoing mail that comes to the mailroom without a cost-center code will be returned to senders so they can put the cost center on it. I have spoken with Mike McFadden, Vice President, Operations, and he has approved this course of action.

Again, if you do not know your cost-center code, you can get it from the Finance and Accounting department website (www.abccorp.com/internal/financeaccounting/costcentercodes) or by calling me (ext. 653) or Mary Beth Morris (ext. 311) in Accounting.

Thank you for your cooperation in this small but important cost-control measure.

cc: M. McFadden
        M. E. Morris

> Format reinforces the stronger tone of this second request.

Sample 14-H: Second request, including threat.

Follow-Up Strategies for Requests

The best way to follow up a written request, especially if a second request doesn't get results, is by e-mail or phone. But if e-mail fails to produce action, pick up the phone. No matter how well you write, a document or e-mail is less personal and easier to ignore than a phone call or a face-to-face meeting. For example, instead of making a third written request, Henry Clavin should call the managers of areas that still don't put cost-center codes on their mail. As a fourth step, he could visit them personally to discuss it.

The Least You Need to Know

- Be specific about what you are requesting in planning and writing your memos. Clearly describe what you need the person to do, in what way and in what time frame.

- Anticipate stumbling blocks and objections and try to defuse them when you make your request.

- Use formatting—including headlines, bullets, and white space—to highlight important information, particularly deadlines and key details, like the time and place of meetings.

- Limit written requests to two memos or e-mails, follow up by phone, and then, if practical, follow up in person for the fourth request.

Writing Up Poor Performance

In This Chapter

- ◆ When to issue a written reprimand
- ◆ Your role and the role of Human Resources
- ◆ How to keep the focus on the performance problem
- ◆ How to get the result you want

As far as I'm concerned, there is no form of business writing more difficult than the *reprimand*. A lot of people must agree, because in almost every company I've ever worked, I've seen cases of poor performance tolerated. They were tolerated because the manager either didn't know what to do, or more often, could not get up the strength to do it.

It takes strength to write a reprimand. It's hard to tell people, in a calm, specific way, that they're not doing their job well. Nobody likes receiving a reprimand, and some people don't know how to respond constructively to one. Giving reprimands is difficult, but necessary at times, so you need to know how to write one.

When Should You Write a Reprimand?

You need to write a reprimand when you've asked a subordinate to change his behavior and he has not done so. Suppose someone keeps arriving late for work. You might ignore it the first time, ask about it the second time, and the third time, tell him that he must start arriving to work on time every day. You should mention that you and other people depend on him to be there on time, and that good business practice demands it.

After one more verbal warning, it would certainly be appropriate to "write him up," as the saying goes. During that final verbal warning, you should warn him of the written reprimand. ("If you're late again within the next 30 days, I'm going to have to write a formal reprimand.")

FYI

A **reprimand** is an order from a manager or supervisor to a subordinate to change his behavior. It can order the subordinate to stop doing something, start doing something, or do something differently. Many people use the term "written warning" rather than reprimand.

The subject of improving employee performance is beyond the scope of this book. Large companies have guidelines and policies for these situations. In a small company, such guidance may come from the head of Human Resources, your boss, or perhaps even the CEO.

Within the context of your organization's policies and procedures, it's usually important to prepare proper documentation in the course of dealing with a poorly performing subordinate.

Remember, you owe someone a verbal warning before moving on to a written reprimand, and if necessary, to termination.

Pitfalls

Although this chapter deals mainly with the termination process, many people do respond positively to written reprimands. I've seen many employees who, having been written up, quickly improved their performance. Indeed, actual performance problems can often be solved through training, coaching, and improving the way work is structured or assigned. The more intractable problems occur when an employee brings a bad attitude, poor work ethic, or personal problems to the job.

The Role of the Human Resources Department

If your organization is large enough to have one, the Human Resources department (also known as HR or Personnel) can be very helpful when you deal with problem employees:

- HR can provide a sounding board and help you get perspective on a difficult employee; HR professionals see these situations all the time and usually take them less personally.
- They know the processes the company has in place to address such situations. This is vital information, because a boss can yell "You're fired!" only in films and TV shows. A company's termination process protects employees from such behavior, and protects the company from most charges and lawsuits involving *unjust termination*.
- HR can review what you write to ensure that it's reasonable, legal, and in line with company policy.
- They can back you up in meetings with the underperforming employee, take some of the pressure off you, and minimize the chances of an unpleasant "scene."

Generally, however, Human Resources won't write your reprimands for you. It's your responsibility as a manager to deal with employee performance issues.

Focus on the Problem

The goal in writing a reprimand is to focus on the problem, not the person. At times, it's easy to become angry at someone who seems uncooperative or uncaring about his job. You may feel that the person is trying to annoy you or wants to be fired. While you may come across such people, most performance problems stem from deeper issues, such as trouble at home, past failures, being in the wrong job, substance abuse, or a poor work ethic.

None of these issues should be the subject of your memo. Don't get into mind reading or trying to be the person's therapist or social worker. You are her boss, the manager on the job. Your role is to signal that she needs to change behavior, not personality. So you must focus on behavior. That means you must focus on facts.

Begin Planning Early

You cannot write an effective reprimand without solid planning. Planning here goes beyond writing an outline: You must gather and record facts very early in the process. Use a memo to the file, as discussed in Chapter 3, to record your facts as you go along (see Sample 15-A).

Memos to the file like this one, or other informal *written* records of what the employee did, when he did it, and what each of you said, are key steps in the process. Don't rely on your memory. Having these facts helps you to write the reprimand by keeping you focused on behavior, and it helps protect you from charges of unfairness.

Regular performance appraisals are another key way of recording lapses in employee performance. Most large companies have formal appraisal systems, and every company needs one. Be sure to review the employee's personnel file and recent appraisals before writing a reprimand.

This kind of fact-finding takes the place of brainstorming when you write a reprimand.

Memo to the file from Timothy Sappington

Re: Dennis Wallace

Date: September 26, 2006

This memo is to note two conversations I had with Dennis Wallace. One occurred today at about 10:15 a.m. The other occurred last Friday.

Dennis has been spending excessive amounts of time on personal telephone calls. I spoke with him about this last Friday, and he first told me "I'm not on the phone that much at all," and then, "I've got problems at home." I told him to please sharply reduce the amount of time he spends on personal calls.

Specific details create an effective record in case problems with this employee continue.

Yesterday afternoon, I received the phone usage detail for last month and analyzed the usage for the five people in my department. Dennis's usage is more than triple that of the next most frequent user. (In fact, the duties of this department, including Dennis's, require few calls outside the building.) Also, he appears to be on the phone as much as ever since I spoke with him about it a week ago.

This morning, I told Dennis that he cannot continue to use the telephone at this rate. I reminded him of our policy of keeping personal calls to a total of 10 minutes a day, and told him that I was concerned about both the expense and, even more, the time taken from his work.

Dennis told me again that he has problems at home. (He and his wife are considering adopting a child and are finding the decision very difficult.)

I told him that I realize that his and his wife's decision is a hard one, but that this is a place of business. I told him that if his phone usage does not return to normal levels within the next week—and remain there—I will have to issue a written warning to him.

Sample 15-A: Memo to the file regarding poor performance.

This kind of memo to the file is not to be shown to the employee. Rather it is to document the employee's behavior, what you have said, and when you said it, for yourself and for later reference in conversations with your boss and Human Resources.

An Outline for a Reprimand

Once you have your facts together and you've decided that the written warning is necessary, you need an outline as shown in the following sample.

To: [Employee's name]

From: [Manager's name]

Date: [insert date of memo]

Subject: Below-standard performance

Statement of the problem

- Specifically describe the overall performance problem
- Note when the problem began or occurred.

Evidence of the problem

- Give specific instances of the problem. (This may take a few paragraphs, or you can use bullets.)
- Mention deviations from company or department guidelines, policy, and expectations.
- Describe behaviors rather than attitudes.
- Note the effect of those behaviors on the operation, on other employees, and on business results.

Steps taken so far

- Mention conversations you have had, prior written warnings, and anything else you've done to help the employee improve.
- Note the degree of improvement (which will be little to zero, given the need for this reprimand).

Your expectations

- Clearly state what you expect from the employee in the future.
- Define the expected performance. (Describe this in terms of behaviors and results, if possible.)
- Mention any assistance that you will provide.

Conclusion and next steps

- Note that, if the employee's performance does not improve immediately and remain at the improved level, further steps—up to and including termination—will be taken.
- If appropriate or necessary, you can give the employee more time to improve, for instance, in cases where additional training is required.

Sample 15-B: Outline for a written reprimand.

This outline includes all the major points you must cover, and in the correct order. You are simply giving the employee written notice that if her performance does not improve and remain at the improved level, she will be subject to further reprimand, possible suspension, and perhaps termination. The entire memo should not run more than two pages, at most.

Tricks of the Trade _____

It's important to note in reprimands that the employee's performance must improve and *remain* at the improved level. Too often, an employee will improve temporarily and backslide after the pressure is off. You may, if you wish or if company policy specifies, state the number of days during which performance will be monitored. For instance, you can say the employee must remain at the improved level for 30 days or 60 days. This does not imply that poor performance is acceptable after that period. Rather, it says that the employee is not being judged by such exacting standards forever.

Pitfalls _____

Do not attempt to undertake corrective action with a poorly performing employee on your own. Talk it over with your boss, and with someone in Human Resources. Ask to see the written policy on reprimands and the termination process, and read it. (HR and your boss may be unaware of an important detail.) Be sure to have your boss and someone in Human Resources examine the memo and approve your course of action.

The Letter Itself: Loud and Clear

By the time you get to the point when you actually need to write a letter of reprimand (as opposed to a warning), you clearly have a performance problem on your hands: The employee has not responded to your requests to improve. Therefore, the letter must be a loud, clear wake-up call for the employee.

The language of such a letter should not be personal. You're not trying to establish rapport. You're not even trying to be persuasive. Rather, you are officially documenting the fact that the employee is not performing up to standards and that this is unacceptable, and cannot be allowed to continue. You are supporting your charges with facts. You are allowing for the possibility that the employee's performance may still improve, but you're also allowing for the possibility that it may not.

Using the Outline

Sample 15-C shows a sample letter of reprimand based on the outline in Sample 15-B and using facts drawn from Sample 15-A.

This kind of memo places the responsibility for improvement directly on the employee, where it belongs. The memo is impersonal and displays no emotion. And it puts the employee on notice that he may face termination if he continues his current behavior. In most companies, this kind of written reprimand is necessary before suspending or terminating an employee for performance problems, except in cases of proven or admitted theft, drug abuse, sexual harassment, and similar serious issues.

To: Dennis Wallace

From: Timothy Sappington

Date: October 12, 2006

Re: Reprimand regarding excessive personal telephone calls

This memo documents the fact that your usage of the company telephone for personal calls is excessive and unacceptable.

I have spoken with you on three occasions regarding this problem, on September 2, 9, and 16, and you have made only marginal improvement. After noting your personal calls during the month of August, I began getting weekly usage reports from our Telecommunications Data Center. Since I first spoke with you about this issue, your personal calls to your home number exceeded a total of 90 minutes on 12 different days and 60 minutes on another eight days. Company guidelines limit personal calls to a total of 10 minutes a day.

Although I understand that you are dealing with a personal situation, you must understand that our company is a place of business. You are incurring excessive costs and taking time and attention away from your work. You must immediately reduce the amount of time you spend on the phone on personal calls to 10 minutes a day or less.

Our conversations on this matter have been largely unproductive. If you need to use vacation time or unpaid leave in order to deal with your personal situation, then you should do so. If you need an adjustment to your working hours, we can consider that as well (although I cannot guarantee it). I have suggested these steps in our talks, but you have been unresponsive.

You must improve your job performance in this area immediately or further remedial steps, including suspension without pay or termination, may be taken.

—— Timothy states the possible consequence of the employee's poor performance in a way that cannot be misconstrued.

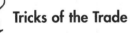 *Sample 15-C: Letter of reprimand.*

Tricks of the Trade

When an employee who has received a written reprimand remains defensive or blames you or the company, and fails to improve right away, things rarely work out well. The best course of action in such situations is swift termination. That means allowing the minimum time for improvement permitted by company policy, closely monitoring the employee's performance, and preparing for any ramifications of the employee's absence, such as increasing work for his co-workers.

What's Next?

Even if you would rather have him out of the company, after he receives this memo the employee has the right to try to improve his performance during whatever period you allow for him to do so. If he does improve and continue to perform at that higher level, he is in the clear, unless he substitutes another unacceptable behavior. If he substitutes another kind of poor performance, you should move quickly (after one verbal warning, at most) to another written reprimand and toward termination.

If an employee improves, it's customary in most companies to note that fact at the next regular performance appraisal. A savvy employee might ask you to document his improvement some time after the letter of reprimand. If this happens, ask for guidance from Human Resources or your boss.

In many cases, unfortunately, you'll find that you have to go to the next step toward termination.

The Final Warning

The next step can be suspension or termination, as stated in the letter of reprimand, or a final warning. In my experience, suspension is rarely used. If the employee isn't improving, suspending him will not help matters. The next step is usually termination. However, in order to be as fair as possible and avoid charges of wrongful termination, many large companies require a final written warning, even after the threat of termination has been given in the letter of reprimand.

Sample 15-D shows an example of such a warning.

Note that the tone of Sample 15-D is impersonal, unemotional, and factual, yet clear and strong. Don't say you're sorry or disappointed. Use the approach of good old Joe Friday on *Dragnet*: just the facts.

Termination Letters

Sadly, some people fail to improve their performance and must be terminated. In a large company, Human Resources usually writes the termination letter. In a small company, however, the task may fall to you.

Keep it short and factual, as shown in Sample 15-E.

To: Dennis Wallace.

From: Timothy Sappington

Date: October 18, 2006

Re: Final Warning: Excessive personal telephone calls

As a follow-up to my written reprimand dated October 12, this memo documents the fact that your usage of the company telephone for personal calls remains at excessive and unacceptable levels.

During this past week, since receiving the written reprimand, your personal calls have totaled five hours and 42 minutes. This is an average of more than 60 minutes per day. The written reprimand mentioned the acceptable limit of 10 minutes, and that was your target.

—— By quantifying the employee's poor performance, Timothy builds a solid case for the next step: termination.

This memo represents a final warning. If you do not immediately bring your level of personal calls to within acceptable limits, further remedial steps, including suspension without pay or termination, will be taken.

Sample 15-D: Final warning.

To: Dennis Wallace

From: Timothy Sappington

Date: October 24, 2006

Re: Termination of Employment

Effective immediately, your employment at this company is terminated. Please remove any personal belongings from your desk and office and vacate the premises as soon as possible.

—— Because the run-up to termination was handled well, the notice of termination can be short and to the point.

The reasons for this step have been well documented in memos to you dated October 12 and 18 regarding your excessive use of the company telephone for personal calls.

We wish you the best in your future endeavors.

Sample 15-E: Letter of termination.

What About E-mail?

Do not document performance problems via e-mails, particularly with the employee. You want hard-copy documentation of your communications with a poorly performing employee, with your signature or initials. E-mails are too easily tampered with, and they are neither a formal nor secure enough medium for such sensitive content.

You can, however, ask for meetings with Human Resources or perhaps your boss via e-mail. However, I would use the phone for most of those conversations.

> **Pitfalls**
>
> Recall that e-mails can be easily misdirected with an absent-minded click of the mouse on the wrong line in an address book. Also, your boss, an HR professional, or even the employee could mistakenly forward an e-mail to another party.
>
> Consider all communications about an employee's poor performance to be strictly between you, the employee, your boss, and Human Resources. Do not discuss an employee's poor performance or remediation with another of your employees or with parties outside the company.

The Least You Need to Know

- Verbal warnings, which you should document in memos to the file, are the first step in working with an employee who needs to improve his performance.

- If the employee does not improve his performance in response to verbal warnings, move quickly to a written reprimand. It's easy to try to put this off, because it's an unpleasant task; however, performance problems usually don't solve themselves.

- All of your writing regarding an employee who needs to improve his performance should be impersonal, factual, clear, and strong. It should also consist of hard-copy memos; e-mail is too informal and not secure enough for these communications.

- Be sure to get guidance from Human Resources and your boss as you go through the process; have them read over your written warnings and letters of reprimand. Consider these documents, and the entire matter, to be confidential between you, your employee, your boss, and Human Resources.

- Get guidance in making a decision to terminate an employee, but don't be talked into keeping a poorly performing subordinate.

Chapter 16

Announcements That Spread the Word

In This Chapter

◆ Knowing when to issue an announcement

◆ What to include and what to leave out

◆ How to announce bad news

Memos that make announcements are one of the chief ways managers at all levels communicate with employees. Human Resources and corporate communications employees also write announcements all the time.

Announcements of the type I cover in this chapter are issued mainly in large organizations. After all, in a small organization, the president can announce new hires and changes in policies at a regular staff meeting, from the shop floor, or even to people individually. However, when you need to get the word out to hundreds or thousands of your fellow employees, you should know how to go about it.

Announcements are not particularly difficult, but like any form of business writing, they have their own requirements. This chapter will show you these requirements and how to meet them.

What's New?

Essentially, announcements tell employees of changes in the organization. Management often uses announcements to make employees aware of …

◆ Management and personnel changes

◆ Policy and procedure changes

◆ Special events

Because they go to groups of people, announcements tend to have an official tone. But they can take a personal or even lighthearted tone in certain instances, such as an announcement for the annual holiday party.

Announcement memos also serve as a key tool for recognizing people and welcoming new employees. When someone joins the staff, it is not simply nice to announce that fact. Your announcement recognizes her existence, welcomes her to the team, and paves the way for people who'll be meeting her on the job.

Similarly, people who work on a particularly successful project or a special event should be recognized. People enjoy being recognized in writing. (That's why most of us like seeing our name in the newspaper, provided we haven't been arrested.)

> **CAUTION** **Pitfalls**
>
> Not making an announcement when one should be made can offend people, leave them feeling uninformed or devalued, or create confusion. For example, I've seen cases when a manager leaves suddenly, either voluntarily or not, and nobody says anything about it to his staff. Or a program or an effort will be ended, and there's nothing said about it. Those vacuums give rise to rumors that distract people from their jobs and make senior management appear embarrassed or befuddled.

E-mailed Announcements: Jewels or Junk?

E-mail can spread the word farther, wider, and faster than any other medium. That makes it an ideal way for communicating announcements. You can adapt virtually any outline or sample in this chapter to an e-mail announcement.

Again, e-mail's ease of use makes it easy to abuse, and announcements do contribute to excess e-mail volume. Particularly in large organizations, people have repeatedly vented their frustration to me regarding announcements about "the bowling league, the golf league, the softball team, the new hire in the copy room, the newest arcane feature of the telecom system, and the fascinating developments in our Canberra office."

Indiscriminate e-mailers say, "Stop whining and just delete it," but the problem isn't the time it takes to stroke the key. The problem is the time it takes to read and assess each sender and subject line, and to decide whether to open it. Once it's opened, the message itself requires the same or even greater scrutiny.

Do your part in the battle against irritating e-mail by asking yourself who needs to know the information you're announcing, using clear subject lines so people can readily delete it, and using separate address lists for the various types of announcements you make.

Tricks of the Trade

Keep e-mailed announcements to a reasonable length. As always, use an attachment if you have a lot of material to communicate, such as detailed new procedures or if you've bundled different material for different readers. If the document is too long, or if you just want to make things easier for your readers, have your Webmaster put it up on your company's website and copy and paste the link to the information into your e-mail. Then in your e-mail, direct readers to the link.

Good Timing

The timing of announcements is important. An announcement issued too late can be an embarrassment. It can make management look uncaring or out of touch, as if the last thing on their minds is keeping employees informed. On the other hand, an announcement issued too early can turn into an embarrassment if the news being announced doesn't happen or if details turn out to be wrong. Pay attention to timing.

For example, if someone new joins the organization, announce he's come on board on his first day on the job. If you send it before then and he winds up not joining, it could be embarrassing. On the other hand, I've seen such announcements go out weeks after the fact, as if it took forever to get around to it.

If the organization will merge with another one, you shouldn't announce it too early: The stockholders need to know first, and, again, it will be embarrassing if the deal falls through. However, when a merger is announced weeks after everyone has been gossiping or reading about it in the newspapers, management appears out of touch or as if it wants the employees to be out of touch.

Pick the right time: not so early that it's before the fact, but not so late that it seems like an afterthought.

When announcing an upcoming annual event such as the company picnic or the blood donor drive, give people six to eight weeks' notice on the first announcement. Do a follow-up two to three weeks before the event, then issue a reminder via e-mail the week before.

Tricks of the Trade

If you have to make an announcement that readers will see as late, acknowledge that fact early in the memo. For example, you can use a first line such as "With apologies to Steve Murphy for the lateness of this memo, we welcome him to Campbell Associates." or "While most of you have read about our recent merger in the newspapers, we'd like to cover several items related to this important event in more detail."

An Outline for Announcements

More than many types of correspondence, announcements follow a fairly formulaic outline. You're really not writing to persuade, unless you're announcing an onerous new policy or the annual blood drive. You don't have to be all that personal, although you don't want to sound like The Ministry of Information. You're basically just getting information across, clearly and efficiently. Sample 16-A provides a general outline for announcements.

From: [Your name, title, and department]

To: [Recipient's name(s) or departments affected]

Date: [Date of announcement]

Subject: [Reason for announcement]

Paragraph #1, Opening

- ◆ Convey the general information—that is, mention the new hire, the policy or procedure change, or the event.
- ◆ Mention who is affected by the change or invited to the event.
- ◆ Note the policy's effective date or the date of the event.

Paragraph #2, Body

- ◆ Provide details about the person, event, or change.
- ◆ Give reasons, if applicable and appropriate, for the change.

Paragraph #3, Body

- ◆ Give additional details, if necessary.
- ◆ Do any persuading, if necessary (for instance, cite the importance of the blood donor drive).
- ◆ Add other paragraphs as needed.

Paragraph #4, Closing

- ◆ Add a closing if necessary (but often it is not).
- ◆ Ask people to join you in the task or event, if applicable.

Sample 16-A: Outline for announcements.

Announcements lend themselves to bullets and to the tactic of setting off key items, such as times, places, and people affected, with white space, underscoring, and bold type.

People Come, People Go, People Get Promoted

Announcing personnel changes is usually straightforward. The most important element, along with doing it timely, is having your facts straight. If you announce incorrect information, you defeat the purpose of the memo and may insult the person you're writing about.

When Someone Joins the Organization

It's fun to announce good news. Sample 16-B announces that someone is joining the organization. The sample follows basic custom for this kind of announcement. The traditional opening line is "Please join me in welcoming …" This is hard to improve on. It's also customary to include some background information:

former employer, skills the person will contribute, and some personal information, with education the most often included item of that nature.

Use good judgment in deciding how much personal information to include. Some people do not want their hobbies or musical tastes disclosed. Very few would want a divorce mentioned or even implied. The best way to ensure that this kind of memo will not offend its subject is to show it to the person, but that shouldn't be necessary if you think carefully about what's appropriate. Take a warm and personal (but not gushing) tone. Don't brag about the employee's accomplishments or go into great depth about the company's expectations of the person.

The audience for such announcements ranges from those who will respond to the person to everyone in the company, depending on how senior the new employee is. As a basic guideline, anyone who will be reporting to or regularly dealing with a new person should receive an announcement when that person comes on board.

When Someone Leaves

Trying to avoid an unpleasant topic, many organizations do not issue announcements when people leave. Meanwhile, the rumor mill spins fast and furious. When anyone in senior or *middle management* leaves, there should be an announcement.

This is one of the few memos in which it's okay to be vague. The reasons for someone's leaving often reflect poorly either on the person leaving (if he was fired) or on the organization (if he found a better position elsewhere). It's best to be obscure about the person's reasons for leaving and future plans, unless he is simply retiring.

The memo in Sample 16-C announces a termination.

FYI

Middle management is the layer of management between senior managers and supervisors. Middle managers usually have managers or supervisors reporting to them, and usually report to senior managers.

To: All Marketing Employees

From: Louise Quant, Vice President of Sales & Marketing

Subject: Ron Geiger, Our New Director of Marketing

Please join me in welcoming Ron Geiger to the position of Director of Marketing. Before joining Reliable Manufacturing, Ron was Manager of Marketing at a Midwest building supplies distributor. Ron's experience with distribution systems and point-of-purchase display brings us the skills we need to further penetrate the retail market.

Ron holds an MBA from Northwestern's Kellogg School of Management and a BA from George Washington University. He has just moved to Middleville with his wife and two daughters and enjoys movies, family outings, and playing blues guitar.

Over the next several days, Ron will be learning more about our company and meeting with each of you personally.

Louise gives just the right amount of information.

Sample 16-B: Announcing a new employee.

To: All Employees

From: Hedrick Jones, President

Subject: Personnel Change

This is to announce that effective tomorrow, Larry Lane will be leaving Amalgamated Ltd. to pursue other interests. For now, the duties associated with Larry's position of Vice President, Corporate Strategy, will be divided among senior management.

Please join me in wishing Larry all the best in his future endeavors.

A short memo is enough to acknowledge someone who was fired or suddenly quit.

Sample 16-C: Announcing a termination.

Most people, reading between the lines of Sample 16-C, will realize that Larry was terminated. The clues are that the change is effective the next day ("effective immediately" would be even more obvious), that Larry's plans are vague, and that he was not thanked for his contribution.

You may be wondering, if everyone knows that Larry was terminated, why not mention it and the reason? The answer is that people's privacy must be protected. Besides, there could be potential legal issues in making such an announcement.

But if the memo is going to say so little, why write it at all? The answer is, to acknowledge Larry's moving on officially and to announce the disposition of his duties.

The memo shown in Sample 16-D announces a more pleasant event.

As a basic rule of thumb, the degree of warmth and personal detail to include in a memo about personnel changes depends upon the person leaving the organization, her length of service, and her reason for leaving.

When Someone Is Promoted

Announcements are particularly important when someone is promoted, because in many companies the promotion doesn't seem "real" to the person being promoted or to her co-workers unless it is announced. Sample 16-E includes the basics of this type of announcement.

The goals of this memo are to announce the promotion, to indicate—subtly and briefly—that it is deserved, and to show that qualified employees who work hard will be promoted.

Pitfalls

When someone leaves for any reason, it creates emotional and operational dislocations. An announcement, even a bland one, at least partly addresses this. Not issuing a memo makes the sense of dislocation seem even worse, especially to those who reported to the person.

Tricks of the Trade

In general, keep memos announcing personnel changes short. Their purpose is to announce changes, not to explain them in depth.

To: All Employees
From: Peggy Gilbert, Vice President, Human Resources
Subject: Thank You, Sheila O'Shay

Please join me in wishing the very best to Sheila O'Shay, who will be retiring from the bank at the end of this month after 37 years of service.

Sheila joined the bank as a loan documentation clerk when we were still First Farmers' Trust and had only two offices. She rose steadily through positions of increasing responsibility in the credit function and became a loan officer in 1992. Sheila's superb business development skills led to her promotion to Vice President of Lending for the eastern district in 1999.

During her career, Sheila also raised four children with her husband Charles, an electrical engineer.

Sheila has certainly earned her retirement, which she and Charles will spend here in Meadowville and at their winter home in Scottsdale, Arizona. We will all miss her.

Those who worked with Sheila are invited to join us for a cake-and-coffee toast for her on Friday the 24th in the Third Floor Conference Room at 4:00 p.m.

——— This subject line captures the spirit of the memo nicely.

Sample 16-D: Announcing a retirement and get-together.

To: All Employees
From: Peggy Gilbert, Vice President, Human Resources
Subject: Promotion of James Neville

Please join me in congratulating James Neville, who will be promoted to Director of Technical Services effective June 14th.

Jimmy joined us in 1999 as a programmer and quickly rose to Senior Programmer, then Systems Analyst, and, most recently, Manager of Technical Support. Jimmy's hands-on knowledge of our systems coupled with his managerial skills and his MBA, which he recently completed in his off-hours, well qualify him for this position.

——— Specific details about the person being promoted bring Peggy's announcement to life.

Sample 16-E: Announcing a promotion.

Announcing Organizational Changes

The most common organizational changes announced are policy and structural changes. Although your major goal is to announce rather than explain, policy and structural changes usually call for more explanation than personnel changes do.

The memo shown in Sample 16-F announces a change that's sure to be unpopular (at least with the managers).

People usually temper bad news with vague language and elaborate buzzwords. This fools no one. In fact, many people lose respect for people who deliver mealy-mouthed messages. Most adults can deal with the truth if it's delivered fairly and personally, as in the following memo.

In Sample 16-F, the threefold message is clear without being harsh: Management can't be rewarded when the company is not profitable; we won't take it out on the employees (not yet anyway); and we have work ahead of us. That's it. It's all there.

Sample 16-G shows an example of a straightforward policy announcement.

To:	All Managers and Supervisors
From:	Mike Cummings, Chief Executive Officer
Subject:	Salary and Promotion Freeze

Mike's tone is appropriate: seriousness and regret, coupled with fairness and authority.

I am sorry to announce that effective immediately and for the rest of this year, there will be a salary and promotion freeze in effect for all management personnel. This freeze does <u>not</u> affect clerical, professional, and technical staff.

The base salaries, job grades, and titles of all managers and supervisors will remain at current levels during the freeze. No new requests for increases or promotions will be considered during this time. Any increases or promotions now in process will be frozen regardless of where they are in the process.

This freeze is necessary because we have not been profitable for the past two quarters and are projecting a loss for this quarter. Although we are taking steps to restore profitability, we cannot in good conscience give raises and promotions to management under the circumstances. I and all of senior management are also subject to the freeze.

Management must accept responsibility for the state of the company and lead the return to profitability. Thank you in advance for joining me in this effort.

Sample 16-F: Announcing a freeze on salaries and promotions.

CAUTION **Pitfalls**

If and when you're in management, or have influence with management, consider the effect that tough policies, such as hiring freezes, budget cuts, and benefit rollbacks, will have on employees. Then consider the effect if only the employees, and not management, are subject to the policies.

One outfit I worked for announced a cost-reduction program, which among other things limited all employees to economy and coach seating on company travel. Within a few days a senior manager flew first class, at company expense, on a visit to a customer. That news got around quite quickly even without a formal announcement, and it did nothing for employee morale or the cost-reduction program.

To: All Sales Personnel
From: Bruce Threadgill, Vice President, Marketing
Subject: Price Increase for Next Year

Effective with orders written on or after January 1st, prices of all our products will increase by 8 percent. Each of you will receive the new price list within the next week.

Management recognizes that this aggressive pricing may hurt the sales of some products in our line. However, we are willing to take that hit in order to earn higher profits on the products that will continue to sell well.

—— Bruce anticipates objections and addresses them directly.

We will hold a series of meetings during the first two weeks of December to discuss strategies for presenting this increase to our customers. The times and places of these meetings will be announced on October 3rd.

Sample 16-G: Announcing a policy change.

Announcements for Special Events

Special events include anything from the annual holiday party and blood donor drive to legal matters, mergers and acquisitions, financial performance, or general news reports about the company.

Recurrent Scheduled Events

Announcements of regular annual events are straightforward, as Sample 16-H shows.

This memo needs to convey the twin messages of good times and safety. Notice that, although I didn't use them on previous samples in this chapter, you can use tools such as indentation, boldface, and headlines in announcements.

Announcing Structural Changes

Employees must be promptly advised of any changes in the organizational structure that can affect them. An example of a memo that does this effectively is shown in Sample 16-I.

To: All Employees at Corporate Headquarters

From: Jamie Fortunado, Vice President, Human Resources

Subject: Holiday Party

It's that time of year again! Happy holidays from all of us in Human Resources.

Here are the details on this year's annual holiday party:

Day and Date: Thursday, December 17th

Time: 7:00 p.m. to midnight

Place: The Boom Boom Room
             444 East 57th Street

A hot and cold buffet will be served from 7:00 to 9:00 p.m. There will be an open bar for the entire evening and dancing to the sounds of DJ Cool Klee on the second floor from 9:00 p.m. to midnight.

Special Note on Transportation

All employees are urged to take the transportation provided by the company from The Boom Boom Room to their homes. Vans will leave for Long Island, New Jersey, and Connecticut at 12:15 a.m. Employees within the five boroughs of New York can take taxis (shared, when possible) and submit their receipts for full reimbursement.

Let's make this the greatest (and safest) holiday party ever! See you there.

Sample 16-H: Announcement of a regular event (company party).

Jamie uses format and tone effectively to get her message across.

To: All Sales Personnel

From: Neil Lemmon, Senior Vice President, Sales

Subject: Reorganization of the Sales Function

Neil states his main message in the first sentence.

This is to announce a reorganization of the sales function effective next Monday, April 3.

Essentially we will be reorganizing Sales along product lines. This will provide greater product specialization than our present regional organization. This change is in response to our customers, who have repeatedly said that we need to improve our product knowledge.

The details will be presented in another memo this coming Friday. Basically, we will collapse our 14 districts and 5 regions into 5 sales departments organized by product line, as follows:

- Copiers
- Commercial photography products
- X-ray and other health-care systems
- Military optics
- Industrial devices

We expect this to be a far more efficient structure resulting in better product knowledge and higher sales.

Sample 16-I: Announcing a change in organizational structure.

Announcements Regarding News Events

Public relations professionals advise companies to be as open as possible during times of crisis. Although the legal staff must often play a role in responding to negative publicity, Sample 16-J offers one basic approach for communicating about it internally.

When addressing news stories, stick with the main point of the story. Be sure you understand how true or false it is and confirm the degree of truth or falsity for the company's employees—to the extent that legal counsel allows. It's not advisable, from the standpoint of communications and morale, to keep employees in the dark. But neither is it advisable to present in a memo details about a legal matter in process.

To: All Employees
From: Lisa Marino, Director, Corporate Communications
Subject: Recent News Stories About Our Company

As most of you are aware, our company has recently been the subject of negative stories in several newspapers and magazines and on radio and television. This memo will clear the air.

The substance of the stories is that our lawnmowers are unsafe and have caused severe injury.

For legal reasons I cannot go into the situation in great detail. However, I can tell you that in all but 2 of the 12 cases, the charges appear to be completely groundless. In two cases it does appear that there may be some liability of some kind on the part of our company.

—— Lisa earns her readers' respect by stating the need to keep details confidential, without appearing evasive.

All of us at Blade Industries remain committed to making the best and safest products that we can. Our products are consistently rated among the highest in safety by independent institutes and in injury statistics. We have every intention of maintaining that record of safety.

Sample 16-J: Internal announcement about negative publicity.

The Least You Need to Know

- ◆ Announcements, by definition, go to groups of people within the company, so a somewhat impersonal tone can be acceptable on some of them.
- ◆ Announcements must be timed properly. It's best to send out the announcement just as the news is happening or soon after it has happened.
- ◆ The purpose of an announcement is to announce a change or an event, not to explain it.
- ◆ Keep announcements short, usually to one page.
- ◆ It's acceptable to use the same language repeatedly in similar kinds of announcements. For example, open with "Please join me in welcoming …" when announcing a new staff member, or "Please join me in congratulating …" for a promotion.

Chapter 17

Media Communications That Draw Great Publicity

In This Chapter

- How to approach newspapers, magazines, and other media
- When to use a press release and how to format one
- What editors and producers look for
- Do's and don'ts when approaching the media

A *query letter* is the term professional writers and editors use for letters that pitch story ideas to newspapers and magazines and to radio and television shows. A *press release* is not really a letter or memo, but rather a special form of writing to the media. However, you should know about press releases, particularly if you are in sales or marketing or in business for yourself, so I include them in this chapter.

Getting publicity has become an extremely valuable skill in our media-oriented society. This chapter will show you how to go about it.

Why Try to Get Publicity?

Publicity is media coverage of your business, product, or co-workers. You can get publicity if you have something that *editors* or *producers* see as newsworthy or as interesting to their readers or viewers. You cannot pay an editor or producer to "run your story." You can, however, pay a *public relations firm* to help you get your story into the media. You can also pay the media to run advertising, but that is not publicity.

The right public relations firm or freelance PR professional can be a big help in getting a story out to the media. But they can be expensive, and you have to work closely with them to get the best results. This chapter will show you how to get media coverage on your own.

> **FYI**
>
> **Editors** decide what stories go into their own publications. They also oversee the entire publishing process, from developing and assigning story ideas to writing and photography to layout, design, and production.
>
> **Producers** decide what stories and guests get covered on a radio or television program. They also oversee all the work necessary to get the show on the air.
>
> A **public relations** (or PR) **firm** works with clients to design and execute a media campaign. This includes targeting publications, editors, shows, and producers; developing story ideas; writing query letters, press releases, and articles; and coaching clients on how to interact with the press.

However you get it, media coverage can be well worth the effort, for several reasons:

- Media coverage can give your company, product, or service a level of credibility that you just can't buy with advertising; people know that advertising is paid for, but an article or news story is taken as objective information.

- You can clip stories and articles from print media and send copies to prospects and customers with a nice note that starts off, "In case you missed it in *The Gazette*, I thought you'd be interested in a recent article they did on a new product of ours."

- Over time, if the media covers you often enough, you might acquire the status of "expert" and then continue getting coverage with relatively little extra effort.

Query Letters That Get Attention

Editors receive query letters every day. At major publications they may literally receive hundreds of *pitches* by phone, e-mail, and hard copy. Since editors are busy and their volume of reading is extremely high, they have to decide quickly what they're going to spend time on and what goes into the "circular file."

Sound familiar? Everyone decides what to read or toss in seconds, so you've got to get attention fast.

How?

You already know the general rules, so I'll just quickly remind you of them:

- Your query has to be well written.
- It has to be professionally formatted.
- It has to address the needs of the reader.

> **FYI**
>
> A **pitch** is a concise written or verbal presentation of an idea for a story, article, interview, or program segment to an editor, journalist, or radio or television producer.

What Editors Need

That last point is crucial. The most common complaint that editors have about query letters is that "the writer obviously never read my publication." Too often, people pitch editors ideas that won't interest their readers, that would offend their advertisers, or that were already covered recently in their publication. Editors toss these letters immediately.

Editors need ideas for articles that will interest their readers, will be acceptable to the advertisers, and have not been done to death, or that at least offer a new spin on an old topic. This means that you must target publications properly and develop fascinating ideas.

How to Target Publications

The publications you want to target are the ones read by the people you want to reach. If you sell high fashion, you want coverage in *Vogue* and *W*; if you sell rock-and-roll CDs, you want your company's artists written up in *Rolling Stone* and *Spin*; if you sell business equipment, you want *The Wall Street Journal* and *Business Week*, and so on.

If you target a publication properly, you'll automatically be on the road to connecting with the editor. That's because you'll be trying to reach the same readers that she's trying to reach.

Now it's obvious that you don't pitch an idea for a piece on the Canadian floor covering market to *Seventeen* magazine and that you don't target *Linoleum World* with an article on how to get rid of zits. However, at a more subtle level, each publication has its own point of view, style, and "voice." Some are serious, some irreverent; some cover personalities, some don't. The only way to get a fix on these aspects is to read a few issues.

Many libraries stock one or more good directories of magazines and newspapers, including *Ulrich's International Periodicals Directory* or *Standard Periodical Directory* for magazines, and *Editor and Publisher International Yearbook* for newspapers. Writer's Digest Books publishes an annual directory, available in bookstores, called *Writer's Market*, which lists hundreds of magazines and newspapers (as well as book publishers). Another source, although it's less readily available (and quite expensive), is *Bacon's Publicity Checker*, also available in a CD-ROM version. A good business library, for example, at a university, will often have a copy of *Bacon's*.

Some of these sources now provide online versions of these directories or other Web-based services. For instance, you can access Ulrich's online products at www.ulrichsweb.com, *Editor and Publisher International Yearbook* at www. editorandpublisher.com/eandp/yearbook/index.jsp, and *Bacon's* online services at www.bacons.com. Online versions of the more dynamic sources, such as *Bacon's*, are updated more frequently than the print versions. However, online services can be expensive. The online world changes rapidly, so it's worth it occasionally to check these online versions of hard-copy sources, and to conduct searches for online sources of media information.

Tricks of the Trade

Every business should have an online, Web-based public relations strategy. This specialized area is beyond the scope of this book, but an online strategy should include a professionally designed website, links to other sites, tactics for becoming visible to search engines such as Google and Yahoo!, and perhaps an electronic newsletter.

FYI

A **byline** tells you who wrote the article in a newspaper or magazine. Sometimes a bio note or author's bio will give a bit of information beyond the name: "So-and-so is president of Speedpar Industries, a manufacturer of automotive products."

When you target publications it's natural to get excited about the big, household names, but it can be a mistake. *Time, Newsweek, The New York Times, The Wall Street Journal,* and other national publications get hundreds of query letters and press releases a week. They also have large staffs that develop article ideas. And they tend to be general in their coverage, interested only in topics with very broad appeal. Given all this, you can often do better targeting local or regional publications that are more tightly focused on the readers you most want to reach.

Your target publications and radio and TV shows, with the names, titles, addresses, telephone and fax numbers, and e-mail addresses of the editor or producer, make up your press list (or media list). Keep this list updated in a computerized database so you can efficiently do mass mailings.

Targeting the right editor or producer is essential. Don't assume that they will pass your material along to the right person in their outfit, and don't suggest that they should or you'll appear unprofessional. When you build your press list, get on the phone and ask whom the best person would be to send ideas or news items to. Many general-interest publications have special editors for investing, small business, new products, technology, education, retail, lifestyle, food, home improvement, and so on.

If you're interested in getting your idea or item into a specific column, write to the editor or author of that column. Sometimes, if the author doesn't have a *byline,* you'll have to call and ask who writes the column. This is especially true for columns called things like "People on the Move" or "Company News" that consist of many short entries.

How to Develop Story and Article Ideas

To develop ideas, get into brainstorming mode (see Chapter 6) and think along typical story lines. These include …

- Event-driven stories, which focus on a recent news item or major event (for example, a visit by a dignitary, a sharp rise or drop in the stock market, or a recession)

- Issue-driven stories, which focus on trends (for example, a wave of layoffs or the aging of the workforce), lifestyles (for example, strategies for time-pressed, two-paycheck households, or successful high-school student entrepreneurs), people's concerns (such as budgeting, retirement, or safety), or other issues

- Personality-driven stories, which focus on people in your organization or those you sell to (for example, your CEO is a skydiver or your largest customer is a French billionaire)

- Internally driven stories, which focus on events within your company (for example, a new product or a reorganization)

If your idea is event- or issue-driven, make sure you find an "angle" for your company or products or services as well as for the editors' readers. Remember, you're writing to get publicity, not for the joy of giving editors great ideas.

If the idea is personality- or internally driven, you need to relate that to a newsworthy event or topic. Editors are not in the business of promoting your company. If you tie something about your company into an event or trend, you justify mention of your company by linking it to something newsworthy.

Developing story ideas takes work. Even professional PR people often find it difficult, and they never stop thinking about it. It comes down to brainstorming and thinking deeply, reading widely, listening carefully, and always seeking connections between your company and the "outside world."

CAUTION Pitfalls

Editors notoriously avoid "puff pieces," which are articles that simply tout your company or its people or products. If you pitch one, you're wasting your time and undermining your credibility with that editor.

Outline for a Great Query Letter

Sample 17-A provides an outline for an effective query letter.

Dear _____:

Paragraph #1

- Lead off with an attention-grabbing opening.
- Tie the idea in with a news item, trend, or general concern of readers.

Paragraph #2

- Explain the article idea.
- Mention that, and perhaps why, the publication's readers will be interested.

Paragraph #3

- Explain why you're qualified to write the article, or, if you're pitching yourself, your client, or someone in your company as a source, to talk about the subject.
- If you are writing the article, mention when you would deliver it, in what form, and any other details.

Paragraph #4

- Add a cordial closing.

⊙ *Sample 17-A: Outline for a query letter to an editor.*

Always be sure to include your contact information.

This general outline will work for articles that you would write, or for ideas that you pitch for the editor to have written by her staff or a freelancer, with you, your client, or someone in your company acting as a source.

Sample 17-B shows a letter for an article to be written by the person doing the pitch. Notice how it follows the outline.

If you have any kind of published article that shows that you can write, include a copy as a "clip" if you are positioning yourself to write the article.

Sample 17-C pitches an idea for a column rather than proposing to write an article.

Jim Rivers Executive Recruiting
400 Water Street
Hannibal, MO 05661
1-800-959-8000

Ms. Ellen d'Amico
Managing Editor
Careers After College
201 Broadway
Cambridge, MA 02139

Dear Ms. d'Amico:

This June, tens of thousands of graduating students will start their careers in business. Yet how many of them are really prepared for the challenges of today's uncertain workplace?

An editor will take a specific proposal for an article more seriously than a vague one.

To help them in career planning and interviewing, I propose a 2,000-word feature article with the working title, "Creating the Chameleon Career." The chameleon career helps people deal with the constant change of today's workplace. It means developing portable skills, constantly gauging the market, and being ready to move quickly from employment to self-employment—and back again.

In my 15 years as an executive recruiter, I've seen what it takes to survive downsizing and recession and to prosper during expansion and growth. I have published several articles in newsletters (see the enclosed clips) and would do a professional job on this piece.

I could have the completed article on your desk within four weeks of your giving me the go-ahead. Please give me your reaction to this article idea at your earliest convenience.

Thank you for your consideration.

Sincerely,

Jim Rivers
Managing Director

Sample 17-B: Request to submit an article, addressed to an editor.

Mr. Mark Darymple
Editor—New Product News
The Gazette
888 Main Street
Deerville, MN 99999

Dear Mr. Darymple:

Our newest product—a high-tech import from Japan—will hit the streets on May 25th. It's The WristPhone: a telephone that's a bit bigger than a digital sports watch and is worn the same way. Because people already wear watches, the product includes a digital watch, but The WristPhone is far more than a timepiece.

Our Japanese partner, CyberPhone Industries, has miniaturized cell-phone technology so that the clarity of communications on this tiny phone equals or exceeds that of most full-size cellular phones. A miniature speakerphone serves as both the microphone for talking and the speaker for listening. While small, the touch-tone pad resembles the one on an ordinary cellular phone and is easily accessible.

The WristPhone will initially be available in one size for men and women and only in black, with a choice of 12 fashionable straps. The retail price of $295 includes a one-year warranty on parts and labor. Billing for calls is through normal cellular-phone service providers at normal cell-phone rates.

If you would like to see a demonstration of this exciting new product, we can arrange one in your office. If you like, we could even let you use The WristPhone for a couple of days so you can review the product. I'm also available for an interview at 1-800-555-9999 ext. 243.

Thank you for your consideration.

Very truly,

Jerry Spengler
Vice President, Marketing

Sample 17-C: Pitch for an idea for a column, addressed to an editor.

— This letter is targeted to exactly the right person.

Whenever you write to the press, aim for an enthusiastic but businesslike tone. Editors resent any hint of a condescending tone or an approach that says, "Here's an idea that's going to blow your readers out of their chairs." Even worse is saying, "If you don't like this idea, we're ready to pitch it elsewhere."

Tricks of the Trade

Be aware that most magazines work with lead times that can be much longer than you might think. For a monthly or quarterly publication, submit article ideas at least three to four months in advance. You can learn about lead times, the readership, and the preferred writing style at the magazine by reviewing the writers' guidelines or guidelines for submissions that most magazine issue. You can usually find these guidelines at the magazine's website or request a copy either via e-mail or by regular mail.

Be careful with simultaneous submissions, which are those that are sent to more than one editor at a time. Most editors don't like simultaneous submissions of article ideas if you intend to write the article. If you're just submitting an idea, that's different. If you do make a simultaneous submission of an article that you propose to write (I don't suggest this), mention it.

Traditionally, most editors prefer query letters, and many still do when they deal with freelance writers. However, many editors also accept, and some prefer, e-mail submissions. This is especially the case when they deal with people they know or people they recognize as professionals. The thing editors seem to agree on is their dislike of phone calls from people they don't know.

The Growing Role of E-mail

Most editors, journalists, and producers are open to short pitches by e-mail. These e-mails need a subject line that identifies the e-mail as a pitch and briefly describes the idea. Do not use vague, pure-hype subject lines such as "Big News," "You Gotta Read This," or "Check This Out." Instead say something like, "Story Idea: Varietal Olive Oils," "Pitch: Robotic Assembly Systems," or "Article Idea: Biologist Succeeds in Business."

E-mail specific individuals, and if they telephone you in response, try to get to know their needs. Ask about the kinds of stories they're most interested in; many editors are actively looking for certain types of articles or pieces covering certain issues or areas.

Sample 17-D is an e-mail pitch to the editor of the weekly food section at a large newspaper.

To: Sherry Tamblyn <sherrybaby@morninggazette.com>

From: Lou Coselletto <lcoselletto@olivenotdrab.com>

Subject: Pitch: The Varietal Olive Oil Trend

Hello Ms. Tamblyn,

As you may know, food and dining enthusiasts now take olive oil as seriously as wine and cheese. They're looking for oils from specific regions, with specific flavors, for specific purposes. Food connoisseurs and critics write tasting notes on the appearance, aroma, taste, viscosity, and finish of imported and domestic olive oils.

I believe readers of your Wednesday "Food & Dining" section would want to know about these olive oils and how to buy, judge, and use them. Therefore, I propose an article on varietal olive oils, based on interviews with importers, retailers, and chefs. I can supply these sources for your staff writer, or write the article and submit it within two weeks.

Contact:
Lou Coselletto
212-558-5800
lcoselletto@olivenotdrab.com
www.olivenotdrab.com

Sample 17-D: E-mail pitch for article idea.

Sample 17-D works because it's specific, brief, and targeted to the right editor. The pitch mentions the editor's readers, makes the trend seem real and appealing, and solves a problem for the editor by supplying sources, or getting the article done on a freelance basis.

Note the contact information, which provides the name, telephone number, e-mail, and website address of the person who pitched the idea. The editor will recognize this as a pitch from a public relations professional on staff at the olive oil outfit or an independent who's working closely with them. Yet the article does not sound like a "puff piece" but like one that will deliver real value to the editor's readers.

Press Releases

The press release, also known as the news release or media release, has its own rules and quirks, but essentially it's a recognized means for an organization to communicate a news item (or what it hopes is a news item) to the media. You can send a press release to several, or thousands of, publications and shows at a time.

Anyone and any organization can send a press release to a newspaper, magazine, radio program, or TV show. As with any written communication, sending it to a specific person is important. However, a press release is not a one-to-one means of communication. It's designed to broadcast a message through the media. Editors and producers understand that it's going to many of them simultaneously.

Press releases used to go out by mail, and often still do. However, the fax machine is becoming the delivery mechanism of choice for press releases. If you have a telephone line, the right communications software, and a computerized database, you can send a press release by fax to hundreds, even thousands, of editors from your personal computer.

In fact, the computer and fax machine have made it so easy to send press releases that they now come flying out of machines all day long. The staggering volume at many publications again raises the question: How do you ensure that your material gets read?

Press Releases That Get Attention

Your press release must be well written, of course, and it must be in the proper format, or it will be dismissed as the work of an amateur.

Getting attention comes down to content. An editor at a nationally distributed newspaper once told me, "Frankly, most press releases aren't really about anything newsworthy. They're about things the company would like to get into the news, but they're rarely about anything that our readers would find interesting." She's not alone in that opinion.

Press releases, by their nature, have to do with your organization. It makes no sense for an outfit to distribute a news item about something not connected with its business. The challenge, then, is to first decide what is and isn't newsworthy, and second, when possible, to develop an angle connected to the outside world. I say "when possible" because it's acceptable to send out a press release that is just company news—if it is significant. If it's not significant, either don't send it out, or first work up an angle connected to the outside world.

Outline for a Press Release

Sample 17-E provides the basic form and an outline for a press release.

For: Name, Address, and Company issuing the release

Contact: The name and phone number of person to contact for more information

FOR IMMEDIATE RELEASE (or the release date)

Headline

Use an attention-grabbing headline.

Paragraph #1

◆ Mention one or two exciting facts in this lead paragraph.

◆ Mention the name of your organization.

Paragraph #2

◆ Add more detail and expand on a fact or two from the first paragraph.

◆ Use a quote from someone in the company or from a more objective source, like a customer.

Paragraph #3

◆ Add more detail, expand on another fact or two, and use another quote.

◆ Mention your organization's line of business.

Close

◆ In the close, try to echo the key fact from the lead and reinforce the basic message, perhaps with another quote.

◉ *Sample 17-E: Outline for a press release.*

Double-space the text and leave a ragged (not justified) right margin. Try to keep the press release to one page. If you go to a second page, type MORE at the bottom of the first page. Then, at the top of the second page, type the name of your business and the word "Continued." Don't go beyond two pages. At the end of the text, type END.

Sample 17-F shows an example of a good press release, using The WristPhone as the subject again. Note the differences between a query letter and a press release.

For: Monarch Mobile Communications
557 Alexandria Blvd., McLean, Virginia 99999

Contact: Jerry Spengler, Vice President, Marketing, 1-800-555-9999 ext.
243

FOR IMMEDIATE RELEASE

WristPhone Set to Shake Up Cell Phone Market

McLean, Va.—Dick Tracy won't need his wrist radio anymore and the cellular phone category could see a shake-up in the months ahead. The $295 WristPhone, which will hit retail stores in the next two weeks, fits on your wrist and includes a digital watch. New nanotechnology from Tokyo-based Monarch partner CyberPhone Industries makes the tiny telephone possible.

According to Monarch President Terry Maltby, "Without a doubt, this technology delivers clarity of sound equal to or better than current cellular phones. This should change the game in cellular phones." Monarch, which makes a line of six different cellular phones, plus several wireless home phones, is the first U.S. company to offer a wristwatch-size phone.

Recognizing that consumers are already wearing watches, the company included a digital watch in The WristPhone. Maltby states, "The phone weighs almost as little as a digital watch. It's nicely styled with a black casing and a choice of 12 different wristbands." The keypad on The WristPhone looks like that of a regular touch-tone phone, only smaller.

Over half a million WristPhones have been sold in Japan. Monarch, the exclusive North American distributor, expects to sell that many in the U.S. and Canada over the next 12–18 months.

END

Quotations in press releases help reporters write their stories.

Sample 17-F: *Press release.*

Try to give the editor everything she'll need to write a short article on the topic. In practice, if a press release gets "picked up" (used in some way by the newspaper, magazine, or show), it is usually as the basis of a short article or as a source of information or a quote in a larger piece. For this reason, it's good to include a quote or two in a press release. Journalists like quotes.

Making Your Own News

If you have the time, resources, and ambition, you can create your own news. I'm not talking about committing a spectacular crime or running for office. I'm suggesting that you launch a survey or conduct a study. Many companies do a study annually or every two years so they have a reason to get into the news periodically. The survey should, of course, be tightly connected to your business.

Some surveys get picked up by major media every year and become mini news events in their own right.

Regardless of the news or item, a well-crafted query letter or press release is your best tool for getting media attention.

Sample 17-G is a press release based on a survey by the fictitious Jim Rivers Executive Recruiters.

For:	Jim Rivers Executive Recruiters
	400 Water Street, Hannibal, MO 99999
Contact:	Jim Rivers, President, 1-800-555-3333

FOR IMMEDIATE RELEASE

New Grads Face Tougher Job Outlook

Hannibal, MO—An annual survey shows that this year's graduating college seniors face the toughest job outlook of the 2000s. The survey of 350 employers, done every year since 1992 by Jim Rivers Executive Recruiters, reveals that most companies are still keeping staffs relatively lean, given the pace of growth in the economy.

This is not to say that there are no jobs for grads this year. "It's just going to be more competitive this year. The slow growth of recent years simply means fewer jobs for recent graduates," said Jim Rivers, president of the company that sponsors the study. Rivers added that job-search skills, such as targeting prospective employers and interviewing well, typically enable qualified grads to land jobs within four months of graduation.

Two paragraphs can be enough if you really have something to say.

END

Sample 17-G: Press release based on a company study.

Do's and Don'ts When Writing to the Media

Do:

- Present an item that can be judged newsworthy.
- Try to write in an interesting but objective manner.
- Give facts, instead of opinion, to the degree possible.
- Use proper form in your press releases.
- Include a quote or two in press releases.

Don't:

- Pitch self-serving "puff pieces."
- Take a condescending or bombastic tone.
- Promise an article (or anything) that you can't deliver.
- Let any typos or factual errors slip through.
- Give up after one or two attempts.

The Least You Need to Know

- If you want attention from the press, build and maintain a well-targeted, computerized media list.
- Use a query letter to pitch article ideas to editors and producers, but send only one article idea to an editor at a time.
- Most editors accept e-mail pitches. An e-mail pitch should be brief and carry an informative subject line that identifies it as a pitch.
- Use a press release to get word out to numerous people in the media at the same time.
- In all of your writing to the media, understand that their concern is not your needs, but their readers' interests.
- If you target the right publications and present good ideas to them often enough, you will eventually get through, but it takes time to learn the right approach.

Sales Letters Are Your License to Print Money

In This Chapter

- ◆ A proven approach to writing sales letters
- ◆ How to talk to the reader about features and benefits
- ◆ How to answer e-mail queries to your website
- ◆ Increasing the chances of getting a response to your sales letter

Although you're probably not a direct-mail pro, there's a good chance you'll have to write a sales letter or something very like one in the course of your career. If you work for someone else, it's a great skill to have in your portfolio. If you're self-employed, you might find prospecting and selling by mail to be a great source of business. That's what I've found as a consultant and business writer.

The topic of direct mail, which includes *mailing lists*, *reply mechanisms*, *collateral material*, and much more, has filled many books. This chapter will show you something basic: how to write a sales letter that opens doors—and wallets and purses and checkbooks.

The Challenge: Getting Attention

If you think there's too much direct mail out there, you're in good company: People in the industry agree. It's a problem for them, and they call it "clutter." Their solution, of course, is not to stop sending out their letters, but rather to get theirs to break through the clutter and grab readers' attention.

At the least, a sales letter has to be well written. If you can make it sparkle or sizzle or skyrocket (what is it about "s" words, anyway?), so much the better. These letters also must speak to the reader in a personal way.

> **FYI**
>
> A **mailing list** is a list of the names and addresses of people who will be the target of a direct mail campaign.
>
> **Reply mechanisms** are ways for the reader to get in touch with you, such as postage-paid return envelopes and postcards, toll-free telephone numbers, and e-mail and website addresses.
>
> **Collateral material** means brochures and other kinds of product literature that accompany the sales letter.

Most of all, you must offer something the reader sees as important. This means that whatever you're offering has to solve a problem, fill a need, save money, or make money for the reader. In fact, your product or service should aim or at least claim to deliver a unique benefit to the reader. This benefit becomes the *unique selling proposition*, something terrific that your product or service, and only your product or service, can do for the reader.

> **FYI**
>
> The **unique selling proposition,** or USP, is a concept from advertising that recognizes the need for a product to stand out from the rest of its kind. Every product should do this, even if it is essentially very much like the others. How can companies do this, when so many products are so alike? It's an exercise in creativity, in which marketing and advertising professionals associate intangible characteristics with the product, which customers come to accept.

The battle for reader attention has led the direct mail industry to develop various bells and whistles to engage the reader. These include so-called involvement pieces that give the reader something to do, such as moving a sticker from the collateral material to the reply card. Although these often work, the most fundamental things you need for success in selling by mail is a good offer, a good letter, and a great mailing list.

A Word About Mailing Lists

As we all know, the reader is king. The people on the mailing list are the readers. Depending on your business, this list can number from ten people up to tens of thousands. In building your mailing list, you actually choose your audience as you would in few other forms of writing for the public. So this step is extremely important. No matter how great your letter is, if it's going to the wrong people, you'll get nowhere.

As a small-business person, I've found that the best way to compile a mailing list is by myself (or through a research assistant), by hand, over time. This means going to the library and searching professional and industry directories, and collecting names from newspapers and magazines. It means writing down website addresses and visiting websites, and gathering contact information from them. It also means keeping the lists of attendees from every event I attend. Then all of these names are entered into my database of prospects. (Often I use the phone to get addresses and titles and so on.) Key point: I don't do large-scale mailings, so this is practical for me.

Tricks of the Trade

If you are a consultant or small-business person, you should definitely consider compiling a computer-accessible list of names and addresses and regularly doing some prospecting by mail. A good word-processing package will enable you to create a table of this information and then merge that list with a sales letter. This is a great way to test an idea you have, to see if it will really work with real prospects.

If you need to do large mailings, say over 1,000 to 2,000 pieces, you may need to rent a list from a mailing list broker. There are several very large ones in the United States, as well as many smaller outfits. They can be found in the Yellow Pages in major cities, or on the web through a search engine. Call and they'll gladly send you a catalog. Often the websites can be quite informative, and even allow you to download names and contact information for a fee.

You can also rent the lists of organizations or publications whose members or readers you want to approach by mail. These lists can be more reliable because they are simply compilations of the members' names and information. List brokers often sell lists of subscribers to magazines that are outdated. However, list selection for direct mail is a subject unto itself, and beyond the scope of this book.

Two Ways to Write a Letter

You can write either a long sales letter or a short one. By "long" I mean more than two pages. A typical format for a long letter is four to six pages on over-sized paper, done so that the letter folds out. By "short" I mean a page or two. One page can be very effective, and stands the best chance of actually getting read. In this book, we deal only with short sales letters.

Short and Sweet Sales Letters

My formula for short, three-paragraph sales letters has not changed for more than 10 years, because it works. The outline in Sample 18-A sums up the formula.

Dear _____:

Paragraph #1

- ◆ Dramatize a problem that the reader can relate to.
- ◆ Use simple language that the reader readily understands.

Paragraph #2

- ◆ Tell the reader that you have the solution to this problem.
- ◆ Explain how your product or service solves the problem.
- ◆ If possible, show that you understand why this problem is important or difficult to solve.

Paragraph #3

- ◆ Ask the reader to place an order or request more information.
- ◆ Tell the reader that you will be in touch.

◉ *Sample 18-A: Outline for a one-page sales letter.*

There's nothing magical about it. It's just the old hard-sell, gussied up:

"Tired of sleeping on that tired old bed? Tired of waking up tired?" (The Problem)

"Then try the new SuperMat Sleep-Easy. Your back will know the difference." (The Solution)

"Visit your local SuperMat dealer today. Check the phone book for one near you." (The Way to Get the Solution)

It works. It's as reliable as ready, aim, fire. (Yes, unfortunately, sometimes you miss.)

Sample 18-B demonstrates this formula in action.

Ms. Wendy Quinn
President
Quinn Distribution
945 Washington Street
Knoxville, TN 99999

Dear Ms. Quinn:

Opening with one or more questions immediately involves the reader. —— Are you disappointed or angry that so much of your money goes to taxes each year? Hardworking business people often don't know that they can lower their tax bills with a few small changes, and often no change, to their operations.

I am a certified public accountant specializing in tax and estate planning for business owners. A number of my clients in the distribution business have found that their taxes dropped dramatically—by up to 25% in some cases—with my tax planning strategies. These strategies are, of course, entirely legal. Some of these strategies may well keep more of your money in your pocket.

Next week, I'll be calling you to arrange a meeting at your convenience. If you give me 30 minutes, I'll give you a new way of thinking about your taxes.

I look forward to speaking with you soon.

Sincerely,

Jack Murray

President

Sample 18-B: A short, sweet sales letter.

What's at Work in This Letter?

Aside from the formula I mentioned in the previous section, several other things are at work in Sample 18-B. Let's analyze them paragraph by paragraph.

In the first paragraph, the *copy strategy* uses a question to dramatize the problem. As I pointed out in Chapter 9, questions tend to engage the reader. If you use questions, don't use more than three in a row, four at the most if they're short, because you might overwhelm the reader. You can use bullets to list the questions and increase white space. Questions are a common copy strategy, so come up with ones that the reader will find really interesting.

In the second paragraph, the writer positions himself as the solution to tax problems. In doing this, he must establish credibility, which he does by mentioning that he's a certified public accountant who has helped clients in the reader's industry. He also quotes a dramatic number—quoting numbers in your copy adds credibility. Numbers impress most people, especially business people. He also tries to ease any of the reader's fears about the legality of these strategies.

The third paragraph tells the reader that Jack will be in touch to make an appointment. The (unstated) action requested is, "Please take my call and give me an appointment." In one sentence he also requests an amount of time and reinforces the core message of the letter by mentioning the benefits again.

The fourth, one-line paragraph in the letter is a cordial closing that rounds things off nicely.

This letter stands a good chance of being read, since it's short and fairly engaging. Unless the reader is paying practically nothing in taxes, she will probably at least take Jack's phone call and listen to his pitch.

FYI

Direct-mail professionals use the term **copy strategy** to refer to the approach that the letter will take toward the reader and the subject. The term "copy" refers to text of any kind.

Pitfalls

A number of copywriting coaches, particularly those selling their services on the web, advocate a highly emotional pitch, but that approach can turn off some readers. Again, it comes down to knowing your audience. For instance, if you're selling a product to businesses, as opposed to consumers, a highly emotional pitch may sound shrill. (You shouldn't totally avoid tapping people's emotions; the best sales writing appeals to both the intellect and the emotions.)

Note that the audience for copywriting training and coaching tends to be writers or aspiring writers. Take it from me; we are an emotional, hopeful group of people. When these copywriters write for other audiences (and some of them do), they usually modify their approach.

Features and Benefits: The Difference and Why It Matters

Tricks of the Trade

Generic salutations like "Dear Client" and "Dear Jazz Fan" are obviously far less personal than those using the reader's name. Whenever it is cost-effective (sometimes it just isn't), have an internal address and a personal salutation inserted by computer. It's not necessary to insert the reader's name into the body of the text.

The major problem in most sales letters written by amateurs is that the copy stresses features rather than benefits.

Here's the difference: *Features* are about the product and service; *benefits* are about the reader and his needs. When you talk about features, you're talking about what you are selling. When you talk about benefits, you're talking about how what you are selling can help the reader.

For example, if you say that something you're selling is durable, that's a feature. The benefit is that it won't break down and cost the customer time, money, and energy. If you say that the software you sell has drop-down menus and a great "Help" facility, those are features. The benefit is that it's easy for the customer to learn and use.

In service businesses like consulting, many sellers tout features without tying them to benefits. Here are some examples of what I mean:

"Acme Consulting Services was established in 1984 to serve the financial services industry."

"Our client base includes some of the largest banks and securities firms in the nation, while our staff of over 40 market researchers, strategic planners, and product development specialists holds more than 25 graduate degrees."

"All of the methods we use on client engagements have stood the test of time, yet we keep abreast of new approaches."

And so on. This is typical of writing that is all about the seller rather than about the reader's needs. The way to avoid writing like this is to focus on how the characteristics of the company can help the reader. Here's how you might rewrite these three points to do just that:

"Because Acme has specialized in financial services since 1984, we understand the problems you face. You don't have to spend weeks and months—and money—teaching us your business."

"Our staff of over 40 includes market researchers, strategic planners, and product development specialists. This versatile group can work with your people in any capacity required to help you reach your business goals."

"Our methods have stood the test of time, which means, frankly, that we do not use our clients as guinea pigs. However, we also keep abreast of new approaches in order to bring you the best of them—the ones that will work in your business."

You see? Prospects often view comments about how great you are or how great your client list is as self-serving. And they *are* self-serving, unless they link to a benefit for the client. Readers care about saving time and money, avoiding loss and frustration, and reaching their financial and business goals. Helping them with those amounts to benefits.

So the way to write about benefits requires translating a feature of your product or service into a benefit, as in the following examples:

Feature	Benefit
The color is red	You'll stand out in a crowd
The motor is strong	You'll enjoy the power at your fingertips
We work quickly	You can give us the project on short notice and still make your deadlines
We're inexpensive	You save money
We deliver high quality	You get it done right the first time
This glass is bulletproof	You'll be safe from gunshots

Whatever it is, if it's a feature worth mentioning, it's worth tying to a benefit.

What About Sales E-mails?

While most people have become tolerant of unsolicited hard-copy direct-mail pieces, that feeling does not extend to cyberspace. Spam or unsolicited sales e-mails won't do your business much good (unless you're a professional spammer, in which case you're on your own).

However, if your business has a website, it should offer visitors the option of e-mailing requests for more information about your products or services. At that point, you have a potential *prospect*, and perhaps a selling opportunity.

Don't use your e-mail response just to repeat the information about your product or service that you already have on your website. Instead use it to establish more personal contact, start *qualifying the prospect*, and set up a phone call.

Sample 18-C is a management consultant's e-mail answer to an e-mail request for more information from a visitor to the firm's website. Note that the response refers to the website, but focuses more on establishing personal contact and learning about the inquirer's needs.

> **FYI**
>
> A **prospect** is a consumer or businessperson who is a potential customer for the product or service you sell. You can identify prospects to approach through the mail or on the telephone by examining your customers and finding other consumers or businesses with similar characteristics. Or a prospect can come to you by calling you or e-mailing you.
>
> A **qualified prospect** is a prospect that you have identified as having three characteristics (or qualifications): 1) a current or near-term need for what you sell, 2) the money to pay for what you sell, and 3) the authority to make the purchase decision.

To: Jim Daniels <jamesrdaniels@microtechologiesinc.com>

From: Tim Mathis <tmathis@tmgresearchassociates.com>

Subject: Answer to Your Inquiry

Jim,

Thank you for your e-mail asking about our services. As you probably saw at our website, we specialize in helping companies of all types identify growth opportunities. For instance, our Marketing Machine‰ finds new customers for your products and services, while our Money Machine‰ boosts sales with creative pricing, packaging, and product line strategies.

I'd like to learn a bit about your needs, and tell you a bit more about how we can help your company grow the top and bottom lines. The best way to do that would be for us to chat briefly on the phone—at no cost or obligation to you, of course.

You can reach me directly at 888-999-5656 during business hours. I look forward to hearing from you, and to filling out the picture that we can only start to convey at our website.

Regards,

Tim Mathis

Sample 18-C: *E-mail response to a request for information.*

More Examples of Good Sales Letters

Sample 18-D shows an example of a sales letter for a business product.

As the sample shows, you are certainly not limited to three paragraphs. This letter employs several tactics worth pointing out:

- ◆ It starts by quoting an independent study. Whenever you can quote a source other than yourself to dramatize a problem, it adds credibility. Testimonials from customers can be particularly powerful.

- ◆ The writer explains how his company can deliver these savings. This helps overcome the reader's natural skepticism.

◆ The guarantee also helps overcome skepticism and sales resistance, and it dovetails nicely with the request for the reader's current prices: Standard Products can't beat a price without documentation, can it?

◆ The letter uses an eye-catching P.S. to flag a deadline. Any time you add a deadline, whether driven by a special sale, free premium, or extra savings, it tends to increase your response rate—the percentage of the pieces of mail you send that generate a response.

By the way, on most mass mailings, a response rate of 1 to 2 percent is considered good. That may strike you as low, but on some mailings, ½ percent is considered a good return. Direct mail is "a numbers game."

Sample 18-E shows a sales letter for a consumer product.

Standard Products Incorporated
900 Lowell Bank Station
Millstone, CT 04587

Mr. Mark Peters
Vice President
Peterson Brokerage Services
245 Lincoln Blvd.
Los Angeles, CA 09008

Dear Mr. Peters:

A recent study by the American Photocopying Institute showed that photocopying costs have risen 7% in each of the past two years. The study showed that the increase is not due to the cost of copiers. Rather, it is the skyrocketing cost of supplies, particularly paper and toner.

I'm writing to you because I can help you cut these costs sharply. In fact, if you own your own copiers or lease at favorable terms, Standard Products Inc. can guarantee that your cost per copy will actually decrease over the next year.

Standard Products can give you this guarantee because we buy in huge volume from various manufacturers and thus win deep discounts. Also, our state-of-the-art distribution network minimizes warehousing and shipping costs. We pass these savings on to you by beating whatever price you're now paying.

Of course, low prices mean nothing without high quality, so we also guarantee the quality of our paper, toner, and other supplies. The copies you get with our supplies will be as good as—or better than—your current copies.

To get these savings, you only have to do one thing: Pick up the phone and call us at 1-800-555-0300. Tell us your current volume of usage and

Effective formatting can save a sales letter from going straight into the recycling bin.

what you're now paying for paper and toner, and we'll fax you a proposal the next business day. (To give our guarantee of lower prices, we do require documentation of your current prices, so be ready to mail or fax us a recent invoice.)

Don't let another year of cost increases rob your profits. **Call us at 1-800-555-0300 today.**

Yours truly,

Leon Davies
President

P.S. If you place an order with us by the 15th of this month, we will take an <u>additional</u> 10% off the price of that first order. Call now and start saving!

Sample 18-D: A sales letter for a business product.

Victory Security Systems
45 Dakota Street
Miami, Florida 00440
1-800-555-6600

Dear Homeowner:

This disclaimer simultane-ously raises the issue and disarms objections. ——— Unfortunately, crime is on the rise in our city and shows no sign of decreasing. I am not, however, writing to frighten you, but to make you feel more secure.

Your Best Protection

Law enforcement officials everywhere agree that a top-quality home security system is your best protection against forcible home entry. Top-quality systems are the only kind we sell at Victory, which means that you get:

- Total protection against forcible entry, whether you are at home or away
- An easy-to-use system that you can set or disarm in the dark with just one finger
- Protection against false or accidental alarms
- Guaranteed three-hour installation and easy 24-month payment terms

We offer a 35-year record of protecting customers in Greater Miami. Our service personnel are bonded, and we can provide numerous local references for your review. Our commitment is to provide only the level of security that you require. However, you must ask yourself: Should I continue without a reliable home security system in today's environment?

Act Now to Protect Your Home and Family

Call us at 1-800-555-6600 today for a complimentary analysis of your home security needs. If you call for this free analysis within the next five business days and show your Victory Security Analyst this letter, he will give you a **free Victory Padlock** on the spot. This is the lock that stands up to the .357 Magnum at close range, as seen on TV.

Don't you owe this call to yourself and your family? Don't you deserve the protection recommended by law-enforcement officials against forcible home entry? Of course you do. Call today and learn how to protect yourself.

Sincerely,

Andrew Victor
President

P.S. Remember: You get a free Victory Padlock just for letting us analyze your security needs.

Sample 18-E: *A sales letter for a consumer product.*

The best writing appeals to both the head and the heart; that is, to the thinking and the feeling sides of the reader. The subject matter in Sample 18-E lends itself to an emotional appeal, which the writer exploits. Whenever possible, try to appeal to basic needs like money, security, and status.

Increasing Your Response Rate

Again, direct mail is a numbers game. Whether you send 6 pieces, 60, 600, or 60,000, the better your response rate, the more business you can do. To ensure that you have the highest possible response rate, be sure you …

◆ Start with an up-to-date mailing list of properly targeted prospects.

◆ Translate each important feature of your product or service into a benefit for the reader.

◆ Make an offer that has some time limit or time factor associated with it.

◆ If possible and appropriate, include a compelling P.S., because people generally read them.

◆ Unless the list proves to be a dud, try a follow-up mailing or even follow-up phone calls to selected prospects.

Provided you can afford the expense, don't give up too fast on direct mail if you believe it can work for your business. Repeated exposure lets people know that you intend to be around for a while and gets them used to seeing your name and your offer. That familiarity ultimately leads to more business.

The Least You Need to Know

- The easiest formula for writing a sales letter is to dramatize a problem, present your product or service as the solution, and ask for action or tell the reader how you will follow up.

- Much of your success depends on selecting or building the right mailing list. Also, after you build a good list, you must maintain it because people and businesses are in constant flux.

- A sales letter must speak directly to readers about how they'll benefit from dealing with you. Don't just tout features; instead, translate them into benefits.

- Enhance your credibility by quoting independent sources whenever possible. If a customer gives you a compliment, ask her if you can put that in writing and quote her in a sales letter. At a minimum, ask if she'll act as a reference.

- To create a sense of urgency, include the element of time ("If you act now …"), offer a special discount, or offer something for free to prompt the reader to act.

Decent Proposals (and Business Agreements)

In This Chapter

- Using proposals to move the sales process forward
- How proposals can be converted to agreements
- The elements of good proposals and agreements
- Protecting yourself in business deals

Most business deals require "something in writing." Something in writing can be anything from a long, formal contract to a short, informal letter of agreement. Deals have to start somewhere, and they often start with a written proposal. In fact, as you'll see in this chapter, the written proposal can become the basis of the final agreement.

The purpose of writing up a business deal, whether for the sale of equipment or for a consulting engagement, is to clarify the responsibilities of everyone in the transaction. Who must do what? When and where? What is the price? What are the terms and time of payment? What is to be delivered? By whom?

This chapter is not about contract law. To deal with that aspect of contracts you need an attorney, and I'm not an attorney. This chapter is about writing clear, businesslike proposals and letters of agreement—which are, in effect, simple contracts.

Is It Worth the Paper It's Printed On?

A *contract* is a legally enforceable agreement between two or more people or organizations. Many people don't realize that verbal contracts are just as legal as written contracts. They are, but without something in writing it's harder to enforce a contract because it becomes "your word against mine." That's why if someone is not willing to put something in writing, it's wise to wonder if they will follow through.

Pitfalls

If you're not familiar with basic contract law and you're writing proposals and signing letters of agreement, either read up on the subject or get advice from an attorney. From the business, as opposed to legal, perspective, many people inexperienced in this area tend either to promise too much in their proposal (in an effort to win the business or please the client) or they sign the client's "normal contract" and find that it works against them.

It takes three things to make a legal agreement: an offer, consideration, and acceptance.

Let's say that you are the one making the proposal, the one selling something or offering to do a piece of work. Your *offer* might be to sell your car to someone or to shoot a video for a company.

Consideration is what you will get in return. Usually this is money, but it could be something that you take in a trade. For example, you could trade your car for a motorcycle of similar value or you could shoot the video in return for free advertising.

Finally, you don't have an enforceable agreement without *acceptance*. This means that the other party has to accept your offer or you both agree to a *counteroffer*. It's usually a good idea to have the acceptance in writing.

Keep these basics in mind when you're writing proposals and agreements: offer, consideration, and acceptance.

FYI

A **counteroffer** is usually the result of bargaining. If you offer to sell your car for $5,000 and the other person says, "How about $4,000?" that person has made a counteroffer.

Tricks of the Trade

You may have several readers for your proposal. In most companies, it takes more than one person to okay a deal. Learn as much as you can beforehand about each person who must "sign off" on your proposal. Early in your sales process, ask "Who would have to sign off on this agreement?" and ask which area of the business they're responsible for or work in. Then try to learn how what you sell would affect them and their operation. In other words, try to learn about their concerns, then try to address those concerns in your proposal, or in conversations on the side.

How to Write an Attractive Proposal

As in most writing, the first step in writing a proposal is to understand your purpose and your reader. The purpose of most proposals is to get a piece of business: You want to sell something, usually to someone at a company (or you probably wouldn't need a written proposal).

That someone is your reader. In the discussions before your proposal, be sure to learn as much as you can about the needs of the people to whom you're selling. That way you can address these needs in your proposal.

The more of the readers' needs that you address in the proposal, the better your chances of making the sale—but watch out. You also have to address *your* needs. It's all well and good to try to meet the customer's need for a low price, but can you make a profit at that price? The customer may need delivery by a certain date. Can you meet that deadline while maintaining your quality standards and not getting burned out?

It's easy to overpromise when writing a proposal. Agreeing to meet an unrealistic deadline is a common mistake. So is throwing in "extras" that the client wants but doesn't want to pay for. When writing a proposal, think realistically about what you can deliver, about how long things take, and about how much profit you'll make if you do what you propose.

The secret of writing an attractive proposal is to do all that you can to meet the client's needs *and* your needs. This means doing some fact finding before writing the proposal. You must learn what the client's needs are and how your product or service can meet those needs. You must learn about the prospect's expectations, how urgent her need is, and about her deadlines. You must also learn your client's views on pricing and quality. Everyone wants high quality at a low price, but that's usually not realistic. Be honest and try to learn whether she prefers low price over high quality or is willing to pay for high quality.

Ask Questions

Your best tools at this point are questions. Before you write your proposal, ask the prospect:

♦ What problem do you want to solve with this purchase? What's the ideal solution?

♦ What's the most important aspect of this deal: price, quality, timing? If you had to pick one as most important, which would it be?

♦ Who will be involved in the decision to make this deal?

♦ Who will be affected by this purchase? What stake do they have in the deal?

♦ How long has this need existed? Is it now urgent? Why?

♦ When would you like to see this completed? What is your deadline?

Ask your prospect for his "wish list," the list of things that he would want you to deliver in an ideal world. Tell him that you probably can't deliver everything on his wish list, but you want to come as close as you can. Then ask him to prioritize the items on the wish list from most to least important. The resulting list will allow you to see what he'd like to get out of the deal, what he sees as most important.

You'll have other questions, of course, depending on your product or service. But these are the basic ones. They are part of any sales process, but they're especially important when you sell by proposal. The more you know about the reader's needs, the better the proposal.

Outline for a Proposal

Sample 19-A is an outline for a proposal. A proposal can run anywhere from one or two pages for a simple deal up to dozens of pages for a complex one.

Introduction

- ◆ Summarize your understanding of the prospect's needs.
- ◆ Mention what you're offering to meet those needs.

Deliverables

- ◆ Describe the equipment you will sell, or, if you are proposing a consulting assignment, the tasks you will perform.
- ◆ Mention any warranties or guarantees in this section.

Time Frame

- ◆ Specify the delivery date or deadline for completing the tasks.

Responsibilities

- ◆ Describe the tasks and items that you and the client are each responsible for under the agreement.
- ◆ Include items such as whether you will deliver the equipment or the client will pick it up, installation, training, follow-up visits, service calls, and so on.

Compensation

- ◆ State the amount you will be paid.
- ◆ Note the terms and schedule of payment.
- ◆ Mention expenses that the customer is responsible for, such as delivery charges, additional equipment, telephone charges, and printing costs.

Conclusion

- ◆ Mention that you are sure the client will be satisfied and you appreciate the opportunity to bid on this business.

Sample 19-A: Outline for a proposal.

A *bid* is an offer by a party to sell goods or services for a certain price. Often a company will request bids from several outfits. This frequently occurs in advertising, construction, and major equipment purchases. Many companies have a policy of getting three bids on any deal over a certain dollar amount, for example, $5,000 or $10,000.

An *RFP* or "request for proposals" is a document put out by an organization to solicit competitive proposals and bids. Often, especially if issued by a government agency, an RFP will ask for great detail in the proposal. If you respond to an RFP, your proposal must address every point in it.

The section heads used in the outline in Sample 19-A—Introduction, Deliverables, and so on—can be the actual section heads in your proposal, or you can change them to better suit your needs.

Sample Letter Proposals

Sample 19-B shows an example of a simple letter proposal for a product. A good-faith payment, as mentioned in the sample under "compensation," is a percentage of the total amount of the sale (usually not more than 10 percent), paid before work begins to demonstrate the buyer's commitment and to put some money in the seller's pocket.

Synergy Systems Inc.
444 Alameda Drive
Palo Alto, California 99999
1-800-555-9999

Ms. Orla McKeon
President
Zip Consulting Inc.
888 Montgomery Street
San Francisco, CA 99999

Dear Ms. McKeon:

Thank you for meeting with us over the past several weeks to give us an understanding of your business and your computing needs. Please convey our thanks to Jim, Marion, and Steve as well.

This letter proposes a solution that we believe will meet your needs for a user-friendly networked personal computing environment that can grow with you as your business grows. The parts of this proposal are:

◆ Introduction

◆ Deliverables

◆ Time frame

◆ Compensation

◆ Conclusion

——— These bullets tell the reader how the proposal is organized.

Introduction

Over the past several weeks, Synergy Systems has met with various members of Zip Consulting to learn about your needs for a personal computer network. This network should enable people in the company to work as a team, provide access to one another's files (except those marked "private"), and link to a time-tracking system for billing. The system must also allow you to send files to clients for review and approval. This letter proposes such a network.

Deliverables: The System, Training, Support, and Warranty

The System

The system will be configured as follows:

These bullets clarify what will be delivered.

- One Acme model 5000 client server
- Eighteen Acme A500 desktop computers with keyboards, mice, and monitors
- Six Acme model 465 laser printers and three Acme C400 color printers
- Synergy Systems series 999 network with all software and support
- Synergy Systems Sweet Suite (including five multimedia packs), plus the TimeTrack system to be linked to your accounting system

The system includes all wiring and full installation and documentation.

Training, Support, and Warranty

Our price includes five days of on-site training by our instructor for all personnel who will be using the system and all personnel that Zip wishes to attend. This means that you are purchasing five 7-hour days of our instructor's time, on-site at Zip.

Synergy Systems will provide support by telephone from 8:00 a.m. to 6:00 p.m. (Pacific time) for one year. We will also provide a one-year parts-and-labor warranty on all components of the system. This means that if any part of the system malfunctions because of a failure in quality or workmanship, we will repair it (or, at our option, replace it) free of charge for one year from the installation date. We cannot, however, reimburse Zip Consulting for any other loss resulting from the failure of this system.

Time Frame

Our proposed installation date would be 10–12 calendar days from the date that Zip accepts this proposal. We will require three days to install and test the system. These dates can be moved forward or backward as you require.

Compensation

The cost of the new system, including installation, training, and support as mentioned earlier, will be $118,000. You will find the cost of the individual components and the applicable discounts broken out on Attachment "A."

Continued support for the second year will be priced at $19,000, which includes all upgrades to the system.

Should you wish to purchase any training and consulting time beyond the five days included in this proposal, you will be billed at $1,200 per day or $200 per hour.

Our terms of payment are 10% of the total as a good-faith payment upon signing this agreement, 40% upon completion of the installation, and 50% within 30 days of completion of installation.

Conclusion

We believe that our proposed network solution represents the best way for Zip Consulting to achieve its goal of creating an interactive work environment with a built-in time-tracking system that feeds the billing system.

Thank you for giving us the opportunity to submit this proposal. We at Synergy Systems look forward to helping Zip Consulting toward its goals with the best in networked systems and support.

To accept this offer, please sign in the space provided below, or if you prefer, in a return letter of your own, and mail it to my attention with a check in the amount of $11,800 for the good-faith payment.

If you have any questions or there are points that you would like to discuss, please call me.

——— Close with an invitation to the reader to call with questions or to talk over the proposal.

Sincerely,

Gar Gartland
President

Accepted by:

_____ Date: _____

Orla McKeon
President

(◎) **Sample 19-B:** *Proposal for the sale of a product.*

How a Proposal Works

When you make a proposal, you formally present your offer and request a decision. Many firms find it a good practice (and a source of cash) to request a good-faith payment, although this is not strictly necessary. What is necessary is to get written approval of a written proposal. It would be nice if we could do business "on a handshake," but I don't recommend it. Settling for verbal approval of a written contract is asking for trouble.

Your prospect may simply sign your proposal and return it, or she may negotiate to modify the proposal. Keep in mind that a proposal is just that, a proposal. Proposals are by definition subject to counteroffers, negotiation, and modification. Some people don't even start seriously considering a deal until they see something in writing; then they begin negotiating. When there's something to be signed, most companies give it serious consideration.

This means that you can expect a bumpy ride on the road to many deals. A proposal will often sit on someone's desk for a while. Sometimes it's because your

Tricks of the Trade

Including an expiration date on your proposal can help you move the sale forward. It can also help you avoid rush jobs. If you don't have a deal by the expiration date, you can then push back the completion date.

deal is relatively low priority; sometimes it's because the person's not comfortable with the proposal and doesn't know how to follow up.

To give him an opening, you can telephone and ask about the proposal. For example, say, "Hello, Jim. I sent you my proposal last Thursday, and I'm wondering if you folks have had a chance to look it over." If he hasn't, at least you may get things moving.

If things seem to have stalled, try saying, "If you're not comfortable with some aspect of the proposal, I'd like us to talk it over. We'd like to do business with you, and if there's anything you feel needs to be addressed we can certainly discuss it."

If he has a problem with your proposal, he may open up at that point. Once it's on the table, you can then perhaps get negotiations moving forward.

Pitfalls

If possible, try to avoid e-mail when following up on a proposal, unless your prospect prefers e-mail or you're dealing with a customer you know well. I've seen several cases where e-mail is subject to misinterpretation, where the tone is hard to manage, or where the lack of the immediate give-and-take of a phone call works against both parties.

Sample 19-C and Sample 19-D show a cover letter and a proposal for a service rather than a product.

Presenting your proposal in modular form, with various tasks and bullets, enables the prospect to clearly see what you offer. It also enables her to negotiate, for example, by saying, "What if we forget about this task, or what if we go with a smaller quantity? How does that affect the price and delivery?" Again, such negotiation is often part of the process.

As you'll see if you contrast Samples 19-B and 19-D with the sample sales letters in Chapter 18, a proposal is not a sales letter. A sales letter opens the door so that you can learn about the prospect's needs and then craft a proposal that meets those needs.

Precision Market Research Associates
111 Sam Houston Drive
Dallas, Texas 99999
1-800-555-2333

Mr. Philip Verakus
Vice President, Marketing
All Brand Motors Leasing Corp.
490 Turtle Creek Road
Dallas, TX 99999

Dear Phil:

Thanks for having Steve and me in on the 12th to learn about your market research needs. I think we have a good understanding of your goals in Dallas/Fort Worth and of the information you'll need in order to create a marketing plan to meet those goals.

As promised, I've attached a proposal for a survey designed to get the information you need. When you've had a chance to review this proposal, please give me a call if you have any questions, comments, or modifications.

Steve and I look forward to working with you on this important project.   —— A positive close creates the right tone.

Sincerely,

Jeff Chu
Managing Director

Sample 19-C: Cover letter for a proposal.

Market Research Proposal

Prepared by:

Precision Marketing Associates
Dallas, TX

Prepared for:

All Brand Motors Leasing Corp.
Dallas, TX

May 2006

Introduction

This document proposes that Precision Marketing Associates (PMA) survey the luxury auto leasing market in Dallas/Fort Worth for All Brand Motors Leasing Corp. (All Brand) in the summer of 2006.

The goal of the survey is to gather information on the following aspects of the luxury car leasing market in Dallas/Fort Worth:

◆ Market share in Dallas/Fort Worth for the major luxury car manufacturers

- Market potential for luxury car sales and leasing
- Consumer and business attitudes toward leasing
- Key factors in the lease versus buy decision
- Consumer and business purchase and leasing plans over the next three years

Tasks and Deliverables

PMA will be responsible for the following tasks and deliverables:

- Task 1: Development of a questionnaire for a 30-minute interview designed to get the above-mentioned information
- Task 2: Development of a randomly selected list of 3,000 consumers and 1,000 businesses in Dallas/Ft. Worth
- Task 3: Completion of 200 telephone interviews (that is, completed questionnaires) with consumers and 100 interviews with business owners or "the person responsible for buying or leasing company cars"
- Task 4: Analysis of the results in a two-hour presentation at All Brand's offices
- Task 5: Detailed written analysis of the results of the survey to be delivered in two parts: one for the consumer market, and one for the business market

Dividing research and consulting projects into phases helps readers clearly understand the process.

Steve Misel and Joan Krupt at All Brand will have input during Tasks 1 and 2 (including approval of the questionnaire developed in Task 1) and will be able to observe interviews in progress during Task 3.

As we agreed, All Brand will not be identified in any way by our interviewers. All aspects of this survey, including All Brand's sponsorship, will be kept strictly confidential by PMA and its employees.

Time Frame

As we agreed, the telephone interviews will be conducted in July and August 2006. We will hold the on-site meeting (Task 4) by the end of September and deliver our final written analysis by October 15, 2006. This means that we will have Tasks 1 and 2 completed by June 30, at the latest.

Compensation

Our complete price for this survey of the luxury car leasing market in Dallas/Ft. Worth, based upon the five tasks outlined earlier, is $34,000.

Expiration Date

An expiration date creates a sense of urgency, or at least potential closure.

We have prepared this proposal in light of our current knowledge of our commitments in the weeks and months ahead. Thus this proposal, including the definition of the tasks and the price quotes, will remain in effect through June 7, 2006.

Conclusion

Given our experience in market research and understanding of your information needs, we at Precision Marketing assure you that we will deliver research that meets your highest expectations.

We look forward to working with you on this important project.

_____ Date: _____

Jeffrey Chu
Managing Director
Precision Marketing Associates

_____ Date: _____

Stephen Misel
President
All Brand Motors Leasing Corp.

◎ **Sample 19-D:** *Proposal for the sale of a service.*

A Letter of Agreement

In many cases, the proposal becomes the agreement when signed by the person authorized to make the deal for the client company. Sometimes, however, you need an actual letter of agreement in order to document a verbal agreement.

Sample 19-E shows a short letter of agreement. Note that the structure of the letter, that is, the section titles and the content, closely parallels that of a proposal.

Party Down Company
999 Wilshire Blvd.
Beverly Hills, CA 02910
1-800-555-9999

Mr. Robbie Manning
888 Beverly Glen
Beverly Hills, CA 02910

Subject: Agreement for Services for October 19th

Dear Robbie:

This letter will confirm our conversation this morning regarding arrangements for your birthday party to be held at 888 Beverly Glen from 10 p.m. to 4 a.m. on Friday, October 19th.

We will provide food and drink as listed on Attachments "A" and "B," as well as live music from the six-piece dance band The Grifters, who will play 45-minute sets on the hour from 10:00 p.m. to 3:00 a.m. We will also provide the services of The Magic Marker, the Santa Monica-based caricature artist, from 1:00 a.m. to 2:30 a.m.

—— Attachments (not shown) contain material that is too long and complicated for a letter.

You will send us the guest list so that we receive it by September 1st. We will mail invitations with RSVPs, as we agreed. See Attachment "C" for a sample invitation and return card.

We will also provide a 200-person tent, and arrange for set-up on the morning of the 19th and breakdown on the 20th. We will supply all decorations (balloons, streamers, favors, noise-makers, and three life-size ice sculptures of you).

Our staff of chefs, kitchen assistants, food servers, waiters and waitresses, bartenders, and buspersons will total 60 people and will begin arriving at your home at about 4:00 p.m. on the day of the party.

Our all-inclusive price for this event will be $45,000 (as detailed on Attachment "D") and payments are due as follows:

It's essential to be clear about what payment is due when, and what portion is nonrefundable.

- ◆ $15,000 nonrefundable deposit with the return of this signed letter
- ◆ $15,000 on October 1st
- ◆ $15,000 on the morning of October 19th

We appreciate having the opportunity to make your birthday this year a truly memorable event.

Sincerely,

Devan Blaine
President

Accepted by: _____ Date: _____

Robert Manning

Sample 19-E: A letter of agreement.

The Least You Need to Know

- ◆ The basic elements of a contract are an offer, consideration, and acceptance.
- ◆ Verbal contracts are just as legal as written contracts but harder to enforce, which is why most business deals require something in writing.
- ◆ A proposal should clearly state what you will do, what you will deliver, what you will be paid, and the time frames for these items.
- ◆ Proposals often become written agreements when countersigned by the person authorized to make the deal for the prospect company.
- ◆ Use a simple letter agreement to document a straightforward verbal deal. In business, it always pays to have something in writing.

Chapter 20

Customer Correspondence That Keeps Customers Close

In This Chapter

- ◆ Writing to customers when you're not selling to them
- ◆ How to deliver "bad news," such as price increases
- ◆ Customer correspondence for crisis situations

In almost any business, it's much easier to keep a customer than to win one. It's also cheaper: Winning a new customer usually costs a multiple of the annual cost of keeping one. Ways of keeping customers vary. In some industries, customers expect to be wined, dined, and given tickets to sporting events. In others, an occasional friendly phone call is enough. But every business should occasionally write to customers—and most do.

The term "customer correspondence" covers a lot of ground. This chapter examines letters and memos about policies, procedures, and product problems; general customer contact letters; and letters to customers to counter bad publicity. We examined sales letters in Chapter 18, and we'll learn about collection letters in Chapter 21. Here, we'll cover most other types of customer correspondence, and ways to ensure that your customer correspondence does the job it's supposed to do.

Why Write if You're Not Selling?

As we saw in Chapter 18, sales letters can bring in business, move the sales process forward, and close the deal. But the letters shouldn't stop when prospects become customers. They might feel abandoned or suspect that your interest has faded now that you have their money. Moreover, regular contact of the right kind builds closer customer relationships.

This is especially true in any business where long-term customer relationships are possible. The more contact you have with your customers, the better they come to know you and your company. Regular contact keeps your name in front of them and sparks the awareness that leads to referrals.

Tricks of the Trade _____

Remember: Your competitors are hammering your customers with sales letters. So nail them down with letters of your own. Smart companies know that customers stray when they feel taken for granted. Even if customers don't respond to, or even read, every letter or e-mail you send, that correspondence still maintains a level of awareness. If you write regularly, they can't say that they never hear from you. (On the other hand, don't overdo it.)

In addition, employee turnover can weaken the bond between you and your customers. By writing regularly, you build a file that tells new people at both companies about the history of the relationship and the way you do business. Which raises another point: There will be policies, procedures, and developments that you'll want to have documented in writing between you and your customers, for both business and legal reasons.

The Role of E-mail in Customer Correspondence

E-mail has become an essential tool in customer relations for several reasons. First, as with all written communications, it's cheaper and faster than hard copy. Second, buyers and sellers e-mail one another regularly in the normal course of business. Third, your customers spend so much time at their computers that you may have a better chance of reaching them by e-mail than by any other means, even with official correspondence.

The drawbacks of e-mail for customer correspondence are its informality and the volume of e-mail that people receive. It's easy for someone to miss your message or give it short shrift if their mailboxes are crammed and they're seeking an e-mail other than yours.

E-mail contact programs such as customer loyalty or rewards programs and newsletters have their place. The first key to success with those vehicles is to deliver actual value instead of incessant sales pitches and "redeemable points" good for a free trip to Angola during mosquito season. The second key to success is to keep them short and clear enough to keep people engaged without having to print them out. Sure, people will print out a rewards coupon that is worth something to them or a truly informative e-mail. But they don't want to wade through hundreds of words to find something useful.

The beauty of e-mail is that it gives you another means of communicating the written word. But to communicate effectively the medium must suit the message. Please see the section "E-mail Reminders and Flags" at the end of this chapter for more on this subject.

Guidelines for Customer Correspondence

Every contact between you and a customer can either strengthen or weaken the relationship. This includes every call a customer makes to your company, every complaint a customer lodges, and every letter, memo, and e-mail they receive from you.

Most customers will overlook the *occasional* lapse in accuracy or professionalism. However, over time the quality of your interactions with your customers will determine the quality of the relationship. The quality of the relationship, in turn, will determine how much business you do with them, how long they remain customers, and how many referrals you get from them (if any).

Tricks of the Trade

Referrals can be your most powerful tool for generating sales. Nobody has more credibility with your potential customers than your current customers. Try to generate referrals by occasionally asking for them, in writing. Also, thank a customer who gives you a referral, preferably in writing. If you truly want to show your gratitude, send a gift or a certificate for a discount on their next purchase.

Think of every written contact that you have with your customers as either adding to, or subtracting from, the *goodwill* you are trying to build in the marketplace. Seen in that light, letters and e-mails to customers are among the most important correspondence you can write.

To build goodwill—and to avoid eroding it—with your customer correspondence, follow these guidelines:

FYI

Goodwill is the stock of positive opinion, feeling, and word-of-mouth between a company and its customers, beyond the actual value of the company's product or service.

- Resist the temptation to try to sell something every time you write to customers. If you're always pitching, they'll tune you out. Instead stick to the reason you're writing.

- Focus on the readers' needs. This can be hard to do when you're trying to explain a complex new policy or procedure. That's because you'll tend to focus more on your company's internal workings than on what it all means to the reader. Always think of the change's impact on the reader.

- Keep in regular touch but don't swamp customers with letters and e-mails. If you send them something every few days, you'll find it hard to get their attention when you really want it.

- Consider maintaining separate lists of groups of your customers' employees, for example the purchasing department, technical department, and end-users. That way, you can direct your messages only to the relevant readers.

- Finally (it can't be said too often) be sure these communications are free from spelling, grammar, and punctuation errors. Otherwise you impress your customers with your sloppiness.

Consider issuing various types of correspondence on different letterhead. For example, letterhead saying, "Important News" could flag exactly that, while less important messages could go on "For Your Information" letterhead.

Tricks of the Trade

Compiling good contact information on the people within a company who approve the purchase of your product, who use it, and who are affected by it is part of good account management. You should gather and track this information over time so that you're communicating with real people rather than "the organization."

Outline for Customer Correspondence

The content varies widely in customer correspondence, depending on the situation, so this outline is more general than the one you'll find for, say, collection letters or cover letters for resumés.

Paragraph #1

- Mention the subject of the letter or memo.
- Tell the reader what or whom is affected.
- Note any actions the reader must take, and any deadlines.

Paragraph #2

- Give more specific details.
- Tell readers what steps you are taking or have taken, if appropriate.
- Detail when and where they should take any necessary action.

Paragraph #3

- Assure readers that you value their business.
- Mention that you will continue to earn their trust.

Close

- Thank the reader.
- Ask the reader to join you in a task or in sharing a sentiment.
- Remind the reader about the most important point or the action to be taken.

Sample 20-A: *Outline for customer correspondence.*

Be sure to use subheads and bullets in these documents. They will flag the most important items, add white space, and allow readers to check things off if they apply to their individual situations.

Nice to Know, Need to Know, or Absolute Must?

Among the myriad nonselling reasons for writing to customers, the first we'll deal with are announcements of changes your customers should know about. I group these into three categories:

- Nice to Knows: Management and Product Changes
- Need to Knows: Price, Policy, and Major Product Changes
- Absolute Musts: Product Problems and Recalls

Bear in mind that not every customer contact has to know about every change or problem. But those who should know must be informed.

Nice to Knows: Management and Product Changes

While they may be important to your company, management changes and minor product changes in your shop are of little interest to most customers. So apply the "So What?" test. Ask yourself: How many people at my company would care about this news if the customer were sending it to us about his company? (You might even ask how many people in your company care about this news!)

Management and minor product change announcements should be crisply informative. There's no need to brag about the new president of your division. You don't need to explain all the reasons for offering your product in four colors instead of six in the future.

A management change or minor product change can be handled as shown in Sample 20-B and Sample 20-C, respectively. These communications could go on company letterhead and be structured as a letter (more personal). Or they could be structured as memos and go on special letterhead labeled "Management Changes" or "Product News." Or they could be sent via e-mail.

First Bank of the South
One Southland Square
Atlanta, Georgia

Dear Customer,

As of June 1, our global banking division will be headed by Marie Poole, senior vice president. Marie, who joined First Bank of the South in 1990, brings 16 years of experience in international banking to this position. Marie will lead our efforts to develop new services for international customers and to align our global cash management systems more closely with your needs.

Marie holds an MBA from Carnegie Mellon and lives in Atlanta.

Also, please join me in congratulating our former head of global corporate banking, Jim Ruel, on his retirement after a 32-year career with FBS.

Sincerely,

Ray Mooney
President & Chief Executive Officer

Sample 20-B: Letter announcing management change to customers.

You usually don't need to explain a management change to customers, but that's a judgment call. If the change occurs in the normal course of business, as in Sample 20-B, you might mention the reason to add some color. If the change is for a negative reason, such as replacing someone who was fired for absconding with funds, you might reassure customers by emphasizing the new executive's expertise, experience, and integrity.

Product News from United Appliances
Consumer Division
4400 Commercial Boulevard
Cleveland, OH 99999

To: All Our Distributors

From: Yoshio Kiyaga, Marketing Director

Re: Discontinued Little Giant Colors

As of October 21, we will discontinue production of all Little Giant products in turquoise and taupe. We will continue to offer the full product line in red, black, forest, and white.

Products Affected

The colors turquoise and taupe will no longer be available for:

- Little Giant Handy Vacs
- Little Giant Blend-Masters
- Little Giant Indoor Grills
- All Little Giant Power Hand Tools

Replacement Parts Available

We will continue to carry replacement parts for all housings, attachments, and controls in turquoise and taupe for these products until June 30, 2007. After that date, we will provide replacement parts only when available from unsold stock.

Why Are We Discontinuing These Colors?

In streamlining our operations, we assessed customer preferences for various product features, including color, by analyzing historical sales. Little Giant products in turquoise and taupe proved to be very slow sellers.

We apologize for any inconvenience this decision causes for you or your customers. Please know that this step will help us to continue to offer Little Giant products at extremely competitive prices.

Sample 20-C: *Memo announcing minor product change.*

Tricks of the Trade

When telling customers about a change in a policy or procedure, focus on what's new. If you discuss the old way in detail, you'll waste readers' time and perhaps confuse them. If you must outline the old policy or procedure, use a separate paragraph or set of bullets titled "Old Policy" or "Former Procedure." Then present the new one with a paragraph or bullets titled "New Policy" or "New Procedure." Or place the points side by side in two columns, so readers can easily compare the differences.

Need to Knows: Changes in Policies, Procedures, or Prices

Changes in your policies and procedures can affect your customers' way of doing business, so this is important correspondence. The change can be anything from a new delivery schedule to stricter government regulations regarding use of your product. The relevant people in your customer organizations need to know about these kinds of policy and procedure changes.

A change in prices, which usually means an increase, can affect customers' costs, budgets, and profitability. Therefore, you need to inform them about the increase well in advance.

Don't make the mistake of viewing a letter about a policy or procedure change as covering yourself rather than truly informing the customer. For instance, suppose a grocer phones a supplier and says, "Your driver left our delivery on the loading dock and raccoons got into the food." If the supplier says, "Well, we sent out a memo saying that we were just going to leave deliveries on the loading dock if the driver rang the bell three times and got no answer," the grocer isn't going to feel better. He's going to feel angry.

The goal is to communicate. So make the memo clear, and get it to the right people. Sample 20-D announces a new procedure to customers.

Continental Corrugated Carton Corp.

Customer Update

To: All Customers in North America

From: Jamie Winston, Chief Operating Officer

Re: Changes to Merchandise Returns Policy

After May 1, we ask that you please use the following procedure for returning damaged goods:

◆ Be sure that one of your employees witnesses the driver breaking the seal on the truck closure. If the seal has already been broken, your employee should note that on the invoice, and check the delivery extra carefully.

- Your employee should refuse delivery of any damaged cartons. If a deck of cartons is partly damaged, he or she may accept the undamaged ones, but should refuse the damaged ones and report the shortage to us.

- Your employee should note the nature of the damage and the number of damaged cartons on the invoice and fax the invoice to us by the end of the next business day.

Why We're Asking You to Do This

We have seen a sharp increase in cartons returned for damages, and receive reimbursement from our carriers only if you follow these procedures. By following this new procedure you will help us maintain the low prices that you expect from Continental Corrugated.

Questions?

As you know, we promptly replace all damaged cartons or credit your account for them. <u>There will be no change to our replacement and reimbursement policy</u>. However, damaged inventory costs our company—and your company—money. Please help us control our costs so we can continue to keep our prices low.

If you have questions or comments about this new procedure, please contact Donna Lambert at ext. 395 or Tim Reese at ext. 390.

Thank you for following this new procedure for damaged carton claims.

Sample 20-D: Memo announcing a change in procedure.

A price change is usually "bad news" to customers, because it's rarely a price reduction. When announcing a price increase, try to set it in a larger context and provide a logical reason (other than increasing or maintaining your own profitability, that is).

Pitfalls

When announcing a price increase, it's best not to discuss the old prices specifically, unless they are very close to the new prices. Better still, if the increase is small, say something like, "This 2 percent increase is the first since 2001."

Superior Metals Incorporated
6000 Mountain Boulevard
Denver, CO 50012

Dear Valued Customer:

Effective on orders placed *after* April 30, prices on all copper products will increase by 7 percent. This increase applies to all products containing at least 50 percent copper, including fittings, sheets, rods, and wire.

This will be our first price increase in two and a half years. During that period the price of refined copper has risen by an average of 6 percent annually. In addition, the prices of the coal, gasoline, and electricity we use in manufacturing and delivering our products rose.

While we regret the need to increase our prices, doing so will help us to continue to provide you with the finest copper products on the market today.

See the Enclosed Sheet

Please see the enclosed sheet for our new price schedule.

Again, the new prices apply to all orders placed *after* April 30. If you have questions or comments about our new prices, please get in touch with your account representative, or contact me directly.

Thank you for your business.

Best regards,

Joseph P. Baumgarten
Vice President, Sales

Enclosure: New Price List

Sample 20-E: *Letter announcing a price increase.*

In Sample 20-E, note the reference to the enclosure, both in the letter and at the end of it. Rather than load up a letter with model numbers, price schedules, or detailed procedures, include them on a separate sheet. Then customers can refer to that sheet until they're used to the new procedure or prices.

Absolute Musts: Product Problems and Recalls

You must, as quickly as possible, warn your customers about any problem you discover about your product or service that can cause physical injury, property damage, or legal liability for them or their customers or suppliers. Note, however, that this type of correspondence generally calls for review by an attorney. That's because you must warn customers in a way that does not create unnecessary legal liability for them or for your company.

Sample 20-F announces a product recall from a manufacturer for a consumer product sold to distributors who then sell it to retail stores.

Green Thumb Manufacturing, Inc.
1500 Milford Avenue
Milford, MO 99999

Urgent: For Your Immediate Attention

To: Our Distributors

From: Manny Cielo

Re: Product Recall—Green Thumb Electric Lawnmowers

If you purchased any Green Thumb Electric Lawnmowers in the second half of calendar year 2005, please do not resell them. Instead, return them to the nearest Green Thumb warehouse, at our expense.

If you have resold any of these mowers, please send the customers' names and contact information to us immediately. As you know, not all customers send us their warranty cards, so we need your help to recall all mowers that have been sold. Note that this recall applies only to Green Thumb <u>Electric</u> Lawnmowers.

What's the Problem?

The nut fastening the blade to the drive shaft may loosen after 50 to 75 hours of use on some machines, due to improperly threaded drive shafts. On these machines, the blade could detach from the drive shaft while the unit is in use. No injuries have occurred, but these units are not fit for use until they have been retrofitted with properly threaded drive shafts.

We have fixed the assembly error, which occurred only at our Milwaukee plant. However, about 4,000 Green Thumb Electric Lawnmowers have been affected. All of these units have been shipped to dealers in the Western District, but we are concerned that some dealers may have reshipped affected machines to dealers in other districts.

Next Steps: See the Enclosed Sheet

<u>Please ascertain whether you now stock any machine with a product number matching those on the attached sheet</u>. If you do, please return the machine to us COD. If you have sold any machine with a product number on this sheet to a consumer or a commercial account, or reshipped it to another dealer, please tell us where it is now, if at all possible.

Thank you for your help in this matter. We apologize for any inconvenience this causes for you or your customers.

Enclosed: List of Recalled Models

Sample 20-F: Memo announcing a product recall.

Customer Contact Correspondence

Contact correspondence includes letters, memos, and e-mail that aim to keep your company's name in front of customers without asking them to buy, do, or remember anything.

Major companies have systematic ways of keeping in touch with customers. These range from customer loyalty and frequent buyer programs (which are promotional programs), to useful newsletters, to useless and sometimes annoying fluff.

Here, I'm talking about correspondence meant to create a more personal, less promotional, bond with customers.

Sample 20-G illustrates what I mean.

McCann Rappaport Savino
Certified Public Accountants
60 Main Street, Mount Ivy, NJ 07648

Ms. Jean Zetelski
President
Zetelski Custom Fabrics, Inc.
421 Main Street
Mount Ivy, NJ 07648

Dear Jean:

Now that tax season is behind us, I want to take a moment to thank you for your business this year and in years past. As a local business, we especially appreciate the opportunity to serve other local businesses like yours. Thank you for choosing us for your tax, accounting, and financial planning needs.

Perhaps only an accountant could appreciate how exciting this tax season has been. With federal and state tax laws changing as often as the weather, it's been a challenging time. But it's been a good time for our community, thanks to growing businesses like Zetelski Custom Fabrics.

We intend to continue to earn your confidence in the years to come, and we thank you again for the confidence you have shown in our capabilities.

Sincerely,

Michael Savino, CPA
Managing Partner

Sample 20-G: Customer contact letter ("Thank you for your business").

Don't overdo this kind of correspondence. People have enough to deal with without digging through reams of flower mail. (See Chapter 25 for more on "flower mail.") But for certain types of businesses at certain times—for example, accounting firms after tax time—a few words of thanks can make a lasting impression.

Tricks of the Trade

A friendly, personalized letter will usually generate more goodwill than a pen, coffee mug, calculator, or calendar embossed with your company name and delivered in a padded envelope. Those promotional items tend to be low quality and, compared with a contact letter, quite impersonal.

When Trouble Comes: Crisis Communications

Crisis communications are among the most challenging tasks in all of business. In large companies, senior executives, the communications staff, and public relations consultants create responses for distribution through the media and often an "Open Letter to Our Customers." In a small business, the president and his staff copywriter, or perhaps the company's marketing consultant (or maybe even you) will craft or collaborate on a response sent mainly to customers. Here we're examining only one aspect of crisis communications—correspondence with customers.

Essentially, your correspondence to customers in such situations should tell your side of the story. This differs sharply from making up a story. Good communication tells the truth. Within that context, you must reassure customers that they can and should continue to do business with your company. This can be a tall order—and it's another area that often calls for legal counsel—but here are a few guidelines:

♦ Admit any obvious problems, but stop short of assuming responsibility if that's a matter for a court to decide (which your attorney will help you determine).

♦ Do, however, assume responsibility for fixing the problem. Develop a workable plan and implement it as quickly as possible. Tell customers the specific steps you have taken and are taking to put things right.

♦ Explain to customers why the problem is isolated, why it won't affect them, and why it won't happen again. (However, do not say this unless you are reasonably sure that it is isolated, won't affect them, and won't happen again.)

♦ If it's an ongoing problem or it could recur, explain that you are working hard to fix it. Explain how customers might be affected and tell them how you will do your best to minimize any difficulties for them.

♦ Thank your customers for their continued confidence in your company and its people and for their patience and support while you are resolving the problem.

Sample 20-H shows a good way to handle bad publicity over a product problem.

FYI

The term **crisis communications** refers to all written and verbal communication issued by a company in response to publicity arising from criminal charges, lawsuits, product problems (including major recalls over severe hazards), and other mishaps. Yet even local businesses can see bad local publicity, over, say, an injury on its property or a lawsuit from a disgruntled customer or employee.

TechnoRama Computing Systems
125 Information Highway
Austin, TX 99999

Dear Customer:

A recent article in *Ohio Business Today* stated that purchasers of our computer and networking systems had experienced "persistent operating difficulties" and "loss of data." I am writing to you to express my concern, and the concern of all of us at TechnoRama Computing Systems, over these problems. I am also writing to set the record straight.

Only four companies among TechnoRama's 280 customers have had problems of the type described in the article. These customers include the two companies that were interviewed for the article and two other corporate customers, who were not interviewed.

What's the Problem?

The problem stems from faulty microprocessors we purchased from a new supplier, whom we have stopped using. As you probably know, Techno-Rama assembles its systems from components purchased from various suppliers. On the basis of tests we conducted on this supplier's components, we agreed to purchase a new generation of processors from them.

Our tests showed that the calculating power of the processors was 25 to 30 percent faster than any competitive processor. Unfortunately, the supplier's manufacturing capabilities did not match its design capabilities. While the processors are fast, they are not reliable, and without reliability speed is beside the point.

Clarification of the Article

Since the magazine went to press we have rectified every problem created by these processors. Although the problems were "persistent" as of the date of the interviews, they have been completely resolved at all four companies—at our expense, of course.

None of these customers, or any other customers, lost data permanently. Our backup systems were fully functional and all lost data was recovered. None of the other 14 customers who purchased systems that included these processors experienced any difficulties.

What We've Done

Here are the steps we've taken to ensure that this problem does not recur:

- We have contacted all customers who purchased systems that included any processors from the manufacturer in question, and replaced those processors with the reliable ones we have long used in our systems.
- We have canceled our contract with the supplier of the faulty processors.
- We have strengthened our component-testing procedures to better evaluate durability, accuracy, and mean time to failure.

Thank You

Thank you for your business, and for the confidence you place in us by using our systems in your operations. We will continue to do our best to earn the trust you place in us with every computer and network we design and deliver.

Sample 20-H: Crisis correspondence to customers.

Pitfalls

There's an old saying: Never pick a fight with someone who buys ink by the barrel. If you have to correct the facts or impression conveyed by a magazine or newspaper article, be calm and factual. Do not express anger, take a sarcastic tone, or impugn the reporter's (or editor's or publisher's) motives or competence. Simply state your case, and leave it with that.

E-mail Reminders and Flags

As I mentioned at the start of this chapter, e-mail can play a supporting role in the kinds of customer correspondence covered in this chapter. Sample 20-I reminds customers of the price increase announced in Sample 20-E earlier in this chapter. Note that the memo includes a message to customers that helps them beat the price increase while perhaps boosting near-term sales.

From:	Joe Baumgarten <jbaumgarten@customernews.superiormetals.com>
To:	Mary Parks <maryparks@unitedproductsgroup.com>
Sent:	April 7th
Subject:	Reminder of Price Increase May 1st

Please remember that prices on all our products with at least 50% copper content will increase on May 1st. Any orders placed by close of business April 30th for delivery by June 1st will be billed at our current prices.

For more details on our new prices and the products that will be affected, please visit www.superiormetals.com/prices/May1.

Regards,

Joe Baumgarten

Vice President, Sales

Sample 20-I: E-mail following up an earlier memo.

Together, hard-copy customer correspondence and e-mails of a nonpromotional, or subtly promotional, nature can help your business stand apart from those that merely pelt customers with e-newsletters and e-mailed sales messages.

The Least You Need to Know

- If the only letters your customers see from you are sales letters and collection letters, they'll get the idea that all you want is their money.

- When you announce a price increase, set it in context by discussing—but not complaining about—your costs and, if it makes sense, the overall inflation rate. Also mention your continued efforts to give them the best products and service.

- You will probably build more goodwill with a personalized letter thanking customers for their business than from "premiums" such as mugs and pens embossed with your company name. Letters are cheaper, too.

- For the type of customer correspondence covered in this chapter, think of e-mail as an ancillary tool. It's too informal and hit-or-miss for conveying new policies and procedures, and product problems and recalls. But as reminders, e-mails help get the word out even for serious matters.

Complaints and Collection Letters That Shine Rather Than Whine

In This Chapter

◆ When you should write to complain

◆ How to keep emotions out of complaints

◆ Complaining to get results

◆ How to write a series of collection letters

Mess-ups are a natural part of life. When you're the one paying, however, chances are you need the responsible business or person to fix the problem fast. Often that means complaining in writing.

When Things Go Wrong

When you pay for a product, you expect to get what you pay for. You expect on-time delivery of the correct item, and you expect the item to perform the way you were told it would. Likewise, when you buy a service, you expect professional conduct and results. That's not always what you get.

In such cases you have two choices: You can ignore the problem or you can complain.

Effective complaining gets results. Complaining to your boss, your co-workers, your spouse, or your neighbor doesn't—unless, of course, they created the problem. Complaining to yourself won't help either. Crying and swearing may give you a sense of release or righteousness, but it won't fix the situation.

None of this will fix the situation because it disregards a basic rule of effective complaining: Complain to the right person. There are other rules. Let's look at them all.

Rules for Effective Complaining

It's natural to get angry when you've been wronged by a supplier, professional, or landlord. That's why it's so easy to become embroiled in costly, time-consuming losing battles. We need rules to guide our interactions with the people causing the frustration. Here are some useful ones:

- Propose a specific solution.
- Keep the moral high ground.
- Complain to the right person.
- Keep good records of all contacts.
- Be persistent.

Let's see how each of these translates into an effective letter of complaint. The rules that follow also apply to complaining in person or by telephone. (I'll cover when to use which medium later in the chapter.)

Propose a Specific Solution

Suppose a new piece of equipment you ordered was delivered this morning. A clerk in the mailroom signed for it without opening the box. When the box was delivered to your office, you opened it to find that the piece of equipment was badly damaged. You called the supplier, who said that you would have to bring it to the nearest authorized service center to have it repaired, but that they will pay for the repairs, which shouldn't take more than a week.

If you're happy with this solution, great, but not many of us would be. After all, the supplier's "solution" creates work and delay for you. In this case, you need to state what an acceptable solution would be and to insist (nicely) that the supplier implement it. Having your own solution in mind before you call gives you a benchmark by which to judge the supplier's solution and keeps you focused on getting things fixed.

Keep the Moral High Ground

Anger and useless (rather than useful) threats will cause you to forfeit the moral high ground. That's what you have when the other person knows you're in the right. Even when someone has not delivered as promised, you'll hurt your position if you take your anger out on others.

Complain to the Right Person

Sometimes we find ourselves amazed at the poor service we receive. It's astonishing to call a company that has messed up your order only to find someone with no sense of sympathy or urgency, let alone sorrow. When you run into a bad attitude, move on to that person's supervisor, quickly. Complaints in writing to the executive levels, including the chairman or president, can be very effective. The executive will pass the problem on, but his name on it ensures fast action.

The right person to complain to is one who is willing *and* able to help you. Occasionally, someone just can't help you. He may be in the wrong department or lack the needed authority. The first step, then, is to identify someone with authority and a willing attitude. Notice I said "person" and not "people." One person willing to champion your cause is better than five people who are mildly interested.

Tricks of the Trade

> If you're getting nowhere with the head of a company, tell him you're ready to go to the relevant regulatory agency. The attorney general's office in most states and in major cities is often responsible for consumer affairs. Also, try the office of consumer affairs if there is one.

If you're dealing with any licensed professional, you can complain (or threaten to complain) to the licensing authority. Doctors, lawyers, ophthalmologists, plumbers, electricians, contractors, and massage therapists are usually licensed by the state. In addition, the local chapter of the American Medical Association and the American Bar Association and similar organizations track complaints about, and sometimes discipline, their members.

Keep Good Records of All Contacts

An important reason to complain in writing is to create a "paper trail" documenting your problem. Keep records of all phone conversations about a problem, and include:

- Name, title, and phone number of the person you're speaking with
- Day, date, and time of the call
- Key points of the conversation
- Exact quotes for promised follow-up steps (or any offensive statements)
- Date and time by which you should have the solution

It's essential to keep pushing for a solution, and that can require persistence.

Be Persistent

When you have a problem, you need fast action. By "be persistent," I don't mean that you should be willing to fight a 10-year war. I mean that you should contact the company involved often over a short period of time. This ensures that solving your problem becomes a high priority for them.

When to Write

The telephone is more personal and faster than writing, so use it first when you need a situation fixed. Complain in writing when you get no satisfaction by talking on the phone or when you'll need documentation.

Writing is also necessary to reach someone at a high level in a large organization. Unless you're a major customer, the secretary usually won't connect you to the chairman or president, but a letter will reach that executive or someone else who can help you.

Another reason to write is to "cc" another party on the document. For example, if you've tried and failed to get a situation resolved, you can "cc" your state attorney general, which might increase the pressure.

Get the E-mails Moving

When you talk with someone, get their e-mail address (and their direct phone number, if you were connected to them). Also get the e-mail address of anyone you are referred to, because the person may be easier to reach by e-mail or be more responsive to e-mail.

E-mail also creates a paper, or at least digital, trail of your communications. I usually send a copy of the e-mail to myself as a cc or blind cc, which I prefer to saving it to the folder of composed messages. That way, I have proof that I sent it, and I get to see it the way my recipients saw it.

Also, if you think it would be worthwhile, you can cc one or more of the people that you've spoken to about the problem. That gives you more visibility—and, okay, makes you a bigger pain in the neck—which may get you more attention.

Analyzing the Reader

Nobody likes receiving complaints, so before you even send your letter or e-mail you know that your reader won't be happy to receive it. The best approach, at least in the first letter, is a strong but reasonable one, with overtones of friendliness, if possible. I say "if possible" because if you're writing because you didn't get results on the phone, your mood is not likely to be friendly. The goal is to persuade the reader to take responsibility for fixing your problem fast.

Outline for a Letter of Complaint

Sample 21-A shows a basic outline with the main elements of a good letter of complaint.

Pitfalls

When complaining, you want the right kind of attention. Don't seek to become a pest unnecessarily. People who are trying to help you, even when they're in the organization that created your need for help, like to be acknowledged for their efforts.

Dear _____:

Paragraph #1

- Cite your relationship with the company—for instance, how long you've done business with them, who recommended you to do so, or the reason you chose them.

- Introduce your problem.

Paragraph #2

◆ Explain the problem.

◆ Cite the steps, if any, that have been taken to resolve the problem.

◆ Document continuing instances of the problem and of failure to solve it, or why you feel the proposed solution is unfair or inadequate. (This may require a separate paragraph.)

Paragraph #3

◆ Tell the company your solution and when you want it implemented.

◆ If it will help your case, and you have identified acceptable alternatives, mention them.

Closing Paragraph

◆ Close as pleasantly and positively as you can.

◆ Mention a specific follow-up step and date.

Yours very truly,

◎ *Sample 21-A: Outline for a letter of complaint.*

A Sample Letter of Complaint

Sample 21-B on the following page shows a first letter following several unsuccessful attempts on the telephone.

The letter in Sample 21-B addresses an all-too-common issue in business: the recurring problem. Recurring problems are the kind you often end up writing about, because by definition they don't get solved with phone calls.

When you write about these problems, propose your solution and leave the time frame regarding recurrence open. For example, it may not be reasonable for Orla to propose that Synergy Systems replace the network if it *ever* crashes again. However, she certainly is right to insist on a new system if there's a crash in the next several weeks, given that repeated repairs have not worked. For the same reason, Orla is smart to be a bit vague about the time frame, although Peter at Synergy Systems may insist on more precise language. In fact, he may reject Orla's solution, but at least she has it on the table.

Another Letter of Complaint

Sample 21-C addresses a different kind of problem.

Notice that the letter shows a personal touch and even some humor. Light humor can lessen the unpleasantness of complaining and win cooperation. Some people will simply avoid angry or irritated people. That's not to say you should never display anger, but rather that you should use whatever tone—light or angry—you believe will get results.

> **CAUTION** **Pitfalls**
>
> Keep letters of complaint short—no more than two pages, and preferably one. You may think that the more you write, the better the results you will get, but it's not so. Focus on the result you want rather than on a person's or company's incompetence.

Zip Consulting Inc.
888 Montgomery Street
San Francisco, CA 99999
1-800-555-9999

Mr. Peter Jordan
Director—Customer Services
Synergy Systems Inc.
444 Alameda Drive
Palo Alto, California 99999

Dear Peter:

As we at Zip Consulting have discussed with you in phone conversations over the past several weeks, we continue to have problems with our Synergy Systems network. We chose Synergy Systems because of your quality and service claims, and we have been pleased with the network—when it works.

Unfortunately, the system still crashes regularly, creating downtime and loss of work in progress. We can no longer continue in this fashion.

As I write this, your repair people are here again to resolve "the crashing problem." This is their fifth visit in the past two weeks (on the 3rd, 5th, 9th, and 11th). This is in addition to some nine hours of phone consultation between your technical people and ours. Each time we have been assured, and twice you have personally assured me, that the problem would not recur. Yet our network has been down since 10:00 a.m. today.

At this point I insist that, if the network crashes again, Synergy Systems replace the network with a new one at no cost to Zip Consulting. While I realize that Synergy Systems is making good-faith assurances that the crashing problem will not recur, I am not optimistic. Our entire former computer system was replaced by Synergy six weeks ago. Therefore, there can be no doubt that the problem resides in the software or hardware or in the installation provided by Synergy Systems.

Orla makes sure her ——— Please understand that today's downtime, repairs, and assurances regarding
message gets through   this network are the last that we will accept. Under the circumstances, I see
to the reader.   replacement of the system if it fails again within the next several weeks as
                           the only fair solution.

Very truly,

Orla McKeon
President

cc: Jeff Chu, President, Synergy Systems

Sample 21-B: Complaint following unsuccessful phone calls.

Correct Copy Center
771 Washington Ave.
St. Louis, MO 99999
1-800-555-5555

Ms. Mary Russo
Credit Manager
Acme Paper Products, Inc.
8080 Main Street
St. Louis, MO 99999

Dear Ms. Russo:

I am writing to resolve, once and for all, a misunderstanding between our companies that began last July. We have been customers of Acme for more than five years, buying $2,000–$3,000 worth of paper from you every month. We want to continue to do business with you, but your collection department is making it tough. A merchandise dispute and billing error (on Acme's part) is threatening to become World War III.

Four months ago, on June 14th, your driver left a shipment of paper on a platform behind our building <u>after hours</u>. We had not requested or agreed to an after-hours delivery. Severe thundershowers that night ruined the entire shipment, valued at $1,688.50.

—— Using humor can make a complaint letter less unpleasant for the reader.

The next day we called your shipping department to tell you that we refused to accept delivery and to resend the order. Someone, presumably from Acme, picked up the damaged paper later that day (June 15th) and on the 16th we received the new order, which we paid for with the next monthly invoice.

Since then, we have received numerous collection calls and letters aimed at getting payment from us for the first $1,688.50 delivery, which we refused. We never accepted the delivery and were never invoiced for it. Acme has not produced signed delivery papers and never will, because we did not accept delivery of the damaged paper.

Yesterday, a David Jameson threatened to stop selling to us if this bill was not paid within five business days. When I explained the situation to him, he said, "All I know is that you owe us $1,688.50. When will I see it?"

Please direct your collection department to stop calling us and sending us letters demanding payment for this shipment. Attached are the original invoices for the past four months, together with copies of our checks in payment of these invoices.

Your folks have an accounting error that you must correct as soon as possible. Thank you for your prompt attention to this matter.

Sincerely,

Steven Barber
Comptroller

Sample 21-C: Letter to a collection department.

An Opener and a Follow-Up

Samples 21-D and 21-E represent two stages in a complaint process.

Note the use of the fax machine on the letters about the heat. Writing provides documentation, but if the recipient doesn't have e-mail or you don't have the e-mail address, the only way to get same-day delivery is by fax or messenger. Overnight service and Express Mail provide next-day delivery in the United States, but in urgent situations that may not be fast enough.

As is the case with written reprimands, when you have to complain in writing, you already have a bad situation on your hands, because talking has not worked. Therefore, you often have to move quickly to strong measures. That is particularly true when safety, productivity, or large sums of money are at stake.

> **CAUTION**
>
> **Pitfalls**
>
> Before you make threats, have your facts straight. Try to find out why your problem hasn't been addressed. Allow for the possibility that there's a legitimate reason for a failure.

February 18, 2006   **By Fax**

Mr. Henry Cheetham
Cheetham Property Management
888 Norway Street
Middletown, CT 99999

Re: Severe Lack of Heat and Communication

Dear Mr. Cheetham:

Short sentences create a sense of urgency.

I am writing regarding the continual lack of sufficient heat in our offices over the past three business days. I have called your office at least twice a day on each of these days. Ms. Stacey has told me that you "are aware of the situation" and that you "are trying to get it fixed." She also told me that she has given you my messages to call me. However, you have not returned my calls.

Both the heat and the communication situations are unacceptable. We must have heat and have it regularly. We are using space heaters, which raise our electricity bill and could conceivably create a fire hazard. As a landlord, you surely realize this cannot continue. As a businessman, you know that not returning my phone calls isn't helping. Whatever the explanation of this situation, I want to hear it. More importantly, I want the situation fixed.

Given the severity of the cold, the interference with our productivity, the increase in our electric bill, and your lack of communication, I am notifying you that <u>we will reduce our next rent payment</u> by an amount that I view as fair unless this situation is fixed immediately.

I await your reply.

Very truly,

Michael Klepper
President

P.S. If you are unable to communicate with me for some legitimate reason, please let me know through Ms. Stacey and advise me what to do.

Sample 21-D: First stage in a complaint process.

February 20, 2006   **By Fax**

Mr. Henry Cheetham
Cheetham Property Management
888 Norway Street
Hartford, CT 99999

Re: Severe Lack of Heat and Communication (Second Letter)

Dear Mr. Cheetham:

This is a follow-up to my letter of the 18th. Given that we still have barely any heat and I have not heard from you, I am taking the following steps to remedy the situation unless I hear from you by 5:00 p.m. today.

First, I will call a heating repair service to restore adequate heat in this office. If the service demands payment on the spot as a condition of doing the work, I will pay them but will expect Cheetham Property Management, as owner and landlord, to be responsible for the bill. If they do not demand on-the-spot payment, I will have them bill Cheetham Property Management.

Second, I will deduct at least one-half of next month's rent in compensation for the time, trouble, electricity, and productivity the lack of heat has cost us.

Third, I will lodge a formal complaint against Cheetham Property Management with the Commercial Building Authority. The complaint will focus on the unsafe, uncomfortable conditions in this office over the past week and on your failure to communicate with us.

I await your reply.

Very truly,

Michael Klepper
President

P.S. Again, if you are unable to communicate with me for some legitimate reason, please let me know through Ms. Stacey and advise me what to do.

Sample 21-E: Second stage in a complaint process.

Using "First," "Second," and "Third" helps the reader focus and remember.

Collection Letters

Collection letters are similar to complaint letters in that both attempt to get someone to do something they should already be doing, in this case, paying their bills.

Credit 101

Most goods and services that move from business to business in the United States are sold on credit. It's a good system, speeding up transactions by making

FYI

A company receives goods on **credit** when they get the goods first and pay later, usually within 30 days. The most common alternatives are to pay when the order is placed or to pay on delivery of the goods. The latter is known as *COD*, meaning "cash on delivery."

sales and shipments move faster and enabling the buyer to see the goods before payment.

Different businesses extend credit on different terms. *Terms* refers to the length of time the buyer has in which to pay and to any special discounts that the seller may offer. While the most common terms are "payable within 30 days," another common arrangement is "2/10 net 30," which means that the buyer can take a 2 percent discount if he pays within 10 days of receiving the invoice. Otherwise, he must pay the full amount of the invoice within 30 days.

In practice, two things—other than paying according to the terms—often happen. First, many buyers pay a bit more slowly than the terms allow. They do this because they don't have the money, or they have it but want to earn interest on it longer. Second, some buyers pay very slowly or not at all.

Once a company is 30 days past due, meaning that they haven't paid the invoice within 30 days of the due date, it usually becomes a collection account.

If you sell services, either as a company, professional firm, or an independent contractor, you also are probably billing your customers and clients after delivering the services. (Although billing monthly or in *progress payments* is always advisable.) That means that you are, in effect, extending credit to them. In other words, you can do the work and then not get paid for it. So you, too, can wind up with collection problems.

The Collection Process

Small companies have a person and large companies have a department that collects past-due accounts. This is usually done by first sending a gentle reminder at the bottom of a second invoice (or the next invoice, if you sell to them every month) and then making phone calls to someone (usually in the Accounting or Accounts Payable department) at the company that is past due.

After the reminder on the invoice, virtually all companies that sell on credit have a series of letters that begin gently and become more aggressive—and, ultimately, threatening—with each letter.

Collection E-mails

Few companies are set up to send collection e-mails the way they send collection letters. Large companies that sell goods usually send an invoice along with the goods being delivered or through the mail shortly after delivery. Also, they need to have a paper trail of invoices and collection letters, because most creditors have a policy of providing written notice to customers with past-due accounts.

E-mail can play a greater role in collections for independent contractors and freelances. They don't have credit or collection personnel and, fortunately, don't have many collection problems. When they do, it's often due to an oversight that just calls for a reminder. Also, the person who hired you for the project knows you and wants to see you get paid, so it's all on a more personal basis than a company selling, say, chemicals or offices supplies.

Occasionally, I've had to send e-mails reminding clients about past due invoices. Typically I send my invoices to the marketing VP or communications director who hired me. That person approves the invoice for payment, and then sends it along to accounting, which sends out my check. Rather than call or write to the accounting department at this point, I simply send my client an e-mail along the lines of the one in Sample 21-F.

To: Sarah Binghamton <sbinghamton@brightpr.com>

From: Tom Gorman <tomgorman@contentbizbooks.com>

Subject: Please help?

Sarah,

Would you help me out please? I've attached, as a Word document, my invoice for the Health Care Now article I wrote for you on how pharmaceutical companies use websites to educate the public.

As you can see by the invoice date, it's now 30 days past due. Would you please give them a jingle in accounting and ask them to expedite the check? Or if you give me the name of the person to call or e-mail, I'll get in touch with them. (Of course, if payment has been sent, please ignore this e-mail.)

Thanks much, and I'm glad the editor was happy with the article.

Best regards,

Tom

Sample 21-F: E-mail reminder of past-due invoice.

These e-mails work for several reasons. First, they actually are gentle reminders. Second, my client now realizes that accounting has been slow in paying someone she knows and hires for projects. Third, I offer to make the call myself, and I remind the client that she and the editor of the publication were happy with my work. Finally, I address the possibility that the client lost the invoice or forgot to approve it, by attaching a copy of the invoice both as documentation and for her convenience.

Of course, the tone in Sample 21-F is far more personal than that used in most collection letters. That's because I've worked with the person more than once, and want to continue working with them. It's also because I know that they will pay me, so I don't have to come on strong. In any event, the person to come on more strongly to would be the one in accounting who's sitting on an invoice that's been approved for payment.

If necessary, after one more reminder to my contact, I call the company and get the name of the bookkeeper or whoever pays the bills. I don't make the problem my client's problem because I like to keep business problems away from clients so we can focus on creative issues. But I would first make sure the client was happy with my work. I would also ask, quite frankly, if the company is in good financial shape.

Sample 21-G would be the kind of e-mail I would send to the bookkeeper if a phone conversation didn't work.

To: Anna Mobly <amobly@brightpr.com>

From: Tom Gorman <tomgorman@contentbizbooks.com>

Subject: Invoice that is 60 days past due

Dear Anna,

I've attached as a Word document a copy of my invoice originally dated over 60 days ago. This project, which was approved by Sarah Binghamton, involved my writing an article for Health Care Now magazine, spotlighting one of your major accounts. Both Sarah and the publication's editor were delighted with the piece and it ran in the June issue.

Given this, I can't understand why I haven't been paid for this work. If there is a problem at your end, please let's discuss it. If not, then please let me know when I will be paid when you receive this e-mail.

I enjoy working with Bright Public Relations, but as an independent contractor, I must insist on being paid promptly, as I'm sure you understand.

Thanks so much for your attention to this matter.

Regards,

Tom

Sample 21-G: Follow-up e-mail to client's accounting department.

If you work for a company that e-mails collection letters, the remaining samples in this chapter can serve as models for them, as well as for hard-copy letters.

Sample Collection Letters

In general, most companies start with a reminder on the second or next invoice. For a regular customer, this reminder should say something such as, "Please consider this a friendly reminder that your account is 30 days past due. If you're having difficulties, please call Jim Russo at ext. 989." For a customer who is less of a known quantity, the reminder should point out the importance of maintaining good credit.

After the reminder, meaning at the 60 days past-due point, most companies have a set of collection letters that go out more or less automatically at the right times. Samples 21-H to 21-M are of increasingly strong collection letters. Some companies, however, begin actual collection letters at 30 days past due.

Dear Valued Customer:

Are you aware that your account is past due?

According to our records, your account is past due in the amount of $1,494.91. Please pay this amount when you receive this letter, if you have not already done so. If you have, I thank you for your payment and ask that you kindly disregard this notice.

— An early-stage collection letter should allow for the possibility that the reader has already sent payment.

Ted Armstrong
Credit Manager

⊙ *Sample 21-H:* *For an account that is 30 days past due.*

Dear Customer:

Protect your credit rating! Your account is past due in the amount of $1,494.91. To protect your credit rating and to avoid delays in having your orders processed, please pay this amount immediately.

— Always mention the amount you are owed.

If you are having financial difficulties, please call me at the number on this letterhead.

Thank you for your prompt attention to this matter.

Very truly yours,

Ted Armstrong
Credit Manager

⊙ *Sample 21-I:* *For an account that is 60 days past due.*

Dear Customer:

Your account is seriously delinquent! Please remit $1,494.91 to the address above immediately.

Your credit rating is a valuable business asset, which you are putting at risk.

Given that our previous requests have not resulted in your paying this bill, we will have to take other measures if we do not promptly receive payment. And again, if you are having financial problems, please call me.

— At 90 days, begin threats of "other measures."

Very truly yours,

Ted Armstrong
Credit Manager

⊙ *Sample 21-J:* *For an account that is 90 days past due.*

Dear Customer:

At this stage, the collection letter should be short and strong. ———

Your account is seriously delinquent and in danger of being referred to our legal department or a collection agency. To avoid these unpleasant consequences, please remit $1,494.91 to the address above immediately.

Very truly yours,

Ted Armstrong
Credit Manager

Sample 21-K: *For an account that is 120 days past due.*

Dear Customer:

Unfortunately, your account is almost six months past due. If we do not receive payment of $1,494.91, we will begin legal action to recover this amount plus expenses or, at our option, we will refer your account to a collection agency.

To avoid one of these unpleasant consequences, please send $1,494.91 to the address above.

Ted keeps his options open. ———

To avoid legal action or referral to a collection agency, you must pay your account in full within 10 days.

Very truly,

Ted Armstrong
Credit Manager

Sample 21-L: *For an account that is 150 days past due.*

Dear Customer:

Your account is six months past due in the amount of $1,494.91. At this point, we have no choice but to begin legal action to recover this amount plus expenses or to refer your account to a collection agency.

Giving the reader limited time to pay may get quick action. ———

The only way to avoid one of these unpleasant consequences is to pay $1,494.91 at this office within 72 hours of receiving this notice.

This is the final notice you will receive from us. If your account is not paid in full within 72 hours, you will soon receive notification of legal action or action by a collection agency.

Very truly,

Ted Armstrong
Credit Manager

Sample 21-M: *Final notice for an account that is 180 days past due.*

Collection Do's and Don'ts

Collecting past-due accounts is no one's idea of fun. Here are some guidelines to make it as effective as possible:

Do:

◆ Keep letters short and impersonal.

◆ Have a systematic schedule for sending collection letters.

◆ Mention the amount every time.

◆ Use words such as "unpleasant" and "unfortunate."

◆ Use phone calls along with collection letters.

Don't:

◆ Imply moral judgment in your letter.

◆ Use language such as "deadbeat" or "fraud."

◆ Make threats that you cannot or will not act upon.

◆ Spend more money on collection efforts than the account is worth.

◆ Harass the debtor.

The Least You Need to Know

◆ Before complaining by letter, complain by telephone. Keep a written record of the time, date, content of, and people involved in every conversation.

◆ Be sure to complain to someone who is willing and able to solve your problem. If the person you're talking with can't help you, ask to speak with his supervisor.

◆ Have a solution in mind and use it as a benchmark to judge any proposed solution to your problem; if the solution is not acceptable, say so and go higher.

◆ Have a set of collection letters that you send on a schedule; use the telephone, too. E-mail can also be useful for reminders, especially if you're an independent contractor, freelance, or small businessperson and you know your clients and customers personally.

22

Rejections, Apologies, and Answers to Complaints

In This Chapter

◆ Acknowledging receipt in a neutral way

◆ Rejecting the proposal, not the person

◆ Dealing delicately with written apologies

◆ Handling customer complaints in writing

Rejection letters are a required courtesy when you must refuse a written request, invitation, or proposal. It may be a request for a donation, an invitation to speak at an event, or a proposal for a new line of products. Whatever it is, your task is to reject it.

Letters of apology are necessary when your organization has somehow offended someone and must now express regret. I divide these letters into two broad categories: letters to answer customer complaints, which should be handled carefully, and letters to apologize for a blunder, gaffe, or offense that you or your company committed.

This chapter will show you how to deal sensitively with each of these writing situations.

E-mail and Rejections, Apologies, and Answers

In general, you probably won't use e-mail for this correspondence unless the request or complaint came to you via e-mail, or you committed the blunder, gaffe, or offense in that medium. The apology in Sample 22-A will show you what I mean.

E-mail is so convenient and fast, however, that if you have the e-mail address of the person you're writing to, you might use the electronic medium even in response to a hard-copy message. For instance, if the sender supplied her e-mail address or suggested that you get back to her via e-mail, it would make sense, and might even be preferable. Sample 22-B, a rejection of an opportunity to participate in a trade show, shows this kind of e-mail in action.

This type of correspondence tends to be short, so it does lend itself to e-mail. In the same vein, you could adapt virtually any of the remaining samples in this chapter and on the CD-ROM to e-mail.

From: Charles Kelly <ckelly@renegadeconsulting.com>

To: Distribution <internal.list2@renegadeconsulting.com>

Subject: Please accept my apology

This past Friday afternoon, I mistakenly sent you an e-mail with an offensive attachment. My mistake was to send the attachment to anyone at anytime, let alone to my colleagues and superiors on company time. As you know from the message that accompanied the attachment, the e-mail was meant for a friend of mine outside the company. But it was offensive in any context, and I deeply regret offending you, people I respect professionally and personally.

Please accept my apology for what I assure you was a momentary lapse of judgment and intelligence. It was a stupid, tasteless "joke" and I assure you that it will never happen again.

I have used this embarrassing situation as an opportunity to re-evaluate the attitudes that would lead me to send that sort of thing to anyone.

Again, I apologize.

Charles Kelly

Sample 22-A: *Apology via e-mail.*

From: Jerry Flipowitz <jfilipowitz@lakesidemotorsports.com>

To: Moira Jones <moira.jones@supremetradeshows.com>

Subject: Sorry, but we can't attend

Moira,

Thank you for your letter personally asking us to attend this year's Chicago Motorcycle Expo, but we've decided to pass on the opportunity this year. I'm e-mailing you because I wanted you to know sooner rather than later, since we've been big supporters.

However, in the past three years, we've spent far more on the exhibit space, and on people to tend to the booth, than we've made in profits from business generated at the show.

We'd like to support the Expo, but we can't justify the expense when we're seeing far better returns on radio and newspaper advertising.

Thank you again for the personal invitation, and good luck with this year's Expo.

Regards,

Jerry Flipowitz

Sample 22-B: *E-mail rejection of invitation to trade show.*

Acknowledgment Letters

An acknowledgment letter works as a good initial response to a request, invitation, or proposal. It lets the sender know that you have received the document and will be evaluating it.

Letters acknowledging receipt of resumés often state, via a form letter, that there will be no further communication unless the organization is interested. Other acknowledgment letters should be individually tailored.

Acknowledging a Resumé

Sample 22-C acknowledges receipt of a resumé.

The letter is short and courteous and places no obligation on the company to communicate further unless they want to interview the applicant.

Unless the company specifically solicited that applicant's resumé, there is no need to say that the company will be in touch after reviewing it. Such a promise accomplishes nothing and only creates more work for the company.

Acknowledging an Individual Request

Sample 22-D is a more individually tailored letter acknowledging receipt of an invitation.

This letter does two helpful things: It mentions the criteria on which the invitation will be judged (an area of great mystery for many people making requests), and it mentions the time frame for a decision—useful information for those lining up sponsors for an event.

Dear Applicant:

Thank you for submitting your resumé to Amalgamated Industries.

The second sentence of the second paragraph makes writing a rejection letter unnecessary.

I have directed it to the proper people in our organization, who, in the weeks ahead, will be evaluating your experience and qualifications in light of our needs. If you do not hear from us shortly thereafter, then we do not currently have an appropriate position. In that case, we will keep your resumé on file for future reference.

Again, thank you for your interest in Amalgamated.

Very truly,

Hanna Gabler
Director of Recruiting Services

Sample 22-C: Form letter acknowledging receipt of a resumé.

Dear Ms. Baker:

A specific comment about the event adds a personal touch.

Thank you for inviting National Auto Parts Inc. to sponsor a car in next year's Rough Rider 1,000. The race certainly sounds exciting.

In the course of its business, National Auto receives many sponsorship requests and proposals. We evaluate each one individually in light of our budgets, business goals, and, of course, the nature and timing of the event. This generally takes about two weeks.

When we have evaluated the sponsorship opportunity you have presented, I will contact you with our decision. Meanwhile, thank you for thinking of National Auto Parts.

Sincerely,

Jackson Campbell
Director, Special Events

Sample 22-D: Acknowledgment of an invitation.

Acknowledging a Proposal Conditionally

On rare occasions, proposals can lead to legal trouble, especially in fields where ideas and creativity are a professional's bread and butter. Take the movies. Trouble can arise when a studio does a film that resembles one someone proposed (or thinks he proposed).

This has led people in certain businesses to be wary of unsolicited proposals. In idea-driven businesses, prudence may require protecting yourself regardless of which side of the desk you're on.

Sample 22-E acknowledges receipt of a business proposal but sets a condition before agreeing to review the proposal.

A *waiver* is a statement in which you give up (or "waive") a right in exchange for something. For example, a record company may waive its right to keep an unhappy artist under contract in exchange for ownership of his previous songs. Or a wrongfully fired employee may waive her right to sue in return for a cash settlement.

> **⚠ CAUTION Pitfalls** ____
>
> If you submit a proposal and there is a condition for having it reviewed, you will need to weigh the potential cost of the condition against the potential gain of having it reviewed and possibly getting a deal. Most companies are not out to steal ideas, but legitimate disagreements do occur, pointing up the need for caution and legal advice.

Dear Mr. Harrison:

Thank you for your proposal regarding an opportunity for the Consolidated Toy Company to invest in your proposed line of motorized insects for children.

As a leader in the toy industry, Consolidated receives many new product proposals. At times these proposals resemble product ideas or actual products that we have in development in-house or with an outside organization or individual. Occasionally, that resemblance can lead to disputes over the ownership of the idea.

Therefore, to protect our interests, we have a policy of not evaluating any business or product proposal unless we have a signed waiver protecting Consolidated from any form of legal action relating to the proposal. Please understand that this waiver completely protects Consolidated should your proposal resemble an idea or product that we are considering or developing.

— "We have a policy" is a useful phrase when you have to enforce a policy.

If you are willing to sign this waiver, please let me know and we will send it to you. (You may wish to consult your own legal advisor in this matter.) When we receive the signed waiver, we will review your proposal and notify you of our decision. If you do not wish to sign this waiver or if I do not hear from you within two weeks of the date of this letter, we will return your proposal without reviewing it.

Thank you in advance for your understanding regarding our policy, and thank you for your interest in Consolidated Toy Company.

Yours very truly,

Richard Worth
Corporate Counsel

◎ *Sample 22-E: Conditional acknowledgment of a proposal.*

Rejection Letters: A Matter of Timing

Ideally, rejection letters should be sent as soon as you have made a decision—but not so quickly as to give the impression that the request or proposal was so laughably absurd that it took you all of five seconds to make up your mind. On the other hand, if you send a rejection weeks (or months) later, it may look as if responding was a low priority.

Worse, if the request is time-sensitive, you may have delayed the other person, particularly if you're hard to reach. For example, invitations to an event—to speak on a panel or to sponsor a table at a luncheon—should be answered quickly. You should answer within a week or two after receiving the request, assuming you received it at least eight to ten weeks before the event, as is customary.

It's okay to take longer in situations where the sender knows you face high volume. A college applicant, job applicant, or author knows that the admissions committee, company, or publishing house has hundreds, or even thousands, of requests to deal with, so they can be tolerant. Nonetheless, six to eight weeks is reasonable in most cases. (College applicants realize that they're all notified at the same time, so this rule doesn't apply to them.)

For business proposals, four to six weeks is considered normal, unless the sender requests a speedier decision. Keep in mind that this chapter is about rejection, not acceptance, letters. If you wait five weeks to tell someone you accept their proposal, you may find they've gotten a deal elsewhere.

If the proposal mentions a deadline for responding, take it seriously—that is, if you're interested in the deal. Although some people use a deadline just to try to generate action, often the deadline is legitimate.

High-Volume Rejection Letters

Because anyone with ink, paper, and a stamp can send you a written request, it's possible to spend most of your day writing rejection letters.

This happens, in fact. That's why so many high-volume rejection letters are *form letters*. Rejection letters from universities to applicants, from personnel departments to job seekers, and (I'm sorry to say) from publishers to authors are impersonal form letters because they cannot devote the resources to writing individual letters.

Rules for Rejection

When you write a rejection letter, keep the following rules in mind:

- Reject the request, invitation, or proposal, not the person who made it.
- Be as specific as you can, but don't go into detail about your reasons for rejecting something.
- Give some encouragement or "leave the door open" if appropriate.

Letters of rejection should be somewhat impersonal. In theory, at least, your rejection of the proposal is not a judgment on the person or organization that submitted it. In practice it might be; but it's unprofessional to let that show. Stay focused on the request. It will help you to stay objective and keep you from moving from an impersonal style to a cold one. Of course, this advice assumes that you are not personally acquainted with whoever submitted the request, invitation, or proposal. If you know the person, your style can be more personal.

FYI

A **form letter** is a letter prepared with standard wording that can be sent to many people. It can be as impersonal as "Dear Applicant," or it can be used as the basis of a more individually tailored letter in which some paragraphs are standard and others are customized to the reader.

Be specific about the reasons for the rejection, so the person knows that you actually considered the request, but not so specific that she can "pick apart" your position and come at you again.

If possible, give some kind of encouragement that leaves the door open. This softens the blow and preserves goodwill between the parties. Remember, you may someday work with that person—or have to submit a proposal to her! Your rejection will be more easily forgiven and forgotten if you're courteous.

Samples 22-F through 22-J show these rules in action.

Letters of Rejection

Sample 22-F is a form letter for rejecting resumés. This letter could be made more personal. For example, it could cite an applicant's specific interest, experience, or skill that was impressive ("Your advertising background was particularly interesting."). Or it could give more specific reasons for the rejection ("We are seeking someone interested in remaining in sales rather than moving to marketing.").

A more individual letter for rejecting a job applicant after an interview can be found in Sample 22-G. How personal or impersonal your style should be depends on your relationship with the applicant. For instance, rejecting a relative of a senior officer of the organization will require a more personal letter than rejecting a stranger.

Sample 22-H rejects a request for a donation. Notice how the writer of this letter manages to convey warmth without departing from the formal style of the rejection.

Sample 22-I, a rejection of an invitation to speak at a conference, uses a similar strategy. In both cases, causes external to the applicant are cited as reasons for not participating.

Sample 22-J, a rejection of a business proposal, is more matter-of-fact.

Dear Applicant:

We regret that the volume of resumés that we receive does not allow us to respond individually to each one.

We do, however, review each one individually. This means that your resumé was reviewed here in Human Resources and then sent to managers in the areas of our organization where there could be a match between your background and our needs.

At this time, unfortunately, there does not appear to be such a match. We will, however, keep your resumé on file and contact you should a potential need for your services arise.

Thank you for your interest in Amalgamated Industries.

Sincerely,

Paul Markham
Director, Human Resources

The use of a form letter is acknowledged, but the reader is assured of individual attention.

Sample 22-F: Rejection of a resumé.

Dear Mr. Malmson:

Thank you for meeting with Mr. Johnson, Ms. Reynolds, and me this past Thursday to explore career opportunities at Amalgamated Industries. Each of us enjoyed meeting you.

Mentioning that some ——— qualified applicants must be rejected softens the blow.

Currently, however, we do not see a fit between your interests and experience and our needs. As you know, we have far fewer positions than qualified applicants.

We wish you all the best in your career. Thank you again for your interest in Amalgamated Industries.

Sincerely,

Paul Markham
Director, Human Resources

Sample 22-G: Rejection of a job applicant following an interview.

Dear Mr. Bennett:

We have reviewed your request for Amalgamated Industries to sponsor a table at this year's Eagle Scout Annual Awards Dinner. We regret that we cannot play a role in this event at this time.

When declining to make a ——— contribution, blame your budget.

Please know that our decision was not an easy one and was based upon internal budget issues rather than on the worthiness of the request or our desire to assist the Boy Scouts of America.

Please accept my best wishes for the success of this event.

Sincerely,

William Greene
Director, Corporate Affairs

Sample 22-H: Rejection of a request for a donation.

Dear Ms. Avery:

Thank you for asking me to be the keynote speaker at the Autumn Gala Conference of the Venture Capital Association of America.

I would truly enjoy having the opportunity to address the participants at this important event, but unfortunately, I cannot, given prior commitments for that week.

Thank you for the invitation, which I was honored to receive.

Sincerely,

Lawrence Jacoby
President

——— Lawrence is intentionally vague about his reasons for turning down the invitation.

⊙ *Sample 22-I:* *Rejection of an invitation to speak at a conference.*

Dear Mr. Dannon:

Thank you for your proposal regarding the opportunity to invest in your contemplated line of automated corkscrews.

We have reviewed the proposal carefully and have decided that, given our current business goals and commitments, we will not invest in this project. I have enclosed the copy of the proposal you sent us.

Thank you for thinking of Amalgamated Industries and please accept my best wishes for the success of your project.

——— Lisa wisely returns the rejected proposal—and documents returning it in her letter.

Lisa Coady
Vice President, Finance

⊙ *Sample 22-J:* *Rejection of a business proposal.*

When rejecting proposals, it's good business practice as well as a matter of courtesy to return the proposal to the sender, as the writer in Sample 22-J does. The sender should have included a self-addressed stamped envelope with the proposal, but even if he did not, it should be returned.

Keep Rejection Short and Sweet

As you see, these letters are all short, straightforward, and courteous, but light on explanation. You may have heard the saying, "Least said, soonest mended." Although rejection in a business situation isn't meant to give offense, there is the possibility that the person at the other end will be offended. At the least, he will be disappointed.

Rejection is rejection, after all, and nobody likes it. The less you say, the easier the rejection will be to accept. Going on about the reasons will sound hollow.

Being complimentary will sound patronizing. Being too apologetic will sound insincere.

When it comes to rejection, keep it short and sweet.

The Sorrow and the Pity

You may need to write a letter of apology when you or your organization offends someone by saying or doing something, or by not saying or doing something. For example, your organization might forget to invite a board member to a function or could deliver the wrong item to a customer, triggering a complaint. Answers to customer complaints are the most common form of written apology in business.

Apologies for a personal offense are best done in the most personal way, meaning in person or on the phone. No matter how personal your style of writing, speaking with someone directly is always more personal.

However, as Sample 22-A at the beginning of this chapter shows, when you offend more than one person (or a multitude) via e-mail, then e-mail will be the most practical and fitting medium of expression.

Letters of Apology

Let's say it falls on you to write a letter of apology after your organization has offended someone. Samples 22-K and 22-L give two examples of how to do this.

The first one, Sample 22-K, should be sent by messenger along with a nice, expensive flower arrangement. When you've made a mistake, there is little to do but admit it and hope that you haven't made an enemy. In fact, a follow-up phone call after this letter would be a good idea in a case like this one. At the least, you'll find out whether your apology has been accepted.

Sample 22-L is an apology for a different kind of mistake.

Again, a simple apology is often all that is required. Very little, if any, explanation is called for. Explanations quickly start to sound like excuses, and excuses have no place in a true apology.

Tricks of the Trade

Always apologize when an apology is called for. When you hear, directly or indirectly, that you or your organization has offended someone, don't brush it off as "nothing" or dismiss it as "their problem if that's the way they took it." Instead, provide the apology.

The only exception I can think of would be when apology equals an admission of guilt and guilt may be decided by a court, as in cases of physical injury or financial loss. For instance, if a passerby is injured on company property, you might seek legal advice before issuing an official apology. This also applies to answering customer complaints, as you'll see in the next section.

Dear Mrs. Chatsworth:

I just learned from Mr. Hillary that you are, understandably, upset that you were not invited to our Annual Toast and Roast, which was held last night.

I apologize for this oversight and take full responsibility for it. My only defense, admittedly a poor one, is that I am new to the job of coordinating this event. I was working from last year's invitation list and did not realize that you had joined our board of directors since then.

—— Every apology letter should contain one sentence of "pure apology"—here, it's the first sentence in the second paragraph.

Your presence was missed, and when I realized that I had neglected to invite you to this event I was, as you may imagine, mortified.

Please accept my apology and forgive my dunderheadedness. I assure you that it will never happen again.

Sincerely,

Terry Daniels
Coordinator, Special Events

◎ *Sample 22-K: Letter of apology for an oversight.*

Dear Mr. Redmond:

Please understand that we did not intend to offend anyone—least of all veterans of the U.S. military—by referring to our Memorial Day Sale as our "D-Day Invasion." It was an unfortunate choice of words for which I take full responsibility.

Without evading responsibility, Scotty makes it clear that no offense was meant.

I am sorry for this irreverent reference to one of the most tragic and heroic events in military history. Please accept this apology from all of us at Main Street Auto Sales, where we will be sure to think our advertising themes through more carefully and considerately in the future.

Sincerely,

Scotty Steward
President

◎ *Sample 22-L: Apology for an offensive choice of words.*

Do's and Don'ts of Apologizing

Here are some do's and don'ts for apologizing in organizational and professional situations (and in most situations):

Do:

- ◆ Admit your mistake and take responsibility for it.
- ◆ Point out that you meant no offense.

- Mention that it will not happen again.
- Send or offer some kind of tangible peace offering, if appropriate.

Don't:

- Try to weasel out of it or offer long explanations.
- Blame someone else (I know, it's tempting).
- Get cute, apologize too profusely, or patronize the reader.
- Blame the person to whom you're apologizing (for example, by implying he is too sensitive).

Answering Customer Complaints

When you receive a customer complaint in writing, you should answer it in writing unless the situation is so urgent that a telephone call or e-mail is indicated.

One very real issue in addressing some customer complaints is how much responsibility to assume. We live in a society in which agreeing that your product was responsible for even a slight injury can land you in court.

Sample 22-M is a letter that offers sympathy (and a free premium) without assuming responsibility.

The letter acknowledges that the little girl got a rash after using the product, but it does not in any way admit or agree that the product caused the rash.

Of course, there will be times when your organization is clearly at fault. Sample 22-N attempts to soothe an angry customer who suffered poor treatment.

When legal liability is a possibility, take great care with wording.

Dear Ms. Mulvaney:

I was sorry to learn that your daughter Kimberly apparently developed a reaction to Just Ducky Bubble Bath.

All of our products are hypoallergenic and thoroughly tested for safety before going to market. It is very rare that one of our products, used according to directions, will injure a user. Thank you for alerting us to this situation.

We regret that Kimberly developed a rash on her back after using Just Ducky, and we wish her a speedy recovery. As a token of our goodwill, please accept the enclosed complimentary samples and coupons for other products of Amalgamated Industries.

Sincerely,

Jack Danna
Director, Customer Service

Sample 22-M: Response to a complaint that shows sympathy without assuming responsibility.

Dear Mr. Martinez:

I was sorry to learn that when you unpacked your recent order from us we had shipped the wrong item. Furthermore, I was upset to learn that when you called us to correct the situation, you received a rude, unresponsive answer.

I can understand your anger and disappointment with this level of service. Please know that it represents a sharp departure from the way that we usually treat our customers.

To ensure that we are shipping the proper item in the future, we have changed our procedures. We now have a final check of paperwork and product by a shipping clerk at the point of departure (rather than in the department doing the packing). We have also reprimanded the employee who treated you rudely and have refreshed his knowledge of the fundamentals of customer service.

As a token of my regret over this entire situation, I have enclosed a new invoice reflecting a 50% discount off the original amount you were billed. Please discard our original invoice and process this one (provided you see this gesture as fair).

— Mary backs up her apology with a tangible way of making the mistake up to the reader.

Again, I am sorry that the level of service you received from us this time was not up to our usual standards. I hope that you give us a chance to "get it right" in the future.

Sincerely,

Mary Glover
Vice President, Sales

Sample 22-N: Response to a customer's legitimate grievance.

When your organization is clearly in the wrong, and especially if you have damaged a customer relationship through costly delays or poor treatment, you must:

- Show that you have taken steps to ensure that the situation won't happen again.
- Try to fully or partially restore the customer's faith in the company.

Most customer complaints are legitimate. It's human nature to foul up now and then. Every organization does. The best companies realize this and understand that the customers who complain do them a favor by pointing out shortcomings. It is the customers who don't complain and don't return, or who complain to other potential customers, who can wreck a business.

Tricks of the Trade

Many good companies encourage dissatisfied customers to complain. One has the following blurb on its invoices: "If you don't like our service, let us know. If you do like our service, let your friends know." That's the best approach to complaints ever.

The Least You Need to Know

- Send written rejections when enough time has passed that you look as if you thought it over, but without thoughtless delay.

- You can be as personal or impersonal in a rejection as the situation requires, but always be cordial and never cold.

- When you have a high volume of submissions to reject (for example, resumés), an acknowledgment letter can replace a rejection letter.

- Respond to written customer complaints quickly, in writing, and with an explanation of how you will avoid similar problems in the future.

- Use e-mail for rejections, apologies, and answers to customer complaints when you received the original message or gave offense through e-mail. Also, use it if the sender indicates that an e-mail answer would be preferred.

Chapter 23

Cover Letters That Open Doors

In This Chapter

- ◆ Using the cover letter for its proper purpose
- ◆ How to get your cover letter to stand out from the rest
- ◆ Conducting shotgun and rifle-shot job searches
- ◆ Suggestions for dealing with online recruiting sites

A *cover letter* is really any letter that accompanies (or "covers") other material. In everyday language, however, it usually means the letter that you send with a resumé. This chapter will show you how to write a cover letter that opens doors, whether you are applying through regular mail or riding the e-recruiting wave. It will also deal with writing to solicit an *"interview for information"* with a potential employer.

Breaking Out of the In-Box

The one and only goal of the cover letter and resumé is to get you an interview. Without an interview, you can't get a job or an assignment; and without a cover letter and a resumé, you usually can't get an interview. Even if you call the hiring authority on the phone, they'll say, "Send me a resumé" before having you in for an interview.

This is partly just procedure, but it's also to save time for the people doing the hiring. Resumés save time by letting companies screen out people who are clearly unqualified. At the resumé stage, therefore, your goal is not getting screened out. During the interview stage, your goal should shift to getting selected.

This is a subtle difference but a real one. Most companies receive so many resumés, they mostly have to screen people out. But they interview few enough people for a job so they can actually select someone.

Four Rules for Cover Letters

Keep the following rules in mind as you write cover letters:

- A cover letter, no matter how well written, can't compensate for a poor resumé.
- A cover letter should reveal your personality, writing ability, and interest in the job.
- A cover letter should be straightforward and brief.
- A cover letter and resumé must be completely free of errors.

Let's briefly look at each of these principles.

A Cover Letter Can't Compensate for a Poor Resumé

Many people seem to believe that the cover letter can explain why they're qualified for the job even though their resumé shows that they aren't. They use statements such as "Although I lack sales experience, I am willing to learn" or "While I have never worked with computers, I am extremely interested in them." If the job qualification is sales experience or a background in computers, these statements highlight a *lack* of qualifications.

It's far better to use the cover letter to bring out any related experience. For example, if you want a sales position but lack sales experience, you should highlight any experience that involved customer contact, negotiation, or proposal writing. If you have it on the resumé, you can say in the letter, "I believe my background in customer service has prepared me well for a career in sales."

See the difference? In one instance, you're excusing a shortcoming—and drawing attention to it. In the other, you're highlighting a qualification for the job.

Be Personal, Write Well, and Demonstrate Interest

A resumé is a fairly impersonal document. You don't mention the words "I" or "we" or "you," and you can't talk to the reader the way you can in a letter. Your cover letter is your chance to reveal the person behind the resumé. So use a personal, but professional, style.

The cover letter is also your main chance to show off your written communication skills. Again, you can only do so much in a resumé, because a resumé is a formula. Yes, there are poorly written and well-written resumés, but a letter is a better vehicle for revealing your writing skills. Make the most of the opportunity.

Finally and perhaps most important, you can use the cover letter to tell the company why you are approaching them. This function of the letter is essential, especially if your qualifications are not exactly as specified in the help-wanted ad or if you're sending your resumé unsolicited as part of a general job search.

If your resumé is unsolicited, you should have a sentence somewhere that begins, "I am writing to you because…" or "I am interested in working at Company X because…" Forcing yourself to finish one of those sentences will help you answer a key question in the reader's mind, since he didn't run an ad.

Keep It Short and to the Point

All business writing should be straightforward and concise. With cover letters the point bears repeating, however, because if you really, really want the job (or if you're desperate), you may write an overly long cover letter. In a moment I'll show you a three- to four-paragraph outline that works.

Zero Errors Is the Goal

Again, it may seem to go without saying that your goal is zero errors. However, I've seen too many errors in cover letters and even in resumés to let this pass without comment. Remember: Because the goal of most readers is to screen people out, any excuse you give them will do. A single error of this nature is excuse enough for many readers.

An Outline for Cover Letters

Sample 23-A is a general outline for a cover letter for a resumé.

Dear _____:

Paragraph #1

- ◆ State why you are writing (if you have been referred by someone, mention it).
- ◆ Mention the specific position.
- ◆ If you have some outstanding qualification for the position, mention it here.

Paragraph #2

- ◆ Discuss your qualifications and experience.
- ◆ Link your qualifications as directly as possible to the qualifications for the job.

Paragraph #3

- ◆ Mention why you're interested in working for the company.
- ◆ Include any experiences, events, or people that brought you to them; this might include your research on the company and the industry.

Paragraph #4

- ◆ Close on a positive, helpful note.
- ◆ Mention a next step, such as your intention to call the following week, if appropriate, or give your telephone number and e-mail address here.

Sample 23-A: Outline for a cover letter.

Use either your personal letterhead or the format for a personal business letter with your own inside address. Don't use your company's letterhead, because you are not writing on behalf of your company. If you are self-employed and have company letterhead, do not use it if you're applying for a position as an employee.

Sample Cover Letters

Samples 23-B and 23-C are examples of letters sent in response to an advertisement. Each follows the outline in Sample 23-A. The applicant in Sample 23-B has the exact qualifications mentioned in the ad.

In Sample 23-B, the writer does not mention his interest in the specific firm. Although there would be no harm in including a sentence or two about this, it's not necessary in this case. Since his qualifications are right on target, the writer's strategy is to use a "soft sell." Sometimes not acting too eager can actually help.

In Sample 23-C, the writer's qualifications are not exactly what the company seeks, so she has to sell herself a bit harder.

John Carlton
444 Fedilis Street
Westport, CT 09999

(203) 555-1111 (home)
(203) 555-8889 (office)

Ms. Jayne Harris
Director of Recruiting
Hot Shop Advertising
555 Madison Avenue
New York, NY 10000

Dear Ms. Harris:

I enclose my resumé in response to your advertisement in *The New York Sunday Times* for a senior copywriter with a specialty in consumer packaged goods.

John draws attention to the best parts of his resumé.

As my resumé shows, I offer five years of experience writing compelling copy for nationally known brands. These best-selling brands include Happy Nut peanut butter, Just Ducky children's products, and Zip Zippity toothpaste and mouthwash. I have worked in all phases of campaign development, from initial concept to final production, and in print, broadcast, and online media.

You can reach me at my office during business hours or at home during evenings and weekends. Thank you for your consideration.

Sincerely,

John Carlton

◎ *Sample 23-B:* *Cover letter by someone with the perfect qualifications.*

99 Pleasant Street
Hanover, NH 09999

Mr. Lyle Emerson
Director of Human Resources
Everclear Spring Water Co.
888 Glen Ellen Road
Portland, ME 99999

Dear Mr. Emerson:

I am writing in response to your advertisement in the Sun for a sales representative.

My interest in Everclear has grown out of a desire to sell for a company that is a leader in its industry. My research tells me that Everclear is such a company and that your sales force is among the best.

> It is generally a good idea to mention specific reasons for your interest in the company.

As my resumé shows, my background includes experience in marketing, market research, and key-account analysis. At Mason Building Products, I worked closely with our sales reps to resolve customer problems while staying focused on the bottom line. I also have first-rate prospecting and closing skills, thanks to successful volunteer fund-raising experience.

I would appreciate having an opportunity to meet with you to discuss the contribution I could make to Everclear. Thank you for your consideration.

Sincerely,

Lorraine Fernald

Sample 23-C: *Cover letter by someone with good, but not perfect, qualifications.*

In Sample 23-C, Lorraine includes a paragraph about her interest in the company to support changing industries and switching from marketing to sales. But she wisely keeps attention focused on her resumé.

When selling yourself, it's better to highlight experience than to go on about how aggressive or bright you are. Such comments sound self-serving, while statements supported on the resumé sound factual. The exception is when you're starting your career and your resumé is too light to offer much support. Then a statement in the cover letter about your energy or ability to learn fast can help.

How to Make a Cover Letter Stand Out

There are three basic ways to make a cover letter really stand out:

♦ Write something that's self-revealing and positive.

♦ Show genuine interest in the company.

♦ Use the right kind of humor.

Write Something Self-Revealing

FYI

Boilerplate language is the conventional language that usually should be included in certain kinds of writing and that changes very little among documents of that type.

To get beyond the *"boilerplate,"* you can say something personal about your background, your reason for pursuing this opening or this company, or your current situation. Just be sure that it is positive. This is not the time to write about your recent divorce, rehab, or unemployment experiences.

Statements about geography are fine. You can mention that you are new to (or would like to return to) an area, or that your spouse is taking a job there.

A career change can be an interesting personal topic. If you discuss it in a positive way, you can begin addressing the barriers to making such a change. For example, if you want to move from a business career to a teaching career, you might say, "My years in management have given me experiences and 'war stories' that will enable me to bring the material to life for students."

A major interest, accomplishment, or life change can help you come alive on paper. Just be sure to connect it to one of the job qualifications. For example, "As an avid whitewater rafter, I know the value of teamwork."

Show Genuine Interest in the Company

The best way to show genuine interest is to research the company. Don't parade a bunch of facts, but show that you know the company by mentioning how you can make a contribution based on what you know.

For example, try to use statements such as, "My experience in testing and rolling out new products could help me to contribute to your product development efforts," or "Given that the company is retrenching, my experience in cost control and outsourcing could be quite useful."

Another way to show interest is to say that you're excited by the possibility of joining the company. Of course, you can say this whether or not it's true, yet it tends to work best when you really feel that way.

Use the Right Kind of Humor

One way to stand out is to use humor, but be careful. As always in business, there is appropriate and inappropriate humor. The standards for "appropriate" can be very tight, particularly when a new hire is at stake.

The first rule of using humor is this: If you can't be funny, don't try. If you're not funny and you try to be, you may do more harm than good. Most of us do have a sense of humor, though, and letting it show can help you connect on a personal level and stand out from the 105 other people who sent a resumé that week.

Humor on paper is largely a matter of tone. With the right tone—ironic, world-weary, lighthearted, whatever—a remark about the weather or a commute can seem funny. With the wrong tone, of course, it all falls flat.

Humor in the following categories tends to be viewed as "appropriate" in business.

◆ The weather: "I look forward to hearing from you, even if Chicago winters can still freeze your eyeballs."

◆ Commuting: "It took me years to escape L.A.'s commutes, but for Paramount I'd hit the freeway on a bicycle."

◆ Insider industry developments: "With loans at a record high and a recession due within a year, I've got my pencils out and I've got them sharp."

Beyond these categories, you're on your own. I grant you, these examples are not knee-slappers. They don't have to be. They just have to show you're human.

> **CAUTION** **Pitfalls**
>
> Avoid "novelty" or "grabber" openings. I saw a letter begin, "As you go through an endless pile of resumés, looking for someone to interview, you now come across someone truly unique." Most business people see applicants who write these kinds of letters as oddballs.

Two Job-Hunting Approaches: Shotgun and Rifle-Shot

Aside from answering ads, there are two basic types of job search. I call them the shotgun and rifle-shot job-hunting approaches.

Shotgun Job Hunting: Target Broadly

In shotgun job hunting, you target companies broadly, send out lots of resumés, and play a "numbers game." If you mail 300 resumés, you may get three to nine requests to come in for an interview. Or less.

The actual number you get will depend on your age, salary, industry, level in the organization, geographical area, and economic conditions. It will also depend on your experience and accomplishments and how well you get them on paper.

Because mass mailing demands a lot of target companies, you have to target them broadly. So broadly, in fact, that you're actually targeting an industry, such as banking or advertising, or a position common to most companies, such as accountant or salesperson. Most people using this approach also target a geographical area, but some go nationwide.

Sample Letters for Shotgun Job Hunting

Samples 23-D and 23-E are letters for situations in which the applicants are mailing unsolicited resumés as part of a shotgun job search. When you're not applying for an advertised position, you have to work harder to get the company

FYI

The **hiring authority** is the person who can hire you. In most large organizations, several people have "input" into a hiring decision, but one person usually has the power to say "yes" or "no." That person is the hiring authority. They're almost always the person the job reports to.

Tricks of the Trade

In many letters, but especially those in which you are selling yourself, it's easy to overuse the word "I." One way to check on this and make it less noticeable is to make sure that you don't begin every paragraph with "I." Also say, "You can reach me …" instead of "I can be reached …" and "Please consider meeting with me to discuss …" rather than "I would appreciate your meeting with me to discuss …"

Since a broadcast letter is not specific to the company that receives it, hundreds can be sent.

to think about you—to consider having you in for an interview or to pass your resumé on to a colleague.

When you're sending an unsolicited resumé to a company, should you send it to the Personnel department or to the *hiring authority?* If you send it to Personnel, there is a chance that they'll route it to the hiring authority—but there is a good chance that they will not.

If, for whatever reason, you can't find out who the hiring authority is, send your resumé to a specific person in Human Resources. However, it's better to mail to the hiring authority or a senior person in the area in which you want to work.

Sample 23-D is a shotgun letter (also known as a "broadcast letter") from a financial analyst doing a mass mailing to Human Resources departments.

In an unsolicited cover letter, don't be afraid to ask for an interview. This is usually phrased in the form of "an opportunity to meet and …" or "an opportunity to discuss …"

The shotgun letter in Sample 23-E has a slightly different spin, because the applicant is just beginning his career.

Dear Ms. Emery:

I am a financial analyst with 24 years of experience in manufacturing. I am seeking a position as a senior financial analyst and have enclosed my resumé for your review.

As my resumé indicates, much of my work has focused on analyzing large investments in productive capacity. These include major projects such as new plants, plant expansions, and acquisitions. I also offer solid international experience, particularly in analyzing the effects of exchange rates, currency controls, and changes in tax policy.

Your company interests me because, given my skills and experience, I want to join an organization committed to international growth. Having known the thrill and challenge of contributing to overseas expansion, I believe I could assist your company in this arena.

I would appreciate your giving me an opportunity to discuss my qualifications and to learn about your needs. If you agree this may be worthwhile, or if you wish to discuss any aspect of my background, please call me at 212-555-9999.

Thank you for your consideration.

Very truly yours,

Susan Haver

Sample 23-D: *Shotgun letter to a Human Resources department.*

Dear Ms. Ozkar:

I am a recent graduate of Pleasantville College's business program, and I am seeking an entry-level position in accounting with a substantial industrial firm.

While earning tuition money during my first two summers of college, I was a part-time assistant to the bookkeeper at the Tammymack Country Club in Glenridge. I also served a summer internship at a local accounting firm between my junior and senior years.

I am considered detail-oriented, energetic, and motivated, and have been told that I have excellent problem-solving skills and that I work well with others.

—— There are graceful ways to mention your strengths.

Your company is among those that I am targeting because of your reputation, industry position, and history of success. I would like a chance to do all that I could to learn your business and contribute to that success in the future.

Please give me an opportunity to meet with you to discuss my qualifications and the role I might play in your accounting function. You can reach me at the above address or at (999) 555-1234.

Thank you for your consideration.

Sincerely,

Mike Cambridge

⊚ *Sample 23-E: Shotgun letter from a recent graduate.*

Rifle-Shot Job Hunting: Target Carefully

In rifle-shot job hunting, you target companies carefully, research them well, decide what role you could play and what contribution you could make, identify the hiring authority, and approach that person. Target no fewer than six companies. Eight or ten is a good number. As you do your research, you'll quickly develop a favorite target company or two, if you don't have one at the outset.

Key tactics in this type of job hunting include interviewing for information and networking. You are really trying to locate unadvertised jobs or jobs that are about to open up. Even better, when this tactic really works you can prompt—or convince—an organization to create a job for you.

For this to work, you must show that you offer value. You must show that you can help the company make or save money by finding new markets, creating new sources of revenue, or making their processes more efficient. It's more likely that you can do that if you've done solid research on the company, know what you can contribute, and show motivation to work there.

Tricks of the Trade

The more research you do on a company, the more confidently you will approach them. Even if you don't actually display a tenth of what you know about the outfit, knowing it will vastly improve your performance in the interviews.

An opening that expresses long-term interest in the company will usually interest the reader.

Sample Letters for Rifle-Shot Job Hunting

Samples 23-F and 23-G are letters written for a focused, rifle-shot job search. Sample 23-F, for example, is by a fairly seasoned middle manager.

Sample 23-G is for a recent graduate on a guerrilla job search. It takes an aggressive approach to the request for an interview. Doing your homework can help get you to this point of self-confidence.

Some businesses, such as law, entertainment, finance, and sales, are more open to an aggressive approach than others. In Sample 23-G, aggressiveness is coupled with a bit of intellectual idealism that, if sincere, will speak to many people.

Dear Mr. Grimes:

I have been following Amalgamated Industries for some time and have long felt that I could someday make a contribution to the company. Now that Amalgamated is moving into the telecommunications business, I believe that day may have arrived.

My interest in Amalgamated grew out of a desire to be affiliated with a growing firm that could consistently reinvent itself. Regardless of economic or market trends, Amalgamated maintains strong growth and a leadership position. Quite frankly, it is the kind of company I would like to work for.

As my resumé reveals, I offer 32 years of management experience in the telecommunications equipment business. This experience has been concentrated on the operations side of the business. As senior operations manager, I have managed plant start-up, retooling, and all phases of operations. Cost control and just-in-time inventory management are particular strengths of mine.

Please consider meeting with me to discuss ways in which I could contribute to Amalgamated's thrust into this exciting business. You can reach me at the above address or by calling (999) 555-3333.

Thank you very much for your consideration.

Sincerely,

Rob Ringelstein

Sample 23-F: *Letter for rifle-shot job hunting.*

Dear Ms. Garribotto:

Having made a study of the major East Coast firms engaged in product liability law, I have of course researched Sparks Manhower & Weeks. I would very much like to be considered for a junior associate position at the firm.

My interest in product liability law is an extension of studies and volunteer work I did as far back as my undergraduate days. The tension between the risks of open capitalism and the need for public safety has always been fascinating to me. I see product liability law as a major way in which our society manages that tension.

Sparks Manhower would offer me an opportunity to play a role in this important arena. In return, I would do everything in my power to contribute to the firm's record of growth and excellence.

After you have had a chance to review the enclosed resumé, I will take the liberty of calling you with the purpose of arranging an interview. Please give me the opportunity to at least meet with you to discuss the potential contribution I could make to your firm.

Many people will respect this kind of aggressive effort.

Meanwhile, thank you for your consideration.

Sincerely,

Rudy Grenoble

Sample 23-G: *Letter from a recent grad on a rifle-shot job hunt.*

Seeking an Interview for Information

You can request an interview for information by writing to a manager in the function you're interested in at an organization you've identified as attractive. By "interviewing for information" you remove pressure from the person you're approaching by asking for information rather than a job. Of course, most executives know that people don't seek information on organizations where they have no interest in working.

Samples 23-H and 23-I request interviews for information, without mentioning the phrase, which is probably preferable. The former is from a young applicant, the latter from a middle-aged applicant.

Ms. Libby Melcher
42 Wilson Terrace
Peoria, IL 99999

Mr. Kevin Barnes
Senior Partner
Marbury, Sloane & Marbury
Certified Public Accountants
599 Main Street
Peoria, IL 99999

Dear Mr. Barnes:

I have several years of experience on the accounting staff at a division of an office supplies manufacturer, and I am exploring the possibility of a shift into public accounting. As you might imagine, I have a number of questions, such as: Is this career move possible, given that I didn't go into public accounting right out of school? Is it too late for me to get on a partner track? Do I have (or could I acquire) the skills needed to become a CPA? And others.

Ideally, I want to discuss these questions with a successful CPA or two. In researching this possibility, I came across your profile at your firm's website and became intrigued when I saw your client list.

Marbury, Sloane & Marbury audits a number of relatively small, publicly held manufacturing companies, which is the type of company I've been working in. You have interfaced with staff accountants at companies like mine, and would therefore be someone well positioned to enlighten me.

Would you be willing to give me 30 minutes of your time to help me with this process? I have done all I can without talking to "someone who knows," and I believe you are someone who does. I'll give you a call next Monday afternoon to try to arrange a meeting with you. Thank you for your consideration.

Sincerely,

Libby Melcher

Sample 23-H: Letter requesting an informational interview (young applicant).

Shirley Reese
411 Third Avenue   Apt. 3-D
Santa Monica, CA 99999

Ms. Kate Frasier
President
Frasier Andersen Art Gallery
2880 Wilshire Boulevard
Beverly Hills, CA 90201

Dear Ms. Frasier:

Several years ago, I decided to leave a successful career of more than 25 years in corporate marketing to pursue my interest in modern art. After moving to part-time status with my employer (Southland Bank), I pursued a Master's degree in fine art at UCLA, and graduated this past June.

Now, I am exploring potential ways to turn my avocation into a vocation, and I wonder if you would be willing to help me.

While I lack the experience and desire to own and operate a gallery, I feel that there may be a match between my former career and my knowledge of modern art. Specifically, I would like to see if there could be a place for me in the corporate art advisory business.

If I understand correctly, some galleries employ or work with art consultants who advise and assist companies and hotels in acquiring art. Your website mentions that you advise architects and commercial interior decorators on acquisitions for their clients. Given this, you may be able to enlighten me.

I would truly appreciate it if you would give me 30 minutes of your time—or let me buy you lunch—and give me the benefit of your experience. I'll call you toward the end of this week to gauge your response to this idea. Meanwhile, thank you for your consideration.

Sincerely,

Shirley Reese

◎ *Sample 23-I: Letter requesting an informational interview (older applicant).*

Both of these samples strike the right note. The writers give good reasons for approaching their quarry and sound levelheaded. They take a low-pressure approach and don't ask for a job in any way. They also mildly flatter the person.

Yet these letters don't always work. Some people don't have the time or inclination to be helpful. Others perceive a ploy to get a job interview. Also, an interview for information usually yields only information (which isn't bad). So you must seek various viewpoints from people in various organizations. That way, you'll get good information while increasing your chances of landing a job.

Pitfalls

Make sure you keep the focus of the interview for information on gathering information. That is, be sincere about learning about the company and the job function. If you're young this is easy to pull off, but if you're older you can do so by positioning yourself as a career changer.

About E-Recruiting

E-recruiting refers to advertising and listings of open positions in various online resources. The major resources include job listing and employment websites, online college and university career centers, online help-wanted listings of newspapers, and the current-openings pages of company websites.

Some e-recruiting sites and vehicles provide limited ways to present yourself. Some allow you to upload only a resumé, while others have a "profile" to complete. Some have electronic forms where you check off your skills and interests, while others allow you to upload a personal statement or even a cover letter.

The more targeted your cover letter is, the more effective it will be, but few online resources allow you to customize your cover letter for specific employers. (Popular sites include www.monster.com, www.hotjobs.com, and www.6figurejobs.com, but the web itself is the best source for current information about online employment resources.)

So except in the information technology industry (and perhaps even there) it's best to think of e-recruiting and online tactics as one of several ways to seek a new position.

Online Cover Letters and Comments

When you do get to post a cover letter or a "comment on yourself" on an employment website, make the most of it. The letter or comment will necessarily be general, and probably short. Sites vary as to how much space they provide for this kind of extra text. If the site permits you to upload or compose a full letter, then follow the cover letter samples in this chapter and on the CD-ROM. If instead you are limited to two paragraphs, describe yourself and your career situation in ways similar to those in Samples 24-J and 24-K.

Tricks of the Trade

When seeking a job, look upon any single job search tactic as just that, a single tactic, and use as many as you reasonably can. This means posting your resumé at online resources and searching their job listings. It also means responding to newspaper ads, registering with an employment agency, and, most importantly, approaching organizations that you would like to work for, whether or not they have advertised a position.

I am a graduate of the Fashion Institute of Technology, and I seek a position as an entry-level buyer or buyer trainee with a sizeable department or specialty store chain. Most merchandise lines interest me, but I'm most drawn to fashion and home furnishings.

With three years as a part-time sales associate and shift leader at Bergdorf Goodman, I am well prepared and willing to relocate. The retail industry now faces huge challenges, and I want to join a team that's addressing them. Please see my resumé for details on my education and experience. Thank you for your consideration.

Sample 23-J: General online comment about yourself (recent graduate/entry-level position).

I am a department store manager with 28 years of experience in all phases of retail operations, seeking a challenging position on the West Coast. My experience includes leading management teams in growth environments, as well as in two turnaround situations where I returned stores to profitability within 12 months.

As my resumé indicates, I oversaw double-digit growth in revenue and profitability at Amalgamated Stores' flagship location in Chicago. I also created in-store employee training programs that won that location first-place, company-wide Mystery Shopper ratings in three of four years. I welcome the opportunity to discuss my experience and your needs at your convenience.

Sample 23-K: General online comment about yourself (experienced applicant).

The Least You Need to Know

- Have the best resumé possible, tailored to the position you're applying for, before you worry about the cover letter.
- The ideal cover letter will reveal your personality, emphasize your qualifications, and describe your interest in the job.
- A "shotgun" letter is a general letter for a mass mailing of your resumé. Letters you write after you research an organization ("rifle-shot" letters) tend to be more effective.
- E-recruiting has opened up another avenue for job hunting, but it's best to consider it just one more avenue.

Chapter 24

References and Recommendations That Help People Get Ahead

In This Chapter

- When *not* to write a reference
- How to respond when someone asks you to write a reference
- Achieving the right style and tone in a reference
- Writing the reference you really want to write

At a supervisory or managerial level, you will occasionally be asked to write letters of reference or recommendation. This is a normal and usually reasonable request, but one that can put you on the spot or in an uncomfortable position. This chapter shows you how to handle such requests and how to write a letter of reference or recommendation.

The words *reference* and *recommendation* are pretty much interchangeable. One difference is that a reference is usually for business purposes—a job reference or a credit reference—while "recommendation" is the word used more often in the academic world. People need letters of recommendation when applying to college, for example.

This chapter also briefly covers letters of introduction. These are not as common as they once were, but they still exist and they are a kind of reference.

Who Is Asking and Why?

The first issue is: Who is asking you for the reference and why are they asking?

The person asking for the reference is your first reader. It's a funny situation because he's asking you for an opinion of himself, presumably an honest one. However, honest opinions are not always what someone really wants. (If you've ever heard the question, "Do I look fat to you?" you know what I mean.)

You will probably be asked to send the reference directly to the institution that requires it. If you don't give a copy to the person who is the subject of the reference, it can leave that person feeling "in the dark." Also, under freedom-of-information regulations, the subject of the letter is often entitled to see his files. To be on the safe side, your best policy is to assume that the subject will see any reference you write for him. It is a (sometimes expected, but not necessary) courtesy to give him a copy.

Reference requests are a bit of a social game. People who ask you for a reference have been asked to supply one by a college, graduate school, employer, club, or lender. It's a social game because no one will ask someone to write a reference if they think they'll write a bad one. Actually, the institution is saying to the applicant, "Do you know two or three literate people who will vouch for you? If not, we don't want to know you either."

But it does go a bit deeper, because there are good references and then there are *glowing* references. A glowing reference is completely and enthusiastically positive. Everyone who asks for a reference wants a glowing one, but not everyone who is asked wants to write a glowing one (or knows how).

Before getting further into good and glowing references, let's discuss negative references.

Tricks of the Trade

It's a good idea to cultivate relationships with a few teachers, professors, and bosses with an eye toward using them as references. You will usually receive the best recommendations from people who feel some personal connection to you or have some stake in your success. People who simply knew you were in their class, or who know that you worked for them, really can't write as good a recommendation.

The idea of "cultivating relationships" may sound a bit calculating, and it may be. But the fact is that you will get to know those people, and they will get to know you, far better than if you didn't go out of your way to establish rapport with them. You do this by asking them for help, helping them when you can, learning about their interests, and getting to know them as people.

What About Negative References?

I'm not going to show examples of negative references because I don't believe in writing them. I would give a negative reference only verbally and then only in special situations. For example, I would want to warn a prospective employer of a violent individual or a compulsive thief. But even then I would do it in a subtle way.

Giving references is mainly a case of "If you have nothing nice to say, don't say anything." There are potential legal issues, including the possibility of you or your company being sued for *libel* or *slander*. Even if you can prove in court that your negative reference is true, it's expensive and time consuming.

Then there is the social aspect. If someone asks you for a reference and you agree to give one, they expect it to be a good one. If you can't agree to give them a good one, then don't agree to give them one at all.

How Do I Refuse to Give a Reference?

Refusing to give a reference or recommendation to someone who asks can be awkward. It's best to handle it honestly, either when they ask or soon afterward.

When someone asks you for a reference and you need time to think over your answer, say something like, "I take writing a reference very seriously so I always like to think about it before agreeing to give one. Let me get back to you in a day or two." If they ask why, explain that it's nothing personal. It's just your policy. You can even say you got burned once, if that's the case. Just don't agree to give a reference that you're not comfortable giving.

To refuse, be straightforward and say something like, "I'm very sorry, but I really wouldn't feel comfortable doing that. I think that, given your performance (or "our working relationship" or "our history together"), you would be better off asking someone else." This can lead to a difficult moment or a conversation you'd rather not have, but it beats giving a reference you'd rather not give.

What if They Didn't Ask?

If someone uses you as a reference before asking you to write one, you still have a right to refuse. In these cases, they put your name on an application as a reference, without first notifying you or knowing whether you would approve of it. If you don't approve, they either grossly misinterpreted your opinion of them or they should have cleared it with you first. In either case, they created the problem and it is theirs to solve. Their best move is to say that you are an outdated reference or you're out of the country, "indisposed," or whatever. In any event, it is *their* problem.

A verbal (as opposed to written) reference is another story. Although it would be helpful to ask you or alert you, someone who worked for you should be able to use you as a reference without asking.

Help, I Need a Reference

We will be looking at situations in which people ask for references, and at samples of written references for those situations. First, however, Sample 24-A provides a general outline for a reference.

> **FYI**
>
> **Libel** means untrue, negative written statements about another. **Slander** refers to untrue, negative spoken statements.

> **CAUTION** **Pitfalls**
>
> To save yourself time and trouble, you may be tempted to tell someone to write their own reference for you to sign. Or they may suggest this. It's a bad idea. It can easily place you in the position of either signing off on a letter that is too complimentary or editing out their over-the-top compliments. Either way it can be awkward.

To Whom It May Concern:

Paragraph #1

- Cite reason you are writing the reference.
- Note the capacity in which you know the individual.
- Mention that you do recommend the individual for the position or, if the reference is more general (such as a character reference), that you know the individual to be a person of good character.

Paragraph #2

- Describe in more detail the capacity in which you know the individual—for example, the number of years, whether he was a colleague or reported to you, and the institution you both served, if applicable.
- Cite the person's qualities and, if possible, give a couple of examples that demonstrate those qualities.

Paragraph #3

- If you are writing a glowing reference, cite more qualities and instances in which those qualities were demonstrated.
- Alternatively, you can supply a couple more examples or an anecdote that evidences the qualities you cited in Paragraph #2.

Closing Paragraph

- Mention again that you recommend the person for the position or membership he is seeking.
- If you wish, say that you "heartily recommend" the person or recommend him "without reservation" or that he "will be a credit to the organization."

Sample 24-A: Outline for a recommendation.

Although it may seem a bit old-fashioned, the salutation "To Whom It May Concern" is still the most appropriate for a reference. You usually don't know the individuals who will be seeing the reference, or even their names. The exception would be cases where the person requesting the reference asks you to address it to a specific individual. Also, the formality of "To Whom It May Concern" actually fits quite well in this type of correspondence.

Employment References

References for employers are the most serious. Employers who check references want an honest assessment of the applicant. Some employers, and some executive recruiters and industrial psychologists involved in hiring key people, will take the person giving a reference through a serious, detailed telephone interview designed to get the truth.

People asked for references know the applicant and usually want them to get the job. They usually have little reason to say anything negative. If they did, they could create legal liability, which is why some companies have a policy of not letting managers supply references. Employers calling for references are directed to the Human Resources department, which will verify only dates of employment, job title, and salary.

Think about it: If you were to say that so-and-so is not a team player or often missed deadlines and it gets back to the applicant who was turned down for the job, you may be sued. Do you have documented proof that they're not team players? How often is "often" when you say they missed deadlines?

It's no joke. Of course, if the person you have been asked to supply the reference on was a fantastic employee, that's another story. But then, what if the person fails or does something dishonest on the new job? Could you be liable? See how involved this can get?

The best advice is to avoid writing employment references. This is easy to do, since most employment references are checked by telephone. Be as bland or as enthusiastic as you want to be, but be careful of negative statements. If a former employee was a real problem and still used you as a reference (some do), the best strategy is to "damn them with faint praise"—give them a polite but unenthusiastic recommendation. The lack of enthusiasm implies a negative opinion. An example would be if you were asked about an ex-employee and said, "He was consistent." You may mean he was consistently bad.

> **CAUTION Pitfalls**
>
> Be careful when writing references if you have a high-profile position. Many business frauds have occurred because the con man presented written references from well-placed people. The best policy is to write references only for people you actually know well enough to evaluate in the capacity in which they will be evaluated.

Blanket Recommendations

It is likely that the only written employment reference you'll ever be asked to write is a general recommendation, also known as a *blanket recommendation*, for future employers, in which you state how you know the person and that you know they are reliable, honest, hardworking, and competent (or excellent). Samples 24-B and 24-C are two examples of such letters.

A departing employee will often ask for this kind of letter because they're not sure where you'll be when they need a reference. Also, they realize that your knowledge and impression of them will probably never be sharper. It's up to you to agree or refuse. You can always refuse to give a general recommendation by saying, "I like to give references on a case-by-case basis."

Sample 24-B is a "glowing" recommendation.

Re: Mary Wares

To Whom It May Concern:

Mary Wares joined Amalgamated Industries in the finance group in 1989. She reported to me, in my capacity as Director of Financial Services, from then until she was promoted to Controller in 1993. In the five years Mary worked for me, first as Assistant Treasurer and then as Treasurer, she was an absolutely first-rate professional in every way.

Mary's key strengths include highly developed analytical and problem-solving skills. She repeatedly displayed an ability to cut to the heart of an issue, clarify our options, and implement the best one. Our treasury function is large and complex, and Mary thrived on both the size and complexity. She brought the same energy to resolving the most minute operational problems as she did to major policy questions.

Mary is an excellent manager of people. That is why I fully supported her promotion to Controller, a position in which she managed 18 senior accountants, and managed them well. (At that point she reported to our then Vice President of Finance, as I did.) Before that, as Treasurer reporting to me, Mary managed four assistant treasurers excellently.

Finally, Mary brings a sharp, but never unkind, sense of humor to the job. She works as long as it takes to get the job done, and displays the team spirit, maturity of mind, and scrupulous honesty so necessary in the finance function of a major company.

I enthusiastically recommend Mary Wares for any position or endeavor for which you may consider her.

Very truly,

Frank Squire
Vice President, Finance

Sample 24-B: *Glowing general recommendation.*

Frank's letter is strong on specifics.

As Sample 24-B shows, you want to say things that are complimentary and related to the person's professional role.

For any written employment reference, you should:

- Mention your relationship to the subject
- Mention how long you've known the subject
- Mention the subject's strengths
- Give examples of the strengths
- Mention what you recommend the subject for

Also, try to point out personal qualities that are useful on the job, such as a sense of humor and energy.

Sample 24-C is a nice, but not glowing, reference.

Sample 24-C is somewhat subdued in its praise. Saying he did a "fine job" does not imply that he was excellent. Adjectives like "hardworking" and "diligent" imply that he showed up and did his job, but was not brilliant and didn't make much effort to go the extra mile. The letter is light on specifics, does not convey great enthusiasm, and is limited to "any sales position." All in all, it gives the impression that Ted was a solid employee but not a star.

To Whom It May Concern:

I have known Ted Marks for the three years he worked for me as a salesperson at Amalgamated Industries. I am the Southeastern District sales manager and I hired Ted.

Ted did a fine job during his time at Amalgamated. He was hardworking and diligent in executing his duties and represented the company well. Customers also liked Ted.

He also performed well in terms of his level of sales, typically making, and occasionally breaking, his quota. His knowledge of our products and how to apply them to solve customers' problems was very good. Ted was good at resolving any difficulties that came up internally at our company, such as late deliveries.

I recommend Ted Marks for any sales position for which you may be considering him.

Very truly yours,

Marcia LaPine

Sample 24-C: Moderate general recommendation.

> **CAUTION**
> **Pitfalls**
> When you write a glowing reference, show the person as balanced. Otherwise, the reader can misinterpret a compliment. For example, unless balanced by another comment, "detail-oriented" may mean "lacking imagination." Similarly, "imaginative" can mean "flighty" unless balanced by a phrase like "but realistic."

Marcia's recommendation is moderate rather than glowing.

Character References

At times you may be asked for a so-called character reference for a friend or an acquaintance. You may not know the person professionally but you may be asked to vouch for their general character. This can come up in the course of someone's getting a loan, being admitted to a club, or even entering a profession (for example, an attorney applying to the bar association). Character references are often handled by telephone, but the need to give one in writing occasionally arises.

Sample 24-D is an example of a character reference for a friend written to a potential lender.

Most character references should mention reliability, stability, sound personal habits, and honesty. When possible, it's not a bad idea to throw in references to the stereotypical middle-class symbols of these qualities, such as marriage, children, home ownership, and sports.

Remember to say how long ———
you've known the person you're
recommending, and in what
capacity.

To Whom It May Concern:

I have known Edwin Runyon for eight years as a friend and as a friend of his family. I can say without qualification that Ed is a reliable and honest person who keeps his commitments.

He is a man who sees his responsibilities clearly and discharges them faithfully. I have seen this in his relationships with his wife, Lorraine, his children, Ed Jr. and Maggie, and his neighbors and friends.

Ed is balanced, law-abiding, responsible, and sober, but he enjoys a good time, particularly on the golf course (handicap: 12).

I recommend Edwin Runyon to you without qualification for any endeavor or responsibility for which you may be considering him.

Sincerely,

Kate Merrill

Sample 24-D: *Character reference.*

Recommended Style for References and Recommendations

Note that the style of references is rather formal. That's as it should be, because you don't know the person you are writing to and your view of the subject—the person you're writing about—is supposed to be objective. Although everyone knows you are not objective, that is how it's supposed to sound.

A formal style also suits the formality of the process. The person asking for the reference is making a formal application, so a formal letter is what the situation demands.

Tricks of the Trade _____

In our economy, references are becoming more important as job tenure becomes shorter and temporary and contract work become more common.

Try to get blanket letters of recommendation when you can, and build a portfolio of work samples, if that's possible in your profession. Although they are not actually "references," letters from clients and customers that attest to the fine job you did for them can be extremely useful.

Academic References

Employees often take a leave of absence (or just leave) in order to further their education in college or graduate school. Although you may not like losing a good employee, there is nothing you can or should do to stop it. The employee deserves your support.

As in Sample 24-E, you want to stress qualities such as intelligence, analytical ability, and hard work.

Always close a letter of recommendation with a clear statement of support. Naming the individual and the institution they're applying to lends a nice touch and emphasizes the strength of your recommendation.

Dear Admissions Committee:

It is with great pleasure that I write to you in support of Clara Goodleaf's application to Harvard Business School.

——— Percival gets the reader's attention right away with a strong opening.

I have known Ms. Goodleaf for all five years that she has worked at Amalgamated Industries. I interviewed her when she applied to the company after she graduated from Smith, and I supported her hire as an entry-level market researcher. Two years later, she was promoted to manager of product development, reporting directly to me. I am vice president of marketing at the home products division at Amalgamated Industries.

Ms. Goodleaf is certainly one of the brightest and most insightful people I have had the pleasure to work with in a 27-year career. Her ability to grasp the abstract issues in a business situation while staying focused on concrete practicalities is unmatched in my experience. Most people can do either one or the other. These twin intellectual abilities are the main reason she moved from an analytical position (at which she excelled) into product development (where she also excelled).

Ms. Goodleaf quickly gains the respect and the cooperation of everyone she works with. This is partly because she respects and cooperates with others, and partly because people are attracted to her ability to focus on what is important and then act.

I have known for some time that Ms. Goodleaf would be leaving the company to pursue a graduate business degree. While as a manager I hate to lose such a qualified staff member, I enthusiastically recommend Clara Goodleaf for admission to Harvard Business School.

Sincerely,

Percival Merrin
Vice President

○ **Sample 24-E:** *Academic letter of recommendation.*

Letters of Introduction

Letters of introduction are mostly a thing of the past, thanks to the telephone. However, I'll cover them briefly because they are a form of reference and they still exist.

A letter of introduction is a recommendation written to a specific individual to get help for the person being introduced. These letters are most often used to introduce someone who is visiting or moving to another city or country to someone there who could be of help.

Sample 24-F is an example of a letter of introduction.

Remember, such letters should be personal in style, since you know the person you are writing to.

22 East Meadow Drive
East Meadow, NY 12222
October 22, 2006

David Ostin
President
DOE Productions
25000 Pacific Coast Highway
Malibu, CA 90265

The inside address is in the personal business format.

Dear David:

The young fellow presenting this letter to you, Joe Hamlin, is the son of my long-time attorney and good friend, Jack Hamlin. I've known Joe since he was in grade school, and over the years have watched him develop into the ambitious, hardworking, intelligent man he is today.

As you realize, I don't know much about your business, but I do know that Joe seriously wants to get into the movies in some beginning capacity. If raw desire and willpower are any qualification for a career in Hollywood (and I've heard they are), this fellow is on his way.

All I ask you to do for Joe to is to give him an hour of your time and see if you can help him in any way. He's a good listener as well as a good talker, and I would appreciate anything you can do to point him in the right direction, help him avoid the classic mistakes, get to see a good agent, and so on.

Thanks much, David. I appreciate it.

Best regards,

Greg Garrison

Sample 24-F: *Letter of introduction.*

What About E-mail References and Recommendations?

In general the process that requires applicants to present written recommendations at most institutions doesn't allow for e-mail, although this will no doubt change. At colleges and universities and, as we saw in Chapter 23, in many, many companies, electronic applications are becoming commonplace. Once any process becomes largely electronic, it generally makes sense to have the entire process electronic, to minimize costs and maximize convenience.

However, colleges and universities still want hard-copy recommendations. That is what they are used to and, perhaps more important, the documents can be authenticated with letterhead and the writer's signature.

But the technology and standards for "electronic signatures" are in the works. Once these digital methods for authenticating documents are widely accepted, we can expect e-recommendations to join the ranks of e-mail. When that occurs, you will still best serve the person you are recommending by following the guidelines and samples in this chapter.

The Least You Need to Know

- Writing references and recommendations more or less comes with the job of being a manager, although it may happen infrequently.

- Unless you can give an enthusiastic and unreserved recommendation, it's a good idea to think it over for a day or two before agreeing to write a reference.

- Employment references can raise organizational and legal considerations, so be careful what you write or say.

- In a reference, mention your relationship to the subject, how long you've known her, her relevant qualities, and whatever you are recommending her for. When possible, give general examples of situations where the person demonstrated the qualities you are citing.

- Use a formal style for most recommendations. Open most of them with "To Whom It May Concern," maintain a level of objectivity, and don't go overboard in praising the person.

Chapter 25

Using E-mail and Thank-You Notes to Network Like a Pro

In This Chapter

- The role of writing in networking and relationships
- Using e-mail to open doors
- When to write a thank-you note
- Keeping in touch with "flower mail"

E-mail provides a convenient way to send quick "thank-you's" to co-workers and contacts. Perhaps that's why it is the primary medium for the personal note—and networking. Almost everyone has an e-mail address, usually one you can easily discover. Approaching people through e-mail can be an enjoyable and very productive means of networking.

The quickness and convenience of e-mail—and telephones—seem to threaten to do away with the traditional handwritten (or even typed or word-processed) personal note. The very rarity of a note, however, makes it stand out all the more. It's a warm way to stay in touch and be remembered.

This chapter will show you how to use e-mail and the traditional note to strengthen your professional network.

An Update on the Art of Networking

Networking has always gone on, but until a few years ago it wasn't a buzzword and wasn't viewed as a big technique for success. Rather, it was based on personal relationships and shared interests or institutions, such as schools, clubs, or professional associations.

For some people, however, networking has become an end in itself. Many people work at developing networks instead of relationships and at gaining contacts instead of friends.

Taking genuine interest in other people is still the best way to network. If you're interested in others, you wind up playing more of a role in their lives and their thinking. When they see a situation that may be an opportunity for you, they'll think of you and call or send an e-mail. If you're out of work, they'll care and want to help. If they meet someone who can help you, they'll mention your name and tell you to call that person.

In other words, there is "networking for success," and then there is cultivating genuine relationships. Writing can help you do either, but it makes more sense to focus on genuine relationships, particularly in the long run.

The Role of Writing

Writing a personal thank-you or other note doesn't take a lot of time, but it takes enough so that many people don't bother. When you take the time to write a note of thanks, support, or congratulations, you're saying that you care about that person. (And you're saying it more sincerely than any greeting card could.)

Over time, the notes you send help forge a chain, just like all the telephone conversations and face-to-face meetings and lunches and drinks and other contacts and gestures. That chain helps form the relationship.

The Role of E-mail

Without a doubt, e-mail has opened a new communication channel, made people more accessible, and made networking easier. Very often I've found, and friends and colleagues have found, that a business relationship begins with an exchange of e-mails.

For an exchange to occur, someone has to send the first e-mail. Examples I've seen of initial e-mails sent just to establish contact include messages to …

- Contact an executive at an organization after visiting its website so you can learn more about what they do (in order to get hired or to do business with them).

- Tell a presenter at a conference that you found her presentation interesting, and would like to thank her and learn how she landed the spot on the agenda.

- Tell an author that you found his book interesting and that you would like to learn how he got it published.

- Thank the writer of a column or article in a publication you enjoy and give him an article idea (Watch out: Staff writers receive tons of these ideas, so make it well researched and well presented).

- Get in touch with an expert (through her website or organization) in order to interview her and learn more about her field.

You can approach just about anyone who has made their e-mail address available at a website, in the biographical note for an article they published, or by other means.

Actually, finding the initial reason to write to an individual presents few challenges. Just ask yourself: Why am I approaching this person? What do I want them to tell me or show me? What, exactly, would I like to learn about their work or organization? If you have that figured out, then you know where you're going, or at least where you'd like to go.

E-mail Openings

Samples 25-A, 25-B, and 25-C show three different ways of casting an initial e-mail approach toward someone with whom you would like to establish a relationship. Sample 25-A approaches an executive at a website about an "interview for information" (a tactic explained in Chapter 23). Sample 25-B approaches an author about how to get published. Sample 25-C approaches someone with whom the writer would like to explore a possible business relationship.

From: Don Chadis <donchadis@aol.com>

To: Dennis Molloy <dtm@advancedadvertising.com>

Subject: Would you help me learn about your firm?

Dear Mr. Molloy,

I've spent several hours at Advanced Advertising's website, and would like to learn a bit more about what you folks do. I've been a copywriter for three years with a mid-size firm in Tacoma and would like to relocate to Seattle.

I would deeply appreciate any information you could give me on the Seattle advertising scene in general, and on the kind of accounts Advanced Advertising works on and the kind of work you do.

My book of samples is in order, but I haven't launched a job search yet. In fact, I'm not yet sure about a move to Seattle. But I am sure I'd like to learn more from someone who knows.

Can I call you later this week with the goal of setting up a time for us to talk for 15 or 20 minutes, either by phone or in person?

I would appreciate any time you can give me.

Regards,

Jill Thompson

⊙ *Sample 25-A:* *E-mail to an executive you don't know.*

To: Kenneth Noble <knoble@comcast.com>

From: Ron Greene <rgreene47@hotmail.com>

Subject: I enjoyed your books

Dear Mr. Noble,

After reading four of your six books, I consider your work an excellent example of how to write investigative business narratives. I am a freelance writer who has published several pieces in trade magazines, but I'm interested in writing business books.

I've read all the major books on how to write a book proposal, get an agent, and so on. What I'm missing is the real-world viewpoint that only a published author can provide. And I would value your views.

Would you be willing to spend 20 to 30 minutes (no more, I promise!) on the phone with me? Specifically, I would like to know how you found your agent, how the publication process has gone for you, and (if possible) anything about the actual money to be made.

Alternatively, we could exchange e-mails. But I would appreciate any time or information you can give me.

Thank you for your consideration.

Ron Greene

Sample 25-B: E-mail to an author you don't know.

To: Rosemary Ryan <mryan@ryancommunications.com>

From: Tom Huf <thomashuf@renegademarketing.com>

Subject: I'd like to chat about a joint venture possibility

Hello Ms. Ryan:

After visiting your website, I see what could be an opportunity for both of us to make money.

I work in marketing consulting and you work in marketing communications. It appears that you write copy for sales letters, brochures, and product literature and help your clients "get ink" in publications. Meanwhile, I conduct market research and help clients formulate their marketing strategies.

I've often seen clients drop the ball on the marketing plan I delivered. They can't write, can't get publicity, and generally can't execute the strategies that I help them develop.

That might be where you come in.

Similarly, you may see situations where the client really has no marketing strategy, or hasn't done research since Lincoln left Nebraska. That might be where I come in.

Pitfalls

Always do your homework before you network with experts or company executives. Read the books and articles about the expert's field. Know the company's website inside out before you approach an executive. When these folks give you their time, they're not doing it to answer questions you can get answered with a Google search.

I think it might be worth it for us to at least talk on the phone for a few minutes. If you agree, let me know via reply e-mail. (There's also a link to my website below.)

Here's to the future.

Regards,

Tom Huf

Sample 25-C: E-mail to a potential business partner.

Where these relationships go is another matter. However, someone has to make the first move. Why not you? And why not by e-mail?

The Thank-You Note

The business (as opposed to personal) thank-you note can be handwritten or word processed and sent through the mail, or e-mailed. Hard-copy versions would go on company letterhead—formatted, of course, as a letter rather than a memo.

A business thank-you note can thank someone for ...

- ◆ A favor you requested.
- ◆ An outpouring of effort or a job particularly well done.
- ◆ A business gift.

Here is an example of each.

Dear Jim:

Thanks so much for driving those materials to the FedEx office at the airport for me last night. I know you were beat and that you wanted to get home, so I appreciate it all the more.

Best,

Mike Ross

Sample 25-D: Thank-you note for a favor.

Dear Pamela:

Just a note of thanks for all your effort on the General Industries project these past couple of weeks. As I think you know, this project would not be on track (or profitable) if not for your hard work and professionalism.

It's great working with you.

Regards,

Donna Laswell

Sample 25-E: Thank-you note for a job well done.

Dear Mr. Herskowitz:

Thanks so much for the beautiful fountain pen that you presented to me after my keynote speech at your convention this past Thursday. It is one of the nicest I've ever seen. I'll remember the occasion—and your generosity—as I use it in the years to come.

I appreciate it.

Best wishes,

Gabriella Mattheson

Sample 25-F: Thank-you note for a business gift.

Pitfalls

As something of a formal practice, thank-you notes do have their little "rules." For example, after a couple has dinner at the home of another couple, the visiting woman should write a thank-you note to the hostess. Again, however, this is following rather formal protocol, and a phone call would be equally appreciated.

Writing a thank-you note is a straightforward matter. There's no need for an outline because the note is short and should genuinely express your gratitude. As with all forms of writing, you should be concise, complimentary, and tasteful.

The need to write a more personal thank-you note often arises in the course of business. These notes are in response to more personal favors or gestures, such as dinner invitations or expressions of support during difficult times. These can be typed on letterhead, but it is often more appropriate to write them by hand on notepaper.

Samples 25-G and 25-H present two examples.

Dear Louise,

Thank you so much for having us out to the beach house this past weekend. John and I—and Jimmy and Jennifer—are all "water rats" from way back, as I think you noticed. That is a beautiful spot you have there, and it was great to get to spend that kind of time with you and Steve.

Warmest wishes,

Joyce Myers

Sample 25-G: Thank-you note for a weekend away.

> *Dear Bill,*
>
> *Just a thank you for your recent note of support and for being such a friend during Kate's recent illness. You and Joan are the greatest. We'll all be seeing more of each other again, when Kate is back on her feet (which should be in another three or four weeks).*
>
> *Thanks again,*
>
> *Jerry*

Sample 25-H: *Thank-you note for a friend's support.*

These kinds of thank-you notes are considered fairly formal by today's standards, but they haven't gone completely out of style. Returning kindness with kindness will never go out of style. These notes have merely fallen by the wayside, probably temporarily, as we hurry on.

Thank-You Letters After Job Interviews and Client Meetings

Believe it or not, people often fail to write a thank-you note after a job interview or a business development meeting with a client or potential client. Always, always, always write a note of thanks in these situations because …

- It's good manners to thank people who give you their time when you ask for it.
- So many people don't do this that you automatically stand out from the crowd.
- You get an opportunity to build a relationship and do a bit more selling.

Conceivably, it might be appropriate to send these thank-you notes by e-mail, especially in the software or another computer-related industry. But even there, I would go with hard copy. The actual letter will stick around longer than an e-mail, and perhaps make its way into the file with your resumé and the interviewers' notes on your performance in the interviews.

Thank You for the Interview

Thank-you notes for job interviews should be on personal letterhead or formatted as personal business letters.

Samples 25-I and 25-J offer examples of one set up on personal letterhead and one set up as a business letter, respectively.

As Sample 25-I demonstrates, you don't have to thank every person you interview with in a session, but it is nice to mention each one. Address the letter to the hiring authority, and extend thanks to each person who interviewed you.

CAUTION

Pitfalls

If the interview went badly, there is not much you can do to fix it in a note. If you made a poor impression you can try to correct it, but raising the issue again may just reinforce the original impression.

Be sure to use the opportunity to reinforce your main message, which should be your major area of interest, your main qualifications, or both. Don't go on and on. Three short paragraphs are enough.

Lisa Russell
9 Deer Hollow
Middleville, IA 99999
(999) 555-1212

Ms. Diane Sollars
Vice President
Campo Company
222 Second Avenue
Sioux City, IA 99999

Dear Diane:

Thank you for having me in for the round of interviews yesterday. I enjoyed meeting you and learning more about Campo. Please convey my thanks to Charles and Donna as well.

Diane scores points by being specific about her interest and qualifications.

I was particularly interested in the national expansion effort that you are planning. That is where I believe I could potentially contribute the most to the company. As I mentioned, I was instrumental in Babbo Corporation's expansion beyond the Pacific Northwest. Timothy Miller at Babbo can tell you more about the role I played in coordinating our nationwide initiative.

Again, thanks for giving me such a clear picture of Campo. It is a company that I would love to join. I look forward to hearing from you soon.

Sincerely,

Lisa Russell

Sample 25-I: Thank-you letter for a job interview.

4 Rubicon Lane
Yonkers, NY 99999
(914) 555-3333
October 10, 2006

Ronald Kerry
Director, Management Information Systems
First National Bank
One First National Plaza
New York, NY 10001

Dear Ron:

Thank you for meeting with me this past Tuesday regarding career opportunities in MIS at First National. Frankly, I was very impressed with your shop and would love to be part of your team.

Although I have never worked in an environment as fully networked as yours, please know that I see the possibility of doing so as motivating, to put it mildly. All of us in technology thrive on new challenges, and I believe that in the course of my career I've shown that the times when I've had to meet a challenge are those when I've contributed the most.

—— Don't be shy: Say why you want the job.

The possibility of joining First National's MIS department is exciting to me. Thanks again for having me in and for your consideration.

Sincerely,

Mike Montgomery

Sample 25-J: Another thank-you letter for a job interview.

Thank You for the Meeting

If you're in sales or running your own business, thank-you notes are extremely important after you meet with a potential client.

Sample 25-K is a letter of thanks after a sales call. This kind of letter should go on company letterhead.

After a sales presentation, thank the prospect for the meeting, emphasize the advantages of your product or service, and nail down the next steps. Never just leave the prospect "hanging" regarding what you're going to do next. Instead, try to create some anticipation.

Sample 25-L is a thank-you from a freelance desktop publisher who pitched a piece of business but was rejected because his price was too high. This would go on letterhead and have an inside address.

Tricks of the Trade

Build bridges; don't burn them. If you are around long enough, you'll find that you'll ultimately do business with many people who wouldn't deal with you at the outset. They will realize that you're going to be around and that you want to do business with them, and they may turn to you when they need a new supplier or decide finally to buy what you sell.

As Sample 25-L shows, you can use a thank-you note to good advantage after a meeting in which you don't get a deal. You can show you're a professional, leave the door open, and reinforce the message that if there's a way to do business with them (without abandoning your position), then you want to do business with them.

Perfect Health Programs Inc.
1000 Commercial Street
Midway, MD 99999
(999) 555-0909

Ms. Becky Jones
President
JMP Inc.
444 Dorset Avenue
Baltimore, MD 99999

Dear Becky:

Thank you for giving me the opportunity to meet with you this morning to discuss your employee health plan needs. Please thank Jim and Merry for me as well.

While the plan you currently have is certainly adequate for your company's needs, we may be able to offer you very competitive coverage with equally fine providers at a lower total cost. And we can do this without shifting more expense to your employees.

Always mention next steps. ——— As we discussed, I will have a formal proposal prepared for JMP by the end of next week. That proposal will show the cost and coverage of both the Gold and the Platinum plans that I presented today, as well as those of your current plan. I know that you will see a clear difference—and, I believe, the advantage that Perfect Health can provide.

Please look for our proposal early the week of the 12th. And thank you for giving us the opportunity to submit it.

Yours Truly,

Jayne Neuberger
Senior Sales Representative

Sample 25-K: Thank-you letter for a sales call.

Dear Kelly:

Thank you for giving me the opportunity to meet with you and tell you about InstaPress Services. Thank you also for your candor regarding the potential for InstaPress to work with you folks.

While I grant you that our pricing is at the higher end of the range, I believe this reflects a higher level of quality and service. I would still like to work with you at some point and show you what we can do.

Should the need arise, please let me know. I would be happy to work on your toughest, most exacting "rush" job, so please keep us in mind.

Sincerely,

—— Leave the door open, even if you lose the sale.

Myra Aronson

Sample 25-L: *Thank-you letter after a rejected bid for business.*

All About "Flower Mail"

"Flower mail" can mean anything from a thank you to any of the various notes we'll cover in the rest of this chapter. (These are also called "bread and butter letters.") I use "flower mail" as the all-purpose term for the many other notes you can write to business contacts, associates, and friends, including:

◆ Congratulations

◆ Support (for example, during legal troubles)

◆ Notes to accompany interesting articles, book reviews, or catalogs

Samples 25-M and 25-N provide short models of, respectively, a note of congratulations and a note of support. These could be formatted as letters on letterhead, sent as e-mail messages, or handwritten on notepaper. I cover notes to send with articles and book reviews in the following section.

Dear Brian,

Congratulations on your well-deserved promotion to District Manager. It could not have happened to a more deserving (or nicer) guy. Although I know you won't need it, I wish you the very best of luck in your new position.

Let's get together so I can buy you a beer some day next week.

To your continued success,

Larry

Sample 25-M: *Note of congratulations.*

Dear Marty,

Please know that I am with you all the way during this difficult time. As the saying goes, "What doesn't kill you, makes you stronger," and I know you'll come out of this stronger than ever.

If there is anything I can do to help you, please let me know.

My very best regards,

Michael Weathers

Sample 25-N: Note of support.

Don't underestimate the power of an old saying during times of trouble. Notes like Sample 25-N are a source of comfort and support to people having tough times, and they are not forgotten.

That brings up a topic related to relationship building and networking: finding reasons to write.

Finding Reasons to Write

If you're in business for yourself, it makes sense to stay in regular touch with your prospects and customers. Often, however, you want to keep in touch in some way other than a sales letter, some no-pressure form of communication that keeps them aware that you exist, but does not ask for a piece of business.

Thank-you and welcome-aboard letters are one way to do this, as demonstrated in Sample 25-O.

Dear Mr. Haines:

Thank you for your recent initial order. Jim McMurray, your account executive, tells me that we stand a good chance of doing more business with you folks now that we have an office in Memphis.

I hope that's the case, and if there is anything that any of us here at Consolidated can do to keep you happy, please let me know.

Sincerely,

Deane Smith
President

Sample 25-O: Note of thanks for an order.

Sample 25-O is a bit more personal in style than the usual welcome-aboard letter, and intentionally so. Too often those letters sound like—and are—impersonal form letters. If you finally get to do business with an outfit after months or years of soliciting them, take a moment to welcome them warmly and get things off on a good footing.

You can only thank someone for becoming a new customer once. So aside from thank-you notes and sales letters, what can you send to customers and prospects by way of keeping in touch?

Many companies use newsletters, but a lot of that material goes unread, and it sure isn't personal. I think that salespeople, small-business people, and free-lancers do better by sending a copy of an article or a book review that the person would find interesting along with a short note, as shown in Sample 25-P. Using e-mail, you can easily send people articles that you find online buy cutting and pasting it into your e-mail, sending the link to the article, or using the "Send this article to a friend" feature that many online publications offer.

Dear Ms. Yudkin:

Here is a copy of an article from a recent issue of Fortune that you might find interesting. It is about a reversal of the recent boom in outsourcing. It seems that many companies are now finding that they can save money by bringing certain formerly outsourced functions back in-house.

The article isn't clear on whether this reversal is due to some real change in the economics of the situation or to a new fad in management thinking.

Either way, knowing that you've always been skeptical of outsourcing, I thought you'd like the piece.

Regards,

Larry Crisp

Sample 25-P: *Note to accompany an article.*

Do's and Don'ts of Thank-You Letters and E-mails

The letters we've been talking about in this chapter are a simple form of business writing, but there are several things to remember.

Do:

- Keep notes short and to the point.
- Write sincerely.
- Realize that, although some people may be surprised or think you're being formal, they'll enjoy receiving notes anyway.
- Use notes to forge relationships and stay in touch.

Don't:

- Write a personal note to someone you don't know well enough.
- Be overly familiar or cute in a note.
- Write a thank-you note for every little thing someone does.
- Expect to get notes in return; you may, but most people don't write them.
- Expect notes to work miracles; they are a small part of building a relationship.

The Least You Need to Know

- Writing thank-you notes and staying in touch by mail can help you build relationships.
- A note of thanks to an employee putting out extra effort is a great idea, because most employees feel underappreciated and many are never thanked.
- Notes of support and offers of help in times of trouble can lead to friendship.
- Writing a thank-you note or letter after a job interview or client meeting is a must.
- Notes should be personal in style. They offer a real opportunity to write it the way you would say it.
- E-mail provides an excellent way to network and to accomplish most of what traditional thank-you notes and notes of support enable you to do.

Part 5

Writing Well in Special Circumstances

In this final part, we examine the challenge of writing well in special circumstances. You may wind up writing for a committee, task force, or team. There's also the possibility that you will be writing for your boss. When writing for a group or for someone else's signature, you face issues beyond the usual ones between you and your readers.

Today, more than ever, there's a greater chance that you'll have to write to non-native English speakers. There are straightforward ways to do this, as long as you consider the sensibilities of those readers as well as their often more limited command of English.

Finally, in today's fast-paced environment you need to think ahead, manage your correspondence (especially e-mail), and use any technological assistance that might help you keep up and stay organized. We look at ways of doing this in the final chapter.

Chapter 26

Writing for Your Boss or a Committee

In This Chapter

- The special challenges in writing for others
- Managing the process when you write for your boss or a committee
- How to deal with multiple editors
- How to edit the work of others

If you work for an organization, sooner or later you'll find yourself writing for someone else's signature. These writing tasks might involve letters from your boss to a client or supplier, memos summing up the work of a project team, or e-mails about the results of a meeting or other group effort.

These writing situations can be tricky. Without the right approach to them, you can spin your wheels through several drafts and still not satisfy anyone. In this chapter, you'll learn an approach that works.

Situations When You Write for Others

Management is the art of getting things done through others. Writing is one thing that others may need you to do. Here are some typical examples:

- Your boss receives a customer complaint and asks you to write a reply.
- Your boss asks you to write a letter confirming your company's attendance at a conference.
- Your boss asks you to write a letter declining to make a donation to a charity.
- You are on a committee investigating safety issues at your company and must write a letter to various managers requesting their cooperation.
- Your company needs a good sales letter to open doors to new clients.
- You are asked to rewrite your credit department's collection letters.

Your boss has a right to ask you to write for her signature. It happens all the time in business. It's an accepted fact of organizational life. While some people will try to shirk the writing involved in being on a committee or team, somebody winds up doing it, and you're somebody. In fact, the better a writer you become, the more you'll find yourself writing for others.

In any of these situations, there are more people involved than you and your readers.

Writing for Bosses

Whenever you write for the signature of others, they have the right to make changes so that the writing sounds the way they want it to sound. So don't be surprised to find your boss editing your writing, changing your meaning, or even criticizing your work.

You may well ask, "If they want to change it, why don't they just write it themselves?"

Good question. But often they don't. Some bosses lack confidence in their writing. Some write poorly and know it. Many feel that reacting to and "fixing" someone else's draft is faster than writing their own. Some just don't have the time, and believe that you do.

Two things can help:

◆ Realize that doing it "their way" is simply part of the process. Don't take changes or criticism personally. The fact is, editorial comments improve most writing, including business writing.

◆ Do all you can to understand "their way" sooner, rather than later, at several points in the writing process. That's what this chapter is mainly about.

Writing for a Committee

You may have heard the expression, "A camel is a horse put together by a committee." This often applies to documents that come out of committees. The more people you must satisfy (other than your actual readers), the harder it gets. So again, you need to do two things:

◆ Realize that you're representing the views of others in this memo, not just your own. This is different from presenting only your view.

◆ Do all you can to learn what others' views are earlier, rather than later, in the process. Again, this chapter will show you how to do this.

Specific Problems in Writing for Others

Here are the major complaints I've heard from people who must write for others:

◆ "I'm working in the dark because she doesn't know what she wants until she sees it."

- ◆ "If they 'fix' it one more time, it'll be broken forever."
- ◆ "It sits on his desk for a week before he gets back to me."
- ◆ "Their edits and comments contradict one another."
- ◆ "I really don't know who I'm writing for."

Most of these problems can be addressed in the following six-step process.

Six Steps to Writing It Right for Others

Whether you are writing for one person's signature or for a committee of 20, use these six steps to manage the process:

1. Understand the goal and the message.
2. Analyze the audience.
3. Get ideas—and agreement—on what to write up front before you start.
4. Write alone.
5. Obtain and enter all edits.
6. Get final sign-off.

Here's how to make these steps work for you.

Understand the Goal and the Message

Whenever someone says to you, "Could you write a letter for my signature on that?" or "Would you please write that up in a memo for us?" be sure you know what "that" is.

Ask two questions:

- ◆ "What goal are we trying to accomplish with this document?"
- ◆ "What do you think is the best approach?" ("What's the best way to say it?")

In asking about the goal, you may find that a letter or memo isn't even necessary. A phone call, e-mail, or a meeting might work better. For example, if the goal is to get input on an issue from several people, the telephone or e-mail would probably be faster.

If you understand the goal, you'll be able to craft a better message. But be sure to get specific ideas on the message—that is, on how best to say it to achieve the goal—from whoever is asking you to write. Ask questions like:

- ◆ "What approach would you like us to take in this letter?"
- ◆ "What do you think the overall tone should be?"
- ◆ "How do you think this memo should present this?"
- ◆ "How long do you think the memo should be?"

Questions like these, and any others specific to your situation, will help you understand the direction to take with the message.

Analyze the Audience

As always, the more you know about the reader, the better. At times you can find yourself writing for readers you know very little about. This may be because the person asking you to do the writing knows very little about the reader. (Could that be why they're asking you to do the writing? Hmmm.) Or perhaps the reader is somehow "off limits" to you.

In either case, get as much information as you can about the reader or readers. Ask the person or people you are writing for the same questions you would ask yourself about your audience:

- ◆ "Who will the reader be?"
- ◆ "What does the reader know—and need to know—about the subject?"
- ◆ "What do we want the reader to do?"
- ◆ "Does the reader know and trust us?"
- ◆ "Is the reader likely to be interested and supportive, or not?"
- ◆ "How can we help the reader?"

The answers to these questions will help you know what to say, just as they do when you write your own correspondence.

Get Ideas—and Agreement—Up Front

The biggest mistake people make when writing for others is to write too much before getting comments from them. In the worst version of this, someone will write the entire memo and then hand it in for comment. Do this only if the memo is very short and you have done a lot of writing for the person who must sign it. Never write an entire piece for a committee without up-front input.

How do you go about getting this input? Draft an outline and show it to committee members, preferably via e-mail so you can store their ideas electronically and, when appropriate, share the ideas among other committee members. Telling people verbally about the approach you'll take and the points you'll cover isn't enough. They can easily give you an absentminded "yes" and then look at what you wrote and say, "This isn't what we talked about."

Most people will give more thought to something submitted to them in writing. So start with a quick outline of the points you'll cover, and send it to them for feedback. Request very specific comments. Don't ask if it "looks good"—it's too easy for them to just say, "Yeah, it looks fine." Instead ask, "What do you think should be added?" and "How could this be improved?" That way, you'll get them to focus and give you some useful ideas.

When you're writing for a committee or team, circulating an outline beforehand is a must. Attach a note as in the following example.

Tricks of the Trade

Sometimes you may have to press a bit to get the information you need. If the person asking you to write is not forthcoming, say something like, "Would it be useful for me to talk with someone else (such as the intended reader of the memo)?" or "Charlie, I'm not terribly comfortable writing without knowing a bit more. What additional background can you give me on this so I get it right the first time?"

To: Distribution

From: John Henry

Re: Request for Ideas on Our Final Memo

Please examine the attached outline for the memo I'll be writing on our recently completed project. This outline shows the points the memo will cover and the order in which I'm thinking about covering them.

Please let me know what points you would like me to add or omit. Also, I'd like to hear any ideas that you might have for improving the sequence.

Please let me know as soon as possible or, at the latest, by Friday the 22nd. If I don't hear from you by then, I'll assume that you approve of this approach.

Thanks in advance for your help on this.

This note is cordial, but it puts the responsibility on each team member to examine the outline and get back to you. This usually saves you from having to chase them for their input. (Notice I said usually; even with this approach, you might have to chase certain people.)

You may find that some of the comments you receive on the outline are in conflict. Try to resolve them in the outline—for example, by including both conflicting points but emphasizing one of them—or get on the phone, perhaps on a three-way call, and resolve the conflict. It's crucial to get the conflict resolved, or better still, to get the team members to resolve it, *before* you begin writing the draft.

CAUTION Pitfalls _____

> Sometimes committee members try to get the designated writer to resolve conflicts among themselves. I've found this fairly often when I've written for a committee or a team: Charlie wants X to be the conclusion and Lou wants Y to be the conclusion. Either person, or both of them, may put you in the position of resolving this difference of opinion.
>
> Getting involved, which can be difficult to avoid, can work for you or against you. If you're a good "politician" and can keep everyone happy, it can work well. If not—and it's often impossible to keep everyone happy in the face of real differences—you can get caught in the middle and make enemies. To the extent possible, try to get the committee members to resolve their differences. Failing that, try to give each different viewpoint equal time and emphasis.

Write Alone

Just as only one person can drive a car, only one person can write a document. What we might call "back-seat writing" slows things down, at best. At worst, it generates disjointed writing and a lot of suffering.

Writing can be tough enough when done alone. Adding co-writers, commentators, and people telling you what to write during the actual writing makes it far tougher.

Actual co-authors usually let one person write a draft alone. Then the other author or authors comment on it or rewrite it afterward. If someone wants to be in the room and take part in the actual writing, you can try letting them. But I would advise against it. Try saying, "How about if I write a draft for your comment? Or maybe you should write the draft. But I would really prefer that we don't try to write the same piece at the same time."

Dealing with others' rewrites can be a chore, but it is easier than having them rewrite your material as you're trying to write it.

Obtain and Enter All Edits

The first edits to enter are your own edits. Before you hand a letter to someone for their signature or circulate a memo for group review, it should be as good as you can make it. No one wants to edit your work for clarity, grammar, and punctuation. They want to focus on content.

Whether you send the document in hard copy or as an e-mail attachment, include a note or e-mail similar to this example:

> **To:**   Distribution
>
> **From:** John Henry
>
> **Re:**   Memo on Group Project for Your Review
>
> Here is a draft of the final memo that summarizes our recently completed project. I've edited it for grammar, spelling, punctuation, and style, but I'm open to comments.
>
> Please pay especially close attention to the content. I've incorporated all the points on the original outline. However, we want to be sure that this is what we want to say and the way we want to say it.
>
> Please get your comments to me by Wednesday the 9th. If I don't hear from you by then, I'll assume that you are happy with the memo as it is.
>
> Thanks for your help.

There are basically two strategies for circulating a letter or memo to multiple reviewers:

1. Distribute a copy to each person for their individual comments.
2. Circulate one copy from person to person in succession for their comment.

Each strategy has its benefits and drawbacks. The first method is fast and gives each person his or her own fresh copy to comment on. However, it leaves you to resolve any conflicting comments. The second method lets each person see and consider previous edits, but it takes longer and may still not resolve all conflicts. Besides, most team members will probably want their own clean copies for review.

Be sure you type <u>DRAFT</u> across the top or bottom of any document that you circulate for comment to remind the reviewers that this is a draft, not the final copy. You can put this in the header or footer of the document in Word or WordPerfect, and even add the date (and time of day, if you wish). Also, if you expect successive drafts or have agreement that three drafts will probably be needed, you can label them DRAFT #1, DRAFT #2, and so on.

This way, if anyone becomes hypercritical about a point of substance or style, you can point out that this is a draft and that you'll fix the problem in the next draft or in the final document. Also, they will recognize the final copy as such when they see that it's not labeled "DRAFT."

Your best bet is to distribute a copy to each member the first time around and try to address all comments in one shot. On many projects, however, this will be impossible. Try to limit the process to two rounds of edits. More than two rounds often creates wear and tear (especially on you) with little added benefit. It may make sense to get comments for the second edit by circulating one copy rather than distributing copies to each person.

Pitfalls

Word and WordPerfect enable you to circulate documents to multiple reviewers for comments, which they can make in different colors so you know who entered which edits. (The "Track Changes" feature facilitates this.) This is another case where technology can be a mixed blessing. When you are working with one or two reviewers, the edits usually don't get out of hand. But I've found that the ease of editing that this feature supplies encourages some reviewers to rewrite documents almost completely.

This software also enables reviewers to make comments outside the text, so that you can click on an edit and learn why they made it or read other commentary on what you've written. (The "Enter Comments" and "View Comments" feature in Word facilitates this.) This feature sometimes creates more work for the writer, especially when writing for a committee.

You can control this by submitting hard-copy documents to the reviewers. That way, they have to handwrite their comments, which is more work, requires more thought, and limits the space they have.

When you tell reviewers that if you don't hear from them by a certain date you'll assume that they're fine with what you've written, you're using what I call a "presumptive deadline." Its purpose is to get them to submit timely edits and to minimize your following up with them. Its purpose is not to cut reviewers out of the process, make them angry, or get you fired. So if a reviewer does not submit his edits by the specified date, remind him about the date by e-mail or phone the day after the deadline. Be absolutely sure to do this with any reviewer whose input is essential or who is senior to you in the organization.

Get Final Sign-Off

After one or two rounds of edits, you should have incorporated all comments and changes. At that point, you're ready to request final sign-off. Circulating one copy with a *circulation list* is a good strategy at this stage. It tells everyone, "Speak now, or forever hold your peace."

FYI

A **circulation list** is a list of names attached to a document. Each person on the list reads the document, then checks or crosses off his or her name, and passes the document on to the next person. For example:

Circulation:	~~J. Keith~~
	~~S. Jones~~
	M. Trankas
	H. Kreitzer
Return to:	Frank Hoban

In an e-mail document, you must supply a list and instruct your first recipient to forward the e-mail and attachment to the second recipient on the list, the second recipient to forward it to the third, and so on.

When circulating a memo for final approval, if you list the most senior person first and he signs off on it, you improve the chances that everyone else will too.

Again, if you're using hard copy, you can attach a note or short memo to the piece itself.

To: Distribution

From: John Henry

Re: Request for Approval of Final Memo

For your approval, here is the final version of the memo summarizing our recently completed project. I believe it does the job, and I enjoyed working on it with you.

Since we want to get the memo distributed as soon as possible, I need your sign-off by Friday the 29th.

Thanks again for your help.

Notice that this memo asks others for their approval in the form of a sign-off, which they should do by writing their initials near their names on the memo. In my experience, it's good to have actual final sign-off or e-mailed approval from each reviewer. If something goes wrong with the memo—if it is poorly received or contains a major mistake or omission—you want the responsibility (or should I say blame?) to be shared. If you have actual sign-off or an e-mail, nobody can say he didn't see the final version before it went out.

Editing Someone Else's Work

What about those situations when you're the one being written for and you're the one doing the reviews and edits? Here are some guidelines:

- Be as clear as possible about what you want said and how you want it said before the writer starts writing.
- Tell the writer all you can about the reader.
- Give the writer thoughtful, timely suggestions on the outline and on each draft. (At the outset, be sure the writer understands that you want to see an outline for a complex or lengthy letter, memo, or report.)
- Take your rightful role in resolving any conflicts with other committee members.
- Correct any grammar, spelling, and punctuation errors you find, but don't change the wording if it is clear and correct. Resist the temptation to do extensive rewrites just because word processing makes them so easy to do.

Here are the three biggest complaints that business writers have about the editing they receive in business (most of which is not from professional editors):

- "They take too long to get back to me with their comments."
- "They change the meaning of what I write."
- "They make changes for the heck of it or to make it sound as if they wrote it."

Be sure to understand that when someone writes for you or for a group you're a part of, it's not going to sound as if you wrote it. Accept that up front and the task will go more smoothly all around.

The Least You Need to Know

♦ In business, sooner or later you will probably have to write for others, most likely for your boss or for a committee or team.

♦ Since writing for others can be challenging, it helps to follow a process for gathering the information you need, agreeing on an approach, and managing edits and rewrites.

♦ The more input you get from the people you're writing for before you start the actual writing, the better.

♦ Remember to ask for comments on the purpose, direction, style, and content of the piece before you start writing.

♦ Give people deadlines and time frames for getting material back to you with their comments and changes. Do this as gently as possible, but be sure to do it, because with the pace of business today it's easy for people to let a document slip through the cracks and hold up its completion and release.

Chapter 27

Writing for Readers Around the World

In This Chapter

- How cultural differences can affect business writing
- How to write for non-native speakers of English
- The ins and outs of British English
- Placing "politically correct" language in context

Over the past 20 years, American business has gone global. Major drivers of this trend include the rise of U.S. *multinational corporations* (MNCs), the influence of foreign MNCs in the United States, and, of course, worldwide communication technology. (They don't call it the World Wide Web for nothing.)

As a result, you may have to communicate with someone who does not speak and write good English. So in this chapter, we look at communicating with people who speak English as a second (or third or fourth) language.

The Language of Business

The universal language of business is numbers. But the second language of business is English. More than 400 million people speak English as a first language and tens of millions more speak it in addition to their native tongue. However, writing in English usually presents greater challenges for non-native speakers than speaking.

Think about it: Many people have trouble writing in their own language, and the problem only worsens if you're not *fluent* in the language you're trying to write in. Similarly, some non-native speakers have trouble reading English. True, they can figure out the message's meaning when time permits, but they can't hear tones of voice and ask for immediate clarification as they could in a conversation.

It Can't Hurt to Be Humble

What are the implications of worldwide U.S. influence and the global use of English?

Well, if you're from the world's largest economy, market, and business center—and if others are taking the trouble to learn your language—it can be easy to develop a superior attitude. (Or what many Americans simply call "attitude.") It can be easy to think that American English usage, and business and social customs, are "the right way" to do things.

It can also be easy for a U.S.-focused tone to creep into your writing. This isn't so much the fault of American writers as simple miscommunication. I only recently realized that a fair amount of my writing (for corporate clients as well as in books) may be read by people who speak English as a second language. As you'll see later in this chapter, if those readers don't know U.S. culture as residents, they'll be mystified by certain expressions. They may also become annoyed at written English that's not accessible to them.

Recall from Chapter 11 that tone arises from the attitude you take toward your material and your readers. If you feel the material is great because it's made in America or that the world has so very much to learn from the United States, then that tone can affect your writing, even without your knowing it. On the other hand, if you're open to other cultures and understand that different, sometimes better ways of doing business exist, then you'll generally avoid a condescending tone. In other words, if you aim to communicate, rather than to show off or appear superior, you'll create no problems.

Avoid Lincoln Tunnel Vision

Most of us at least occasionally employ cultural references in speech and writing that only people like us will understand. Some of these references arise from corporate culture. For example, only people in your company, and perhaps some major customers and suppliers, will know that the acronym CPSD means "Consumer Products and Services Division."

Other cultural references spring from sports, music, films, politics, and geography. Sports references are a good example. Most sports fans in Western nations follow soccer, which they call football, rather than American football. So references to touchdowns, pass interference, and so on may be lost on them. The same might go for curveballs (baseball), slam dunks (basketball), and slap shots (hockey). While American sports draw overseas audiences, they have not permeated those cultures.

American cultural references often relate to U.S. currency. Sayings such as "put in your two cents," "a penny for your thoughts," "bet your bottom dollar," "get off the dime," "stop on a dime," "two bits," "big bucks," "c-note," and even "millionaire" may not make total sense overseas. (Someone with a million Japanese yen has less than ten grand—uh, that is, 10,000 dollars.)

American expressions may also confuse foreign readers. Examples include "a dog's breakfast" (a hodge-podge or mixed bag), "low man on the totem pole" (someone with low status or seniority), "behind the eight ball" (running late on a project), "that dog won't hunt" (a losing proposition), "let the cat out of the bag" (give away a secret), "shake a leg" or "get the lead out" (get moving), and "hang up his/your/our jock(s)" (quit a job or an effort).

Geographic references such as south of the Mason-Dixon line, upstate, downstate, uptown, downtown, and midtown can confuse foreigners and even nonlocals. Even references to north and south can have readers reaching for the nearest atlas, if they have the time and an atlas. City nicknames, such as the Big Apple (New York), Beantown (Boston), Motown or Motor City (Detroit), Chi-town (Chicago), Twin Cities (Minneapolis and St. Paul), the Bay Area (greater San Francisco), and Lost Wages (Las Vegas) may also be lost on non-U.S. residents.

Pitfalls _____

Avoid any and all references to politics. Never assume that the person you're writing to is a liberal, conservative, or moderate, supports or opposes military action, or favors certain economic or public policies. Indeed, the topics of "politics, religion, and other men's wives" were traditionally considered off-limits in after-dinner conversation, which used to occur between men, in the drawing room, over brandy and cigars. (Harrumph!)

Pitfalls _____

Every business wants to be seen as friendly and approachable. (Well, maybe not desperately hip nightclubs.) When you deal with non-U.S. customers, suppliers, and banks, use words and cultural references that they'll find familiar. At a minimum, omit those that only Americans could understand. Otherwise, you may appear less open to doing business. You may also appear provincial when you would rather appear worldly.

Writing to Non-Native Speakers

When they lack fluency in English, non-native speakers will understand more of your writing if you use the techniques I've recommended for all written communications. The most important among these are to …

- State your point clearly and early in the document.
- Use short words, sentences, and paragraphs.
- Stick with active voice most of the time.
- Use proper punctuation.
- Maintain a businesslike style.

Unless you know your readers, be a bit more formal than you would for U.S. readers and native speakers. Also, be polite; use "please" and "thank you" freely. Avoid long explanations whenever possible; when they're necessary, organize your major points carefully and use bullets for subpoints.

Additional Refinements

A few additional refinements will help you to get your point across more effectively to non-native English speakers and understand their points.

- Europeans write dates differently than Americans. For example, where Americans write September 23, 2007, Europeans would write 23 September 2007. Similarly, instead of 9/23/07, Europeans write 23/9/07. Most readers will probably understand the American convention, but you should be aware of the European one.

- It's not necessary, but you can use phrases that your overseas correspondent uses, even if you might not ordinarily use them. These include expressions such as "Regarding yours of the 15th," and "We are in possession of your letter dated 12 May 2006," which Americans consider old-fashioned, but are still taught to some non-native speakers.

- Do not imitate grammatically incorrect usage. For instance, many non-native English speakers drop articles or use them incorrectly. Don't mimic such practices, even if you think it might make your reader feel comfortable. Someone at the other end may see it as patronizing or insulting.

- Write about events, plans, and recommendations in terms of action. Tell your reader who did what, who is doing what, or who will do what by when.

- Phrase requests in polite but direct terms. For instance, say, "Will you please give us your answer by the end of April?" rather than "We would appreciate hearing about whether we'll be moving ahead by the end of April." (The latter is ambiguous: Would we appreciate hearing by the end of April, or would we appreciate moving ahead by then?)

Take particular care to write in concrete terms. One of the last things students of a foreign language learn is the ability to express and understand abstract thoughts and subtle feelings. If you write in terms of such thoughts and feelings, you may confuse your readers or leave yourself open to misinterpretation. However, these comments don't apply when you're writing to someone you know will comprehend your thoughts and feelings.

Observe the Formalities

Although the whole world is speeding up, the pace of business life in the United States is still faster than in most other nations. Most Americans will forgive, or at least understand, abruptness or even an occasional lack of manners due to this fast pace. But in certain other cultures, people expect some interaction on the phone before being placed on hold and feel slighted if you don't read their business cards before you pocket them.

As always, it's best to know your audience. If you don't know them, you can't go wrong by observing a few formalities. By that I mean:

- Using "please," "thank you," and "you're welcome" often. For example, when you reply to foreign writers, thank them for their letter or e-mail early in your message, preface most requests with "please," and acknowledge any expression of gratitude they make toward you.

- Don't use pressure or try to rush the reader into a decision. Be clear but not too forceful. In many countries, particularly in Asia, people strongly dislike high-pressure tactics. Often they must deal with many layers of approval, or they simply take a while to make decisions.

- Avoid a bragging tone by supporting statements and claims with examples, figures, and references. Try to be as factual as possible, particularly in sales, marketing, and deal-related correspondence where we all tend to "puff" the merchandise.

- Recognize cues from your audience and consider adapting to their pace and business practices. If you're American, try not to leave yourself open to the classic criticisms that non-Americans level at Americans. These include: "They're all rich and wasteful," "They're too aggressive and move too fast," "They become too familiar too early in the relationship," and "They talk too loud."

Do the British Speak English?

It's often said that the United States and Great Britain are "two nations separated by a common language." It's a joke of course, and, thank heavens, not true. Although there are many differences between American and British English, they are virtually all minor (except perhaps for pronunciation, but, fortunately, this book is about the written word). The differences occur mainly in vocabulary and spelling.

In vocabulary, for instance, Americans and the British differ on the following terms:

American	British
apartment	flat
elevator	lift
inventories	stocks
line	queue
luxurious/high-end	posh
mail	post
revenue	turnover
run (for election or re-election)	stand
stock (common stock/preferred stock)	shares (ordinary shares/ preference shares)
vacation (on vacation)	holiday (on holiday)

Spelling differences also abound:

American Spelling	British Spelling
analyze	analyse
check	cheque
color	colour
criticize	criticise
defense	defence
dialog	dialogue
liter	litre
maneuver	manoeuvre
neighbor	neighbour
traveler/traveled	traveller/travelled

And those are just a few examples.

Minor differences in usage also occur. For example, in the United States, people say, "John was taken to the hospital," or "Diane will be in the hospital for two weeks." In the *United Kingdom*, people drop the "the" and say, "John was taken to hospital," or "Diane will be in hospital for two weeks." (The British would point out that Americans say, "John will be back in school next week," rather than " … back in the school." But, as the British also say, "there it is.")

FYI

The terms **England**, **Great Britain**, and **United Kingdom** can be confusing. Many people use Great Britain (or Britain) and the United Kingdom (UK) interchangeably, which is no crime. However, Great Britain properly refers to England, Wales, and Scotland, and United Kingdom refers to Great Britain plus Northern Ireland. England means the actual country of England, which shares borders with Scotland and Wales. Use the term British to refer to the people of Great Britain and English (or British) for inhabitants of England.

Be aware that many people who speak English, notably Australians, Indians, Jamaicans, and Bermudians use "British English." So do Canadians, although mainly in spelling. Each country has its own differences in vocabulary, spelling, and usage, even if they all have roots in British English. At the same time, American vocabulary, spelling, and usage are continuing to spread even in those nations.

Is Politically Correct, Correct?

The issue of political correctness may arise in writing for domestic or foreign audiences. *Politically correct* language is controversial, so I'll tread lightly here and present both sides. I am not an academic, politician, or linguist—just a working writer, and that's the perspective I offer.

The term politically correct (or PC) is often used satirically or negatively. At its best, politically correct language respects people's differences, sensitivities, and equality. At its worst, such language saws the limb it sits on out from under itself. It does so by making such a big deal about differences, sensitivities, and equality that it becomes something of a joke.

Politically correct language refers to people, usually people who have been subject to real or alleged discrimination, in terms that they as a group have developed or find acceptable. So, for example, homosexuals are "gay" (or homosexual) and not "queer," and black people are "African American" or "people of color" and not "Negroes."

The underlying reasoning is threefold: First, people have the right to label themselves rather than accept labels from others. Second, people who are in some way different from the majority don't want to be perceived in terms of those differences, but rather as people. Third, language informs our thoughts and opinions, and negative words reinforce negative stereotypes and images. Therefore, PC language tries to be respectful or at least neutral in the way it describes people.

These concepts extend to nations and nationalities as well. For instance, in the past 30 years or so, many formerly colonial nations in Southeast Asia and in Africa have renamed themselves. Siam became Thailand, Ceylon became Sri Lanka, Burma became Myanmar, and Rhodesia became Zimbabwe. Similarly, American Indians are now called Native Americans, Eskimos are called Inuit, and people once called "Orientals" are called Asians.

Political correctness can be carried too far. In one perhaps apocryphal case, a university supposedly maintained two bins for waste paper: one labeled "white paper" and one labeled "paper of color." Similarly, a PC term for people with disabilities—"physically challenged"—gave rise to jokes about short people being "vertically challenged" and so on. Therefore, as always, language should be used with common sense and good judgment.

Gender-Neutral Language

The issue of gender-neutral language sometimes arises in business. For instance, the term chairperson or salesperson, or chairwoman or saleswoman, has replaced chairman and salesman in many organizations, which makes sense. Yet attempts at purely gender-neutral writing, such as constantly using "he or she," "his or her," or the unacceptable "his/her" (or, worse, "s/he") usually leads to clumsy, distracting sentences. Two solutions are to use the masculine and feminine pronouns interchangeably or to use the gender-neutral plural pronouns—they, them, and theirs—which can itself become awkward.

> **CAUTION** **Pitfalls**
>
> Although you'll often see it, I advise against using plural pronouns with singular nouns to maintain gender neutrality. It's grammatically incorrect to write, "When you need a support person's help, call them at extension 345." Yet it's clumsy to say, "When you need a support person's help, call him or her at extension 345." So you can try the plural, "When you need support people's help, call them at extension 345," but that's not accurate because the reader needs only one person's help.
>
> I might say, "When you need a support person's help, call 345." But that doesn't work every time. And it leaves you to work these situations out case by case, which is what we all have to do. For the record, in this book I've switched more or less randomly between masculine and feminine pronouns.

Global E-mail and Global English

People who communicate in English internationally are seeing a convergence around U.S. usage in e-mail, which is replacing hard-copy letters and memos globally as well as in the United States. As in the States, e-mails tend to be shorter and more frequent, and often omit capital letters and standard punctuation. Under these circumstances, the fine points of usage can get lost.

Nonetheless, many people around the world retain a more formal approach to the written word. Many others will more readily understand and buy into correspondence that uses straightforward language and respects their differences. Some people view local differences as charming or valuable, in and of themselves, and they may resist communication that does not acknowledge those differences.

Thus your mission whenever you write, for the guy across town or the chap across the ocean, remains the same: ensuring that your readers will absorb the knowledge, act on the requests, or agree to the plan that you are communicating.

The Least You Need to Know

- If you're American, it can be easy for a U.S.-focused tone to suffuse your correspondence. Be aware of this and, if necessary, adjust your wording and usage when writing for international readers.

- When writing for non-native speakers of English, state your point clearly and early in the document (usually); use short words, sentences, and paragraphs; and stick with active voice, proper punctuation, and a businesslike style.

- At its best, politically correct language respects people's differences and equality. At its worst, it can be carried to comical extremes or restrict the expression of ideas and opinions.

- American usage can generate resentment among people who applaud cultural differences. Writers who want to do business worldwide should consider those sensibilities in their correspondence.

When You're Under the Gun

In This Chapter

◆ Managing your on-the-job writing workload

◆ Writing under pressure

◆ Using technology tools to stay organized

To write clearly is to think clearly, and vice versa. But today's heavy workloads and rapid pace often don't leave much time for either. As a business writing workshop facilitator, I often heard people say that they just didn't have time to write. I would point out that people have been writing business correspondence for centuries. Surely the writers of yore had the same number of hours in a day that we do.

Maybe so, the workshop participants would say, but we have more writing to do. And look at the conditions we face: dozens of competing demands in a deadline-driven environment, usually without the help of secretaries. I saw their point.

So in this chapter, we'll examine ways of dealing with these challenges.

Keep Your Head While Others Lose Theirs

To write well when you're under the gun, you must either ignore the gun or take it as inspiration. Doing either implies that you actually have the ability to bang out a letter or memo quickly, which you should be able to do with the instruction and the examples I've provided—and with practice. But there's another way: You can make sure that the gun rarely points your way.

Here are five strategies for managing the writing side of your job so you don't wind up under the gun in the first place:

1. Think several moves ahead—then plan and act accordingly. Do the last-minute-Jakes of the world forget that Christmas falls on December 25th or that U.S. tax returns are due by April 15th? Maybe, but more likely they ignore such eventualities. Don't take that approach on the job. For instance, when you define the scope of a project, think about the amount of writing you're creating for yourself, and be sure it's worth it. If it is,

create a prospective outline for the final write-up (and change it when needed), gather material as you conduct the project, and, if possible, enlist co-authors to draft certain sections as well as a reviewer or two.

Tricks of the Trade

Just as a good cook or housepainter cleans as he goes, you should gather and organize material for your final write-up for a project as you conduct the project. If you have an outline, you can save relevant material, comments, and resources in hard-copy or electronic files for each major topic. Then when you sit down to write the final memo or report, you have much of the material at hand.

2. Set reasonable reader expectations. In many situations that arise in a normal workday, you can promise a reader a "brief memo," a "short e-mail," or a "one-pager" on a subject, then deliver as promised. Many writers tell readers far more than they need or want to know.

3. Master the basics. If you try to write fast without a grasp of basic sentence structure, grammar, and punctuation, you'll either slow yourself down to a crawl or write badly. When you're learning the basics you have to take time to look up words and points of grammar (at the editing stage, not the drafting stage!). But when you have them down pat, you'll write faster, more clearly, and with more confidence.

4. Try to cover one topic per letter, memo, or e-mail. Your readers don't want to plow through endless tracts of text any more than you do. Separate issues into future documents with statements like, "This plan involves changes to our accounting methods, which I'll cover in a separate memo." Just use clear subject lines so people can keep all of the memos and e-mails on a subject together.

5. Limit the number of readers, to the extent possible, because the more readers, the more work (and "feedback") a document can create. Bear in mind that the productivity of any workgroup is in inverse proportion to the number of members in the group.

Getting Out of the E-In-Box

Some people I interviewed for this book often receive over 100, and sometimes over 200, e-mails a day. When I ask what the irrelevant, work-related messages were about they all said something like, "Oh, about some meeting or something going on in another department or stuff from management or Human Resources that has nothing do to with me." Assessing and deleting these messages drains productivity.

Why do people send e-mails so indiscriminately? Mainly because they can, but also because they can then say, "Don't you read your e-mails? Gee, we sent one out two months ago about construction workers invading your department around now." This is tantamount to public notices of divorce or bankruptcy buried in the classified ads in the newspaper. They fulfill a legal requirement, but nobody reads them.

All you can do is your best, but here are six tips for minimizing incoming e-mail:

1. Never open unsolicited junk e-mail. You will wind up on lists for more unsolicited junk mail.

2. Delete your name from e-newsletter lists when you haven't read at least one of the past three issues.

3. Delete (without opening) offers from retailers, credit card companies, movie theaters, car dealerships, and other outfits that believe that once you've contacted them you want to hear from them regularly. If they send too much useless stuff, ask to be removed from their list.

4. Set up specific e-mail accounts for your personal, professional, and special interest correspondence. The latter might include accounts for e-mail related to charities, civic groups, clubs, hobbies, or side businesses you're involved in.

5. Unfortunately, e-mail provides an obvious in-box, but no real out-box. Create "out-boxes" in the form of multiple folders in your e-mail accounts to store and manage your messages. Just be sure your account has enough storage to handle the volume. That shouldn't be a problem. For instance, Microsoft's Hotmail, which is free but supported by advertising, provides 250 megabytes of storage. For an additional $19.95 per year, you can get 2GB (gigabytes, or one billion bytes) of storage. Clearly, computer memory has become the least expensive commodity in the e-world.

6. Finally, don't send out e-mail that's going to (a) clog others' in-boxes for no good reason, or (b) cause useless e-mail to flow in your direction.

Prioritizing Your Writing Tasks

Most of us prioritize our writing tasks the way we prioritize all tasks—by their degree of urgency. As the time management consultant Alan Lakein pointed out more than 20 years ago in *How to Get Control of Your Time and Life*, most of us allow the urgent to crowd out the important.

What's the difference? Urgent tasks cry out for immediate attention, but important tasks relate to your major goals. A voice mail from a client or your boss asking for a return call that same day may or may not be important, but it's certainly urgent.

And that's the problem: Thanks to the electronic leash, urgent matters arise constantly, but it's often hard to know how important they are. Also we want to preserve business and personal relationships, and not returning e-mails and phone calls—even "unimportant" ones—can undermine relationships.

You need ways to manage the flow of correspondence and messages coming at you, and ways to triage them by urgency and importance. Deal with the urgent, important ones first, but also with the important ones that never seem to become urgent, such as planning for retirement.

Here are five ways to do that:

◆ Train colleagues not to expect instant answers to routine e-mails and voice mails. Let them know that you're unreachable sometimes. If you respond to everything that comes at you as it comes at you, then you're not prioritizing your tasks. That virtually guarantees you will miss or not complete some important things.

◆ To get blocks of time for important tasks, have your voicemail greeting inform callers that you're out of town, then stay in the office and work on them. (This seems obvious to me, but I know people who think it's impossible and give up their weekends instead.)

◆ Return e-mails and phone calls at the same times every day. Two or three times a day, set aside ten minutes to half an hour to answer messages, perhaps in the morning, at midday, and toward the end of the workday. If you can't answer or don't have time to answer an e-mail then and there, write an e-mail saying when you will answer it, as shown in Sample 28-A.

To: Kim Clarke <kclarke@acmeindustries.com>

From: Steve Kline <skline@acmeindustries.com>

Subject: Your recent e-mail

Kim,

Thank you for this e-mail. I agree that this situation needs attention in the near future, but I can't give it the thought that it requires right now.

I'll send you an e-mail by close of business Wednesday outlining what I believe we should do next.

Regards,

Steve

Sample 28-A: Reply e-mail about a future reply e-mail.

◆ Schedule times for important or potentially long phone calls. Key point: Be sure you schedule a time for the call to end. Mention that you have a meeting or another call to make right after the time allotted for the call in question (see Sample 28-B).

To: Paul Welsh <paulwelsh@renegadeassociates.com>

From: Jack Entrup <johnentrup@renegadeassociates.com>

Subject: The issue you raised

Paul,

Thank you for your e-mail below. This is definitely an important issue. Could we discuss it on the phone late afternoon tomorrow (Tuesday) or Wednesday?

Would 4:00 p.m. work for you on either of those days? If not, would another time after 2:30 p.m. some day this week work for you?

My mornings and lunchtimes are jammed this week, but I'd like us to discuss this ASAP.

Thanks again.

Best,

Jack

Sample 28-B: Reply e-mail to schedule a phone call.

♦ Take time to recharge. Many people let their jobs devour their weekends, holidays, vacations, and brains. As a self-employed, full-time writer, I've found that downtime is essential to remain creative and avoid burnout. Also, if you have a spouse or family and want to keep them, know that although they're often not urgent, they sure are important. Remember: Nobody on his deathbed ever said, "I wish I had spent more time at the office."

Create Systems That Support You

What do I mean by systems? A system is a set of equipment and a plan of action for executing specific tasks. The tasks are usually repetitive, but may not occur in the same way every time. Having a system means you don't have to reinvent the wheel, or even think about the wheel, when a situation comes rolling your way. To construct a system, you need hard-copy and electronic in-boxes, out-boxes, storage areas, files, and folders, and a schedule for reviewing, sorting, responding to, weeding, and otherwise dealing with their contents.

The problem with most systems of organizing correspondence is that people try to adopt the system, rather than adapt the system to their needs. As a result, they use the system for three days and then revert to chaos. While laziness and inflexibility play a role in chronic disorganization, the right system can help you sort, store, and retrieve documents, even if you use it only once a week.

Electronic File Backup Options

Your two main options for backing up files are disk media or Internet services. Disk media let you save files to high-capacity disks that you can take offsite (unless you work at home, which complicates things). The most practical options are Zip drives, which use high-capacity disks and special drives, or CD-RW disks, which work in the *compact disk (CD)* drives that come with most new computers. You can learn about Zip drives and disks, which currently offer much greater capacity than CDs, at the manufacturer's site, www.iomega.com.

Online storage offers virtually unlimited space, but for a monthly or annual fee. This option is becoming especially popular for storing photos, video, and filmed material. Few business writers will need this kind of space, but for documents the real advantage is offsite storage of your files, on the computers of the company providing the service. That's great, given that many of us don't bother to take disks home with us after work. Besides, those disks can be lost or stolen. And where do you keep your backup files if you work at home? You can learn about online storage at www.iomega.com/istorage, www.xdrive.com, or www.ibackup.com, all of which are sites of companies that provide online storage for a fee. Streamload, America Online, and Apple also offer online storage.

The importance of these backup solutions depends on the kind of writing you do, your work habits, and the importance of your files to your business. Of course, if you work for an organization, you no doubt have a technology department (or person) to take care of these issues.

> **FYI**
>
> The three main types of **compact disks (CDs)** are CD-ROM, CD-RW, and CD-R. ROM means "read only memory," which indicates that you can read data on the disk but not write any new data onto it or make changes to the files on the disk. RW means "read/write," which means you can write data to the disk, read data on the disk, and repeatedly rewrite data to the disk. R means "recordable" and these CDs are used mainly for recording music.

> **CAUTION** **Pitfalls**
>
> If you're self-employed or have a home computer, it's easy to pass up new technology that most companies adopt and make available to their employees. Or you may resist new technology because you hate to spend time, money, and effort updating your system. However, new technology is often worth the expense. For instance, if you're using small plastic ("floppy") disks, antique versions of Word or WordPerfect, and dial-up Internet service, you're probably undercutting your writing productivity.

Use Mail Merge for Mass Mailings

As you probably know, if you're a freelance, an independent consultant, or a small-business owner who mails letters to hundreds or thousands of people—or who plans to—mail merge will help you get the word out. To use mail merge, you create a mailing list in a table in Word or WordPerfect or in Microsoft Excel, and a letter to send to people on the list. Both the mailing list and the letter can be used repeatedly. (Put a new date on the letter!) You create a letter with an inside address and salutation similar to the example in Sample 28-C, and it goes on your company letterhead.

Your Company Name
Street Address
City, State Zip Code
Telephone # Fax #

[insert date]

«MrMs» «First Name» «Last Name»
«Recipient's Title»
«Company»
«Street Address» «Suite #»
«City», «State» «Zip Code»

Dear «MrMs» «Last Name»:

[Begin typing letter here, or copy and paste text of letter here]

Sincerely,

[Your name]

[Your title]

Sample 28-C: *Mail-merge setup for a sales letter.*

When you run mail merge, the program sorts through the mailing list and extracts the correct information from the list and plugs it into the proper spots in the address and salutation. The result is a letter that looks exactly as if it were created only for that reader. By the way, mail merge has become very easy to use in Word and WordPerfect.

Want to Be a Dictator?

Do you want to give dictating a try? You can, but you'll probably be talking to your computer instead of a secretary. Speech recognition software (or voice recognition software) now selling for 150 dollars or less enables anyone with Word or WordPerfect to have their spoken words instantly translated into text on the screen.

I own ScanSoft Dragon NaturallySpeaking, which is one of the two leading brands. The other is IBM ViaVoice, which I haven't used. The software does what it claims to do, but you must invest time to "train" it to spell certain words as you say them, because many words sound similar and people's pronunciation varies.

The software lets you create e-mail directly in your e-mail program or in Word or WordPerfect to paste into your e-mail. This may be the most practical application, given that e-mail is inherently conversational. You can also dictate anywhere, because the software can recognize your recorded voice. Thus you can dictate correspondence into a portable tape recorder in your car or at the airport and enter it into your computer or laptop later. Or you can talk into your personal digital assistant, because the newest releases of the software can interface with a PDA's e-mail capabilities.

Tricks of the Trade

On the web you can find reviews of speech recognition software and comments and discussions about various brands at www.eopinions.com. You can learn about the software itself at www.scansoft.com/naturallyspeaking and at www-306.ibm.com/software/voice/viavoice.

Investigate this software if you're interested, but many people find it's not worth the effort. I've found that I can write short letters faster than I can dictate, but I haven't tried it on longer pieces. It's possible that I could dictate them faster than I can write, but I haven't really tried. Also, I enjoy writing, although if something rendered me incapable of typing, I would learn to dictate like those executives in the movies. I can, however, report that the software does work, installation is easy, and integration with Microsoft Word is fairly seamless.

Keep on Writing

The various types of business correspondence covered in this book have been around in one form or another for decades—in some cases, centuries. Even as our workloads grow and technology develops, written communication will remain an important part of business and organizational life. Aside from a grasp of the basics of good writing, the keys to success in this area are managing your writing priorities and making technology your ally rather than your enemy.

Like most skills, business writing develops with experience and application over time. As you progress in your career and encounter various writing situations, you will find that they present a consistent set of demands: You must tell readers, clearly but with some sensitivity, what you want them to know or do. You must convey the importance of knowing or doing it. And you must alert them to any relevant time frames and next steps.

I trust that this book and the CD that accompanies it will help you in these very worthwhile endeavors. For guidance on using the CD, please see the appendix.

The Least You Need to Know

- Gather material in the course of the project, enlist other writers if possible, and aim to deliver a clear and concise final document.
- You must actively manage your response to the calls and correspondence that comes your way every day. Take special care to distinguish between the urgent, but unimportant, and the truly important.
- Create systems for capturing, storing, and retrieving your correspondence and for backing-up your files.
- Look into speech recognition software if you dislike writing, have trouble typing, or believe it could boost your productivity.

Working with Your CD-ROM

The CD-ROM that came with this book includes all of the outlines and samples in the book plus hundreds of additional samples of all types of business correspondence. These outlines and sample documents can help you write virtually any type of business correspondence. They can also help you become a better writer in far less time than you could if you started every document from scratch.

Accessing the Samples on the CD-ROM

To access a specific sample on the CD-ROM that came with this book:

- ◆ Load the CD into your CD drive, and wait for the menu to appear.
- ◆ When the menu "Chapters and Types of Correspondence" appears, click on the type of document you want to access.
- ◆ When the menu for that type of document appears, you will see a brief note on that type of correspondence and a menu of outlines and samples.
- ◆ Scroll down through the menu and click on the sample you want to access, and you will be linked to it immediately.

When the sample appears, you can use it in any number of ways, as I explain in the following sections.

Using the Samples on the CD-ROM

Here's how to use the outlines and samples on the CD.

Use Outlines to Understand the Structure

An outline provides the structure, or a suggested structure, for the content of a document. It suggests the things to include in the first, second, and third paragraphs and so on, but not the exact words to use.

Use an outline to understand a document's goal and general content and how it should be organized. Also, use it as a guide while you are actually writing. After you copy an outline into your word-processing software, you can write directly into it, following the content guidelines as you go. An outline gives you the most flexibility in writing your own documents.

Use Samples for Layouts, Key Phrases, and Wording

The samples on the CD do not have preset margins, spacing, and font sizes, which is a feature of true templates for a specific brand of word-processing software, such as Word or WordPerfect. However, unlike Word or WordPerfect templates, these samples show you how to format the document—*and the phrases and words to use.*

The differences among software brands and releases are too numerous for these samples to include style settings for all brands and releases. Yet you can copy these samples into Word or WordPerfect or into an e-mail message area, and use them as templates.

When you face a new writing situation, first review samples of the relevant type of letter, memo, or e-mail to see how it's done. Note the format of the document and the content and sequence of the paragraphs. When does the letter present its main point or ask for action? Where is the information that supports the writer's major points? How does the memo open and close?

When you understand the type of correspondence you are writing, copy the most appropriate sample into your word-processing software and use it as the basis for your document. You can use the samples as a starting point or simply incorporate the structure and wording directly into your documents. (Although this book is copyrighted, you have the publisher's permission to use these samples for your correspondence, but not to republish them!) You can also mix the language in two or more samples, if you wish.

To customize the sample to your situation, you must, of course, modify the language and add your own wording. You can, up to a point, use the samples word for word. But it's best to use them as a framework and a jumping-off point for your own writing. Also, be sure to insert the correct date and your recipient's name and address into your document.

Create Your Own Templates

You can make your own templates in Word or WordPerfect by using *style settings* and your software's template creation feature to define formats for the types of correspondence you write. Or create templates by saving documents that you have found effective and customizing them to future situations.

Pros and Cons of Samples and Templates

On the plus side, samples and templates can help you write quickly by providing the structure and even the words that you need for specific types of correspondence. They can also show the differences among the various types of correspondence and distinctions in wording, style, and tone within a type of correspondence.

FYI

Style settings in Word or WordPerfect templates determine the documents' format and structure. Those templates include the program's settings for margins, font sizes and styles, effects such as bold or italics, and headers such as FAX or Memorandum. They also specify areas in which to write certain things, such as the recipient's name and your message.

On the minus side, samples and templates can become a "crutch" if you rarely deviate from them and don't develop confidence in your own writing ability. They may also lead readers to question your originality if you repeatedly use the exact same language in various situations.

Always remember that to communicate you must address your readers directly, keep their needs in mind, and tell them what's in it for them, while being clear and courteous.

Index

M

N

Check Out These
Best-Selling
COMPLETE IDIOT'S GUIDES®

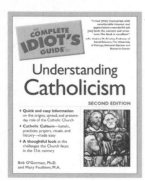

Understanding Catholicism
SECOND EDITION

Bob O'Gorman, Ph.D. and Mary Faulkner, M.A.

1-59257-085-2
$18.95

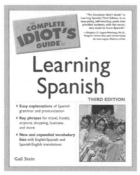

Learning Spanish
THIRD EDITION

Gail Stein

0-02-864451-4
$18.95

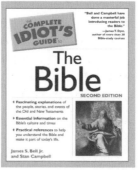

The Bible
SECOND EDITION

James S. Bell Jr. and Stan Campbell

0-02-864382-8
$18.95

Being a Groom
SECOND EDITION

Jennifer Lata Rung and Mark Rung

0-02-864456-5
$9.95

Grammar and Style
SECOND EDITION

Laurie E. Rozakis, Ph.D.

1-59257-115-8
$16.95

Playing the Guitar
SECOND EDITION

Frederick Noad

0-02-864244-9
$21.95 w/CD

Personal Finance in Your 20s & 30s
SECOND EDITION

Sarah Young Fisher and Susan Shelly

0-02-864374-7
$19.95

Knitting and Crocheting
SECOND EDITION
Illustrated

Barbara Breiter and Gail Diven

1-59257-089-5
$16.95

The Perfect Resume
THIRD EDITION

Susan Ireland

0-02-864440-9
$14.95

Buying and Selling a Home
FOURTH EDITION

Shelley O'Hara and Nancy D. Lewis

1-59257-120-4
$18.95

Low-Carb Meals

Lucy Beale and Sandy G. Couvillon, M.S., L.D.N., R.D.

1-59257-180-8
$18.95

Calculus

W. Michael Kelley

0-02-864365-8
$18.95

More than *450 titles* in *30 different categories*
Available at booksellers everywhere

ALPHA